Theology and Literature

Theology and Literature: Rethinking Reader Responsibility

Edited by
Gaye Williams Ortiz and Clara A.B. Joseph

THEOLOGY AND LITERATURE
© Gaye Williams Ortiz and Clara A. B. Joseph, 2006.

First published in 2006 by
PALGRAVE MACMILLAN™
175 Fifth Avenue, New York, N.Y. 10010 and
Houndmills, Basingstoke, Hampshire, England RG21 6XS
Companies and representatives throughout the world.

PALGRAVE MACMILLAN is the global academic imprint of the Palgrave Macmillan division of St. Martin's Press, LLC and of Palgrave Macmillan Ltd. Macmillan® is a registered trademark in the United States, United Kingdom and other countries. Palgrave is a registered trademark in the European Union and other countries.

ISBN-13: 978–1–4039–7198–2
ISBN-10: 1–4039–7198–6

Library of Congress Cataloging-in-Publication Data

Theology and literature : rethinking reader responsibility / edited by Gaye Williams Ortiz and Clara A.B. Joseph.
   p. cm.
Includes bibliographical references and index.
Contents: On reader responsibility: an introduction / Clara A.B. Joseph and Gaye Williams Ortiz—Some dilemmas of an ethics of literature / Liebeth Korthals Altes—Only irresponsible people would go into the desert for forty days / David Jasper—The ethics of biblical interpretation / Robert J. Hurley—Samuel Beckett's use of the Bible and the responsibility of the reader / Spyridoula Athanasopoulou-Kypriou—On trial / Lewis Owens—Bible and ethics / Johannes Nissen—The playwright, the novelist, and the comedian / Dirk Visser—Dialogue in Gandhi's Hind Swaraj or Indian home rule / Clara A.B. Joseph—Responsibly performing vulnerability / Erik Borgman—The "Indian" Character of modern Hindi drama / Diana Dimitrova—Film and apocryphal imitation of the Feminine / Elizabeth Philpot—Revolting fantasies / Alison Jasper—Literature as resistance / Dirk De Schutter.
   ISBN 1–4039–7198–6
   1. Religion and literature. 2. Religion in literature. I. Ortiz, Gaye. II. Joseph, Clara A. B.

PN49.T4446 2006
809′.93382—dc22   2005057422

A catalogue record for this book is available from the British Library.

Design by Newgen Imaging Systems (P) Ltd., Chennai, India.

First edition: May 2006

10 9 8 7 6 5 4 3 2 1

Printed in the United States of America.

CONTENTS

NOTES ON THE CONTRIBUTORS

Liesbeth Korthals Altes, University of Groningen, the Netherlands: Liesbeth Korthals Altes is head of the department of Arts, Culture and Media at Groningen University (NL), where she holds the double chair of General Literature and of Modern French Literature. She has published works on modern French and francophone literature (Duras, Genet, Huysmans, Tournier, Djebar), on narratology (mainly the representation of values, irony, and voice), and the relation between literature and ethics.

Erik Borgman, University of Nijmegen, the Netherlands: Erik Borgman is the author of *Dominican Spirituality: An Exploration* (Continuum, 2001) and *Edward Schillebeeckx: A Theologian in His History* (Continuum, 2003) and coeditor of *Literary Canons and Religious Identity* (Ashgate, 2004).

Diana Dimitrova, Department of Religious Studies, Michigan State University: Diana Dimitrova received her Ph.D. in Indology and English from the University of Heidelberg. She has taught courses in South Asian Religions, Literatures, and Languages at the University of Frankfurt, McGill University, and Emory University. At present, she is teaching at Loyola University, Chicago. Her current research deals with gender and religion in Hindi drama.

Robert Hurley, University of Laval, Quebec, Canada: Robert Hurley is a professor of New Testament Exegesis and Religious Education at the Faculté de théologie et de sciences religieuses at Université Laval in Quebec City, Canada. His analyses of New Testament texts and secular "wisdom literature" proceed from insights derived from affective stylistics, a radical version of reader–response criticism. While the themes of justice and politics attract him in the biblical sphere, questions of spiritual discernment, imagination, and creativity occupy a central place in his analyses of children's literature.

David Jasper, University of Glasgow: David Jasper is Professor of Literature and Theology at the University of Glasgow, Scotland. He has published widely in the field of theology and the arts, and his latest books are *The Sacred Desert* (Blackwell, 2004) and *A Short Introduction to Hermeneutics* (WJK, 2004). He was the founding editor of the journal *Literature and Theology*.

Alison Jasper, University of Stirling, Scotland: Alison Jasper is a lecturer in Religious Studies at the University of Stirling, Scotland. Her publications include "The Shining Garment of the Text: Gendered Readings in the Prologue of John" and "Recollecting religion in the realm of the body (or Body©)" in Anderson and Clack's *Feminist Philosophy of Religion: Critical Readings* (Routledge, 2004). Her current research is in the areas of body, feminist theology, and the teaching of religious studies.

Spyridoula Athanasopoulou-Kypriou, University of Manchester, United Kingdom: Spyridoula Athanasopoulou-Kypriou holds a Ph.D. in systematic theology from the University of Manchester where she also lectured on Christian anthropology and on Religion, Culture, and Gender. She is now tutor of religious studies in Athens, Greece. Her publications include various articles on Samuel Beckett (for example, "Beckett's Not I and/or the art of living," update in *Samuel Beckett Today*/Aujourdh'hui is, 2005, and "Beckett Beyond the Problem of God," *Literature and Theology* 14.1 [2000]: 34–51), and on theology and her research interests are in the field of literature and theology and Eastern Orthodox theology. She is currently working on Eunomius' and Gregory of Nyssa's understanding of language.

Johannes Nissen, University of Aarthus, Denmark: Johannes Nissen is associate Professor of New Testament Exegesis at the Department of Biblical Studies, University of Aarhus, Denmark. He has authored a number of books and articles, especially in New Testament and mission, Bible and ethics, and hermeneutical issues. His recent publication in English is *New Testament and Mission: Historical and Hermeneutical Perspectives* (Verlag Peter Lang, 1999; 2002; 2004); he is also coeditor of *New Readings in John: Literary and Theology Perspectives* (Sheffield Academic Press, 1999). He has recently published a major book in Danish on Bible and Ethics: called *Bibel og etik. Konkrete og principielle problemstillinger* (Aarhus University Press, 2003).

Lewis Owens, Canterbury Christ Church University College, Canterbury, England: Lewis Owens received his Ph.D. from Cambridge University on the religious philosophy of the Greek writer Nikos Kazantzakis. He is the author of "*Creative Destruction: Nikos Kazantzakis and the Literature of Responsibility*" (Mercer University Press, 2002) and several articles on Kazantzakis in international peer-reviewed journals. Current research includes the fiction of Abram Tertz and the life and work of Dmitri Shostakovich. Lewis Owens is currently President of the U.K. Shostakovich Society and currently teaches Philosophy of Religion at Sidney Sussex College, Cambridge.

Elizabeth Philpot, University of Göteborg, Sweden: Elizabeth Philpot is a doctoral student at the University of Göteborg, Sweden, working on the dissertation: *Apocryphal Images in North European Art (i.e. Norway, Sweden, Denmark and Great Britain)*. Her publications include the following: "Judith and Holofernes: Changing Images in the History of Art" (essay included in *Translating Religious Texts*, ed. D. Jasper, Macmillan Press, 1993), "Mary Magdalene—Saint or Sinner? The Visual Image" and also "The Triumph of Judith—Power and Display in Art" (two papers in *Talking it Over: Perspectives on Women and Religion 1993–95*, ed. Jtly, St. Mungo Press, Glasgow, 1996), "The Fourth-Century Mosaics of the Roman Villa at Lullingstone in Kent" (essay in *KAIROS Studies in Art History and Literature in Honour of Professor Gunilla Åkerström—Hougen*, Paul Åström förlag, 1998). [Reviewed by Isabelle Morand, *Revue des Études Anciennes*, Vol 101, 1999, pp. 605–606], and "Susanna: Indecent Attraction/Fatal Exposure" (essay in *Believing in the Text*, ed. David Jasper and George Newlands with Darlene Bird, Bern: Peter Lang, 2004).

Dirk De Schutter has published articles in English and Dutch on nineteenth and twentieth century philosophy (Hegel, Nietzsche, Heidegger, Arendt) and literature (Hölderlin, Barth, Banville, Saramago, Celan). He translated Derrida's "Violence et métaphysique" and essays by Arendt into Dutch.

Dirk Visser, University of Groningen, Amsterdam: Dirk Visser is a lecturer in English. He is currently completing his Ph.D. dissertation on the ethics of theatrical representation at the University of Groningen. Some of his publications are: "The Trouble With Larry: *The Normal Heart* Revisited," in *File*, III.1 (May 1994), "*Angels in America*: Theater tussen Queer en Kitsch," in *Homologie*, XVIII. 1 (January 1996), and "Communicating Torture: The Dramatic Language of Harold Pinter," *Neophilologus*, LXXX. 2 (April 1996).

THE EDITORS

Gaye Williams Ortiz is an author and educator, formerly Head of Cultural Studies at York St. John College and presently a professor in Communication Studies at Augusta State University, Georgia U.S.A. In 1997 she coedited (with Clive Marsh) *Explorations in Theology and Film* (Blackwell). She now lives in the United States, and is vice-president of SIGNIS, the World Catholic Association for Communication. She was the organizer of the International Society for Religion, Literature, and Culture conference in York, England in 2002. Her most recent published work includes "Jesus, Mary and Joseph! (Holy) Family Values in Film" in O'Kane, *Borders, Boundaries and the Bible* (Sheffield Academic Press, 2002); "The Catholic Church and Its Attitude to Film as an Arbiter of Cultural Meaning" in Mitchell and Marriage, *Mediating Religion: Studies in Media, Religion and Culture* (T&T Clark, 2003); and "Passion-ate Women: Female Presence in *The Passion of the Christ*" in Plate, ed., *Re-Viewing the Passion* (Palgrave Macmillan, 2004). Her Ph.D. dissertation for the University of Leeds was on the relationship between the Catholic Church and the film industry.

Clara A.B. Joseph is an Assistant Professor in the Department of English at the University of Calgary, Canada where she teaches undergraduate and graduate courses in literary theory, Gandhian literature, postcolonial literatures, and Christian literary works of India. Her coedited book of essays *Global Fissures: Postcolonial Fusions* is forthcoming with Rodopi, Amsterdam. Her recent publications include, two coeditions with Janet Wilson of *World Literature Written in English* (*WLWE*) special issues are as follow: *The Postcolonial and Globalization* 39.2 (2002–2003) and *Rethinking the Postcolonial and Globalization* 40.1 (2002–2003), and articles such as "Why Indeed Must Anything be Left of English Studies?" in *English Studies in Canada*, "Nation Because of Differences," in *Research in African Literatures*, and "Rethinking Hybridity: The Syro-Malabar Church in North America," in *South Asians in the Diaspora: Histories and Religious Traditions* (Leiden, Netherlands: Brill, 2003).

On Reader Responsibility: An Introduction

CLARA A.B. JOSEPH AND
GAYE WILLIAMS ORTIZ

Contemporary theories of reading have been heavily determined by new criticism, Russian formalism, and structuralism, and their influence continues, variously, in New historicism, post-structuralism, as also in postcolonialism and cultural studies. In general, the millennial academic tendency is often marked as "postmodernist," positioning the reader, the author, and the work as "text"—at once constructed and relative. Within this theoretical (and practical) worldview, questioning becomes an engaging and reiterative performance and undecidability the norm. Hence, to resurrect the function of the reader in terms of responsibility, the duty-bound ability to respond, in such a situation becomes more than a simple resurrection of Roland Barthes' structuralist substitution of function of the reader for the reader. Instead, it contemplates the ethics of action and reaction, of *dharma* (duty) and *karma* (action-reaction) in short, of consequences for an act done casually—reading.

Those who read, write, and teach literature have a fundamental responsibility. If this sounds like old-fashioned ilk, it probably is. And we want to rub it in on the sixtieth anniversary of the extraordinary display of creativity in terror and destruction (World War II) that tells us, belatedly or perhaps not, that it is not enough to create. As all wars, and not just world wars, have repeatedly proven, creativity and innovation are not in themselves blessings. The quickest way to stun your enemy with a deathblow may have all the wonder of speed and accuracy and, yes, even style, but if we have begun to categorize it as "art" we need an urgent second look at that word.

As an acronym this word indicates three inherent aspects: Author, Reader, Text. ART. Critics and theorists have been squabbling over each of these terms. Variously, they say that it is time to get rid of the term "Author" and to acknowledge that there is no coherent individual who intends to write and actually fulfills that intention. Moreover, they continue, the Reader can never get at the original intention of the author anyway. In fact, they patiently explain, there is no reader—the reader is simply the reading process which is a writing process and, do not forget, there is no author either. In a widely known instance, theorist and scholar Roland Barthes contemplates "The Death of the Author." Both the Author and the Reader declared devoid of what has in some circles been referred to as the human person are now textualized. The last element, the Text, is thus not only the words on the page or the paint on the canvas, but very much a continuation of the "writing process" (the dead Author) and the "reading process" (the late Reader), so that, in the words of the late Jacques Derrida, there is nothing outside the text.

Derrida may not have intended it so, but highly influential academics have found it quite convenient to move into a game of deconstruction (a word that not for no reason rings of destruction). If the author, reader, text, and the world are text, then the chief function of academics in the arts and the humanities is to engage in a game of indiscriminate undermining, be it parables or child pornography. The aim is to lay bare the contradictions and then sit back and watch the structure shatter—deconstruct. This, highly imaginative (we will add), methodology in itself is supposed to be sufficiently ethical. This vision of the molecular even when devoid of the whole is claimed to be holistic. To go beyond such smithereens into any redemptive meaning is deemed unethical because authoritarian, something upon which the Fathers of such a church—Michel Foucault and Friedrich Nietzsche—would equally, if variously, cry anathema.

But then unexpectedly, out of the pile of deconstructed rabble, wriggles out the exploited child, destroyed but not deconstructed. Scarred mentally and spiritually, broken and bleeding, this child's silence and absence are the demonic presence that a postmodern world has yet to encounter. The presence of this child as a human person too gets debated, as in recent court cases that resulted in the Supreme Court of Canada reading into laws on child pornography certain "improvements" that basically said that child pornography is alright provided these are imagination-based and for personal use, and that videos/photos of consenting sexual activities of those who are fourteen years or older can be had for private use. The Supreme Court of Canada has thus defined art (since the court had already decided that child pornography earned certain exemptions for artistic merit) as both a personal and private affair, implicitly something that can be purely imaginary and therefore without real-world and public consequences, but in case there is an impact it would not really matter because such an impact would be personal, private. That a pedophile Canadian tourist in Asia thus got away with a minimal sentence (a respectable four-month house arrest) is here of no public or global consequence.

If the theory is one of indiscrete undermining, the court's decision is comprehensible: the individual artist as the writerly process and the reader(s)/audience as the readerly process were/are simply working on the text, yes, children. Such an "artist' " intention is, after all, invalid where the key term is intentional fallacy, referring to the "error" of resorting to the purpose of the author for an understanding of the text in the reading process. Where intention cannot be proven, the court rests its case. This is perfectly logical.

But is it responsible? And do literature and the arts have a responsibility?

To answer this question without a nonanswer, we turn to: the "Letter of His Holiness Pope John Paul II to Artists, 1999." Acknowledging, through the Book of Genesis, holding high the status of a human being as created in the image of the Creator, and resorting to his own mother tongue Polish in which there are close lexical connections between the word for creator and craftsman, the Late John Paul II declares: "the human craftsman mirrors the image of God as Creator." He goes on to note:

> None can sense more deeply than you artists, ingenious creators of beauty that you are, something of the pathos with which God at the dawn of creation looked upon the work of his hands. A glimmer of that feeling has shone so often in your eyes when—like the artists of every age—captivated by the hidden power of sounds and words, colours and shapes, you have admired the work of your inspiration, sensing in it some echo of the mystery of creation with which God, the sole creator of all things, has wished in some way to associate you.

The experience of artistic creation is an ultra-modest but exhilarating reflection of the divine gift of the "mystery of creation." Yet, there is a difference between creator and craftsman—the former creates out of nothing, the latter out of something. Thus the artist is not God but a subject of God who experiences the divine spark of truth, beauty, and goodness in a significant way. Recognizing that "to be an artist" is not "to be moral" or vice versa, John Paul II underscores the revelatory power of a literary piece or an artistic object: "In shaping a masterpiece, the artist not only summons his work into being, but also in some way reveals his own personality by means of it."

This proposition is in blasphemous violation of postmodernist deconstructionist theories and methodologies. In fact, poststructuralists may argue that this is the quintessential comeback of an oppressive clerical logocentricism ("humanism") that ought to have vanished with the Renaissance and the Englightenment. By insisting on the *presence* of an integrated and responsible human being whose essence lies supposedly in a greater and that too metaphysical *Presence* John Paul II has clearly detextualized the key players of ART. Such detextualizing would hold the advocates of "artistic merit" accountable to not just the artists (in their supposedly private and personal world) and their right to freedom of expression but, to put it simply, to children, women, and men (including the artist)—human persons. John Paul II's invocation to a " 'spirituality' of artistic service" challenges the artist to be motivated by a sense of self-giving responsibility to society, rather than by any desire for glory or profit.

Further, to suggest that artists are "ingenious creators of beauty" is problematic within poststructuralist thought where all essences, indiscriminately, deconstruct like computer images in virtual reality, with little consequence. Once again referring to the opening chapter of the Book of Genesis, John Paul II notes that God saw that all was good in what was created. The Greek term, *Kalokagathia*, refers to not just beauty but to "beauty-goodness." Plato's definition is introduced to illustrate: "The power of the Good has taken refuge in the nature of the Beautiful." In short, even God could not escape the aesthetic satisfaction inherent in creation and its simultaneous expression as goodness. Emphasizing that the aesthetic is ethical, John Paul II summarizes the relationship between the two aspects as follows: "In a certain sense, beauty is the visible form of the good, just as the good is the metaphysical condition of beauty." He, thus, locates beauty as the outside and goodness the inside of that outside. Where some might be suspicious of essentializing either beauty or goodness, John Paul II moves to an understanding of the worth of not just art but of creation itself in terms of beauty-goodness.

In a similar vein Mahatma Gandhi, in an interview with a student of Nobel laureate Rabindranath Tagore, examines the relationship of beauty to truth. Capitalizing truth to signify God, Gandhi argues for the priority of "Truth" over beauty. Accordingly, if beauty is to be found it has to be sought in Truth, never vice versa. The relevance of truth for creation lies in the search for meaning, so that creation thus presents meaning, not meaninglessness, not however for its own sake but by pointing to the ultimate purpose of creation—God. All good art is thus Truth-directed.

When the artist's role is thus defined in terms of truth, beauty, and goodness—of a vertical relationship with God and a horizontal relationship with the world, the Supreme Court of Canada's ironic, if not pathetic or rather tragic, better still—irresponsible—categorizing of a certain kind of child pornography as art reflects on the popularity of some artistic and literary theories that make a disproportionate case for the game aspects of art and literature, as well as on a highly profitarian society that stands to gain by such a position. Virtual reality is the ideal cocoon for a postmodern technological society as it is for deconstructionist methodologies that lack discrimination, for this world can pretend to be without consequences. Deconstructing screen images make an interesting game, and profit for corporations. What is equally interesting is that both such a methodology and such a society embrace secularism with a vengeance, dogmatically—for example, a mercenary Santa Claus would be the center of Christmas season. The lack of ethics, in such a case, could be perceived in any reference to God or to the religious basis of philosophy, and not in the fact that the children of the world are being exploited, abused, killed by "artists" who cannot keep their pants up. This, indeed, can be the ethics of only Virtual Reality.

The question of reader responsibility, induced by a subtle and complex set of factors that include history, society, gender, protocol, knowledge, expectations, and assumptions, is what our contributors attempt to address. However, no matter how specialized their own particular area of study, the theorists on display here have effects that carry beyond their original field. Those writing here are concerned with and excited by the production of meaning in the context of the response of the reader. But even though their areas of specialization are diverse they reflect the growing interest in the ethics of the reading process; more than ever this means that they are not so much concerned with the end product of a reader's interpretation but the process whereby this conclusion has been reached. When a reader tries to figure out what a text is "about," as Jonathan Culler suggests, the answer to that question is not as important as "what you do with the details of the text in relating them to your answer" (Culler 1997, 65). Erik Borgman, one of our contributors, has said that ethics can be defined as a "hermeneutics of reality and the human condition" (2002 Conference of the International Society for Religion, Literature and Culture). If, therefore, literature can be a source of ethical reflections, then the reading of literature as a source of ethics can mean that the reader shares in the text's responsibility to reality and not virtual reality.

That emphasis on reality echoes the deeply held belief of a writer from the American South who spent a lot of time and energy discussing how she hoped readers would engage with her fictional writings. Flannery O'Connor wrote that to read a work of fiction is "to plunge into reality" (Kilcourse 2001, 20). She seemed to reject the image of a reader as "escaping" into a book or as passively taking in what s/he is reading; rather, O'Connor argued that it required "skill and courage" to read fiction, and so part of what she tried to do was to educate her readers as to how to read and understand fiction. As a writer who was not only a devout Roman Catholic but who was fascinated with how divine grace works within human life, she bemoaned a perceived "absence of a religious culture to help these readers interpret the deeper meaning of fiction" (16). She believed that readers who were willing to have their "sense of mystery" deepened by contact with reality did not have to be particularly sophisticated, but they did need to be somewhat discerning in their choice of reading. Sometimes blunt in her attempts to raise the aspirations of Southern readers, Kilcourse quotes her description of a talk she gave to a ladies' club: "The heart of my message to them was that they would all fry in hell if they didn't stop reading trash" (16). Her desire for her readers was that they experience a shock: the ability of literature to shock, she said, was in the same vein as the parables of Jesus in the New Testament, which "reverse audience expectations" while revealing a hidden truth (39).

O'Connor's wish was that she could in some way re-create in readers the joy that she said literature engendered in her. That desire, rather than an obsessive desire to determine what readers made of her writings, is commendable but perhaps, in the end, naive. So too, we could add, is the famous statement by Umberto Eco: "The author should die once he has finished writing. So as not to trouble the path of the text" (Eco 1983, 7). Any writer who puts her imagination to work on that quote would take care never to complete her work! Yet, as Gary Radford points out, there is a complex interplay between three factors of inter-pretation: linguistic and cultural knowledge and "your history of previ-ous interpretations of other texts (Radford, 2002, 7)." The lack of any real control by the writer of how the reader reads and uses the text s/he has written is a product of not simply words nor the author's intentions, Radford says; what also is key to the reading process is the comprehension achieved through previous interpretations of the many texts read by the reader. Once we begin thinking back to what we have read this past year—let alone what we've read since we could read as children—it gives us an inkling of how complicated this process of reading can get.

The essays in this collection respond to the same question: "How to read?" Yet, many of them also consider the "Why?" question. In pondering intention and purpose, the essays bring refreshing and provocative responses to well-established theories. The essays are dialogical while they remain reluctant to offer a single model of reading or reader responsibility.

In "Only Irresponsible People would go into the Desert for Forty Days," David Jasper's close reading of Jim Crace's novel *Quarantine* poses an important theoretical question: "what does it mean for fiction to be true, and might a different fiction, different typologies, different metaphors, reveal a different yet still coherent and valid truth which does not contradict difference?" Jasper hits the nail on the head in thus bonding issues of literary representation with those of ethical reading. In "Some Dilemma of an Ethics of Literature," Liesbeth Korthals Altes traces with sophistication and care mainly two current practices of ethical reading of literature. Altes discusses literary theorists Martha Nussbaum and Andrew Gibson as practitioners of opposing methods that have their uses and disadvantages: Nussbaum's forecloses prematurely on matters of morality; Gibson's opens endlessly and playfully to question everything. The essay further makes a case for the possibilities and advantages of an in-between method (between Aristotle and postmodernism) of a responsible reading of literature. The arguments that take the author to the in-between method are much needed in any serious discussions on the relationship of literature and ethical theory. As if in conversation with this essay, Robert Hurley considers the ethics of exegesis, in "The Ethics of Biblical Interpretation: Rhetoricizing the Foundations," and examines the practice of Schüssler Fiorenza and Stanley Fish. With Fish's anti-foundationalist and rhetorical practice of reading as a reader-response literary critic, Hurley dismisses Fiorenza's insistence on a "legitimate reading."

Mahatma Gandhi's spiritual and political treatise, *Hind Swaraj or Indian Home Rule*, a book that could be placed in the hands of babes and yet was censored by the colonial government, urges a holistic understanding of literary representation, argues Clara Joseph. By tracing the fictional dialogue in Gandhi's work, Joseph, through theories of Jurgen Habermas, discovers the reliance of Gandhi in this early work on the dialogue of the Bhagavad Gita and argues for a Gandhian theory of literary representation that requires the writer/reader to be a satyagrahi or seeker of truth. Similarly, in "The Playwright, the Novelist and the Comedian: A Case Study in Audience Responsibility," Dirk Visser examines the literary representation of anti-Semitism that arose in the Netherlands at the Book Week of 2000 and proceeds to examine the question of the relationship between truth and beauty. Through a close analysis of four events—(1) the show of the comedian Freek de Jonge; (2) Rainer Werner Fassbinder's play *Der Müll, Die Stadt und Der Tod* (Garbage, the City and Death); (3) actor Jules Croiset's self-staged kidnapping; and (4) Harry Mulisch's novel *Het Theater, De Brief en De Waarheid* (The Theatre, the Letter and the Truth)—the essay offers a clear and convincing argument for the need of an audience with a heightened sense of responsibility.

Spyridoula Athanasopoulou-Kypriou's "Samuel Beckett's Use of the Bible and the Responsibility of the Reader" is an intriguing piece that deftly examines the manner in which Beckett makes biblical allusions and concludes on the impact of this manner on the reader. The author argues that Beckett, by using denotation rather than connotation and perhaps a positivist philosophy, forces the reader to acknowledge that it is the reader, rather than the writer or the text, who produces meaning. Similarly, in "On Trial: Mikhail Bakhtin and Abram Tertz's address to 'God,' " Lewis Owens examines the literary theories of Mikhail Bakhtin and Abram Tertz to argue that they are critical responses to the demands of Soviet Socialist realism. Owens daringly and convincingly suggests that their theories of dialogue further signify the importance of open-endedness (versus closure) in an understanding of God.

But ethical responsibility can be found in the very narrative structure. This is the topic of the next essay. Erik Borgman's literary analysis in his essay, "Responsibility Performing Vulnerability: Salman Rushdie's *Fury* and Edgar Laurence Doctorow's *City of God* read through the Lenses of the Frankfurt School and New Political Theology—and Vice Versa" leads to the astounding argument on how literary narratives can undertake a religious function, and how theology is illumined through literary analysis. Borgman's reading notes that by highlighting the multiplicity in cultural and media images, *Fury* opposes monotheism. Borgman, however, is quick to point out that neither monotheism nor polytheism matters in *Fury* where, precluding Derridean meanings of multiplicity, it is rather the superior need for love and understanding that overpowers the narrative. Similarly, *City of God* posits the search for God, rather than any finding of God, as itself redemptive so that the city of God-seekers is a religious space. For Borgman, Doctorow's theme comes close to that of a problematic Political Theology.

In certain ways contemplating on the literary space as also the religious space, Diana Dimitrova examines representations of women particularly in the plays of Upendranath Ashk. Through textual and contextual analysis she argues that Ashk was influenced by Ibsen but that Ashk's portrayal of women points to a "feminism" that is not entirely Western. She further examines the findings of Girish Karnad who locates modern theatre in India in the context of authorial ethics and audience responsibility. The next two essays deal with filmic approaches to the topic. Elizabeth Philpot, in "Film and Apocryphal Imitation of the Feminine—Judith of Bethulia" ponders the absence of a feminist film on the biblical Judith. She maintains that the silent movie, *Judith of Bethulia*, by privileging spectacle fails to reflect the feminist movement of the time. Similarly, in "Revolting Fantasies: Some Kristevan reservations about popularist cinema," Alison Jasper examines how the film adaptations of *The Silence of the Lambs* and *Interview with the Vampire* can be analyzed using Julia Kristeva's theories on revolution. Finally, Dirk De Schutter, brings to us the wisdom of Hannah Arendt who draws the ever important distinction between fiction and the fictitious. His essay, "Literature as Resistance: Hannah Arendt on Story Telling" explicates on Arendt's caution to the general reader.

The value of the interdisciplinary nature of theory is evidenced in this collection of essays. The original impetus for this edition lay in the International Society for Religion, Literature and Culture which was established in 2000, and the essays in this book which began as conference papers for the Society's 2002 conference in York, England. It is primarily focused on research from North America and northern Europe, particularly Holland, the United Kingdom, and Scandinavia, but the Society also has links with societies in South Africa, Japan, and Australia. The name of the International Society combines three academic areas that have become increasingly identified as interconnected disciplines: religion, literature, and culture.

Although to the academic community reading this book today this may be an obvious and fruitful interconnection, it was not always that way. By way of example, Alister McGrath, in his anthology of Christian literature, begins his Preface by signaling the ambivalence with which Christians have regarded literature. On the one hand, literature was seen by some Christians as an ally in the presentation of a "Christian vision" as well as a legitimate tool of cultural interaction. McGrath mentions the anonymous *Cursor Mundi* (*c.* 900 CE), in which it is argued that "since people enjoy reading secular literature so much, it makes sense to present religious truth in literary forms" so as to give the reader enjoyment and spiritual nourishment (quoted in McGrath 2001, xii). The opposite view, however, regarded literature not only as alien to the Christian faith but as an instrument of deception (this ambivalence is evident in much the same way with polarized Christian views of film). Since the recognition and analysis of the Bible as a form of literature was not common until fairly recently (McGrath cites Wordsworth's literature, which "increasingly adopted the characteristics of religion" as being important to this development), this long-existing "disconnect" that distinguished between reading the sacred and the secular is understandable but still somewhat surprising. Opening up the Bible to scrutiny as a literary text, however, is only one part of what has become a wholesale school of interpretation of genres of "Christian literature." Is the question of how the reader interprets "Christian literature" dependent upon its function as shaped by the author's own set of Christian ideas and values (or even a non-Christian author's critique of Christianity)? Or is Christian literature "Christian" because it fulfils the needs of the Christian reader? Can we then identify (or appropriate) the writings of Gandhi as "Christian" because they inspire or challenge the reader to live a life more fully Christian?

In all, the essays deftly draw links between issues of ethics and literary/cultural criticism while also examining interventions of the religious or theological. Through literary analysis, biblical exegesis, and theoretical hypothesis, individual contributions reconsider the responsibility of the reader and the author as also the process of reading as well as the structuring of the text in context. The collection showcases theory and practice at the juncture of literature and theology and within international contexts. These essays make a comprehensive, thought-provoking, and valuable contribution to current scholarship in the analysis of literary and religious narratives and theories through mainly three significant features: first the encounter with world faiths or world literatures, second an explicit literary cum theological discourse, and third a strong focus on the ethics of reading and representation.

In this book academics from different parts of the world respond to shared theoretical issues of reading theological and literary works, making the collection a valuable resource for any academic discussions on what it means to read religious and secular narratives. The essays variously bring together literary and scriptural narratives and theories to examine related issues of ethics—ethics of reading and ethics of representing. The work is significant for its several essays that critique many prominent literary theories and especially theories of the reading process and of reader-response. This international collection of essays that strides literature and theology through literary theory will be attractive to major university programs in the faculties of humanities, culture and communication, and the fine arts around the world. An attractive feature of the edition is that several of the contributors are well-established authors with a high reputation; other contributors are in early or mid-career who bring to the collection fresh and, often, intellectually provocative views.

The strength of the edition lies in the international-oriented and multidisciplinary application of reader-response theories that straddle theological, cultural, and literary boundaries. Further, it refuses to privilege the post-structuralist interpretation of the text even when actively engaging with such a mode. While Jasper's (also Hurley's) essay in our collection maintains a post-structuralist position, several others (such as Altes or Athanasopoulou-Kypriou) advocate an in-between theory of reading; others (e.g., Borgman, Joseph, etc.) challenge post-structuralist games of undecidability. We hope that the multiplicity of theoretical positions, presented in a style that is at once sophisticated and clear, makes the collection sufficiently open-ended yet well-oriented to the problem of reading processes as also to issues of representation of narratives.

The edition can be used as a text book in courses that bring together ethics and literature—a growing field because of increased attention to critics such as Martha Nussbaum and Edward Said. Graduate as well as upper-level undergraduate courses in literary theory and criticism, hermeneutics, methodology in literary studies and religious/theological studies, gender studies, philosophy, critical studies, cultural studies, film studies, and twentieth (twenty-first) century theories of the reading process can easily incorporate this edition, particularly as the essays showcase a combination of hardcore theory and hands-on application on literary and cultural texts. Additionally, the edition's strength in bringing together international scholars who discuss works from various parts of the world—South Asia, northern Europe, North America—makes this edition desirable in postcolonial studies as also in the study of world literatures and cultures. The format of the book with its overall categories: A Theory of Ethical Reading, Reading and the Biblical, and Reading and the Literary, and the format of individual essays with abstract, key words and, in most cases, subtitles, should direct the reader quickly and smoothly to topics of interest.

Our thanks and appreciation go to the contributors to this book for attempting to draw us into the debate about reader-response within an ethical framework of activity, keeping in mind the "plunge into reality" that O'Connor urges readers to make and the possibilities and pleasures, and the responsibility, that literature can engender in its readers.

Works Cited

Borkman, Erik. "The Statement for Conference 2002: York." Minutes of the International Society for Religion, Literature and Culture, November 8, 2002.

Culler Jonathan. *Literary Theory: A Very Short Introduction.* New York: Oxford University Press, 1997.

Eco, Umberto. *Postscript to the Name of the Rose.* Trans. William Weaver. New York: Harcourt Brace Jovanovich, 1983.

Gandhi, Mahatma. "Interview." In *The Collected Works of Mahatma Gandhi.* Vol. XXV. New Delhi: Publication Division, Ministry of Information and Broadcasting, Government of India, 1967. 247–256.

Kilcourse Jr., George A. *Flannery O'Connor's Religious Imagination.* New York: Paulist Press, 2001.

"Letter of His Holiness Pope John Paul II to Artists, 1999." May 12, 2005 at <http://www.vatican.va/holy_father/john_paul_ii/letters/documents/hf_jp-ii_let_23041999_artists_en.html>.

McGrath, Alister. *Christian Literature: An Anthology.* Oxford: Blackwell, 2001.

Radford, Gary P. 2002. Beware of the Fallout: Umberto Eco and the Making of the Model Reader. Available from the World Wide Web <www.http://themodernworld.com/eco_papers_radford.html>.

PART 1

A Theory of Ethical Reading

CHAPTER ONE

Some Dilemmas of an Ethics of Literature

LIESBETH KORTHALS ALTES

Introduction

What can an ethical approach to literature mean, and how does it relate to the autonomy art and literature have achieved through the nineteenth and twentieth century? The current "ethical turn" goes from fairly straightforward moralism (literature has to represent certain values and attitudes as desirable), through clarificationism (literature, in representing conflicting views on human affairs, triggers a critical reflection on, and a weighing of, values), to an ethics of/in literature as a radical deconstruction of morality itself. This essay discusses mainly two approaches: relying on an Aristotelian notion of ethics, Martha Nussbaum defends the moral function of literature, which not only fosters flexibility and pluralism but also positively teaches "how to live the good life"; quite differently, on the basis of a poststructuralist *bricolage* combining Levinas, Derrida, Lyotard, Blanchot, and feminist ethics, Andrew Gibson reads literature precisely for the ethical experience of radical undecidability it offers. However deep the differences, both approaches run the risk of reducing literature to a preset idea about what ethics actually is: by locating literature's ethical dimension either (exclusively) in the familiarization of the strange and clear moral guidance, or (as exclusively) in the experience of strangeness, of absence of meaning, and the evanescence of the self. Ethical criticism, in my view, needs to address precisely the dialectical tension between the two, and ponder the different ethical functions literature can have, for different readers in different contexts.

Key Words

Ethics and the novel; reading experience; postmodern ethics; narrative identity; otherness; undecidability.

★　★　★

> Les oeuvres d'art ne valent rien comme réponses au nihilisme, elles valent tout comme questions posées au néant.
>
> [Works of art are of no worth as answers to nihilism, they are worth everything as questions to nothingness.]
> Lyotard, *Moralités postmodernes*, 1993, 151. (my translation)

Is it "time to go back to Leavis," that is, to a moral commitment in literary criticism? This is how Andrew Gibson provokingly opens his reflection in *Postmodernity, Ethics and the Novel*, of course before insisting on all that separates his own "ethical" from Leavis' "moral" reading of literature. Since the 1980s, the question seems to have acquired new relevance, with the ethical turn in literary studies. After the initial and seminal publications of that period,[1] ethical criticism has gained momentum in the 1990s.[2] The ongoing discussion on the legitimization of the humanities, and of literary studies in particular, in postmodern multicultural societies, confers a sense of urgency and relevance to the reflection on the ethical function of literature and the arts.[3] But what can an ethical approach to literature mean, and how does it relate to other functions of, and approaches to, literature?

Art, Morality and Ethics

The autonomy of the arts with respect to dominant morality, religion, and politics is an important privilege more or less acquired in most democratic societies, which however remains very fragile. As Bourdieu and others have argued, art as an institution became increasingly independent since the eighteenth century. On a philosophical level, Kant's characterization of the aesthetic as "disinterested" has been deeply influential in the conception of the autonomy of the arts. However, the relationship between art and morality is intricate and hardy. Even a movement like *L'Art pour l'art* (*art for art's sake*) can be argued to defend a higher conception of ethics, autonomous in the sense that it is free from bourgeois norms. Moral transgression in art generally presupposes a "common" morality as its operation ground, and often legitimizes itself as a new, alternative morality (see, e.g., Bataille's *La Littérature et le mal*, which attaches to the imperative of transgression a high moral norm of authenticity). No representation of human affairs, aesthetic or otherwise, can really avoid having a moral or ethical dimension, even if it is in the negative. The question is only what role and how central or peripheral it comes to play in the interpretation and evaluation of art, in our case, literature.

Leaving aside for this occasion the autonomist or aestheticist standpoint that literature has nothing to do with morality or ethics, one could project the current "ethical turn" on a scale that, as mentioned in the beginning of this essay, would go from straightforward moralism (literature has to represent—ultimately—certain values and attitudes as desirable), via clarificationism (literature, in representing conflicting views on human affairs, triggers a critical reflection on, and a weighing of, values), to an ethics of/in literature as a radical deconstruction of morality itself.[4] Two approaches occupying rather different positions on such a scale are discussed here, exhibiting between them some of the dilemmas and pitfalls of ethical criticism: relying on an Aristotelian notion of ethics, Martha Nussbaum defends the moral function of literature, which not only fosters flexibility and pluralism but also positively teaches "how to live the good life"; quite to the contrary, with his postmodern *bricolage* combining Levinas, Derrida, Lyotard, Blanchot, and feminist ethics, Andrew Gibson reads literature precisely for the ethical experience of radical undecidability it offers.

How can literature be related to either morality or ethics? For clarity sake, I start with the distinction, common but by no means generally accepted, between *morality* as a set of personal or collectively shared principles of conduct, norms, and values, which stresses individual choice and responsibility in concrete situations, and *ethics* as the reflection upon moral issues. As Geoffrey Harpham writes: "Ethics places imperatives, principles, alternatives on a balanced scale, sustaining an august reticence, a principled irresolution to which, nevertheless, the limited and precise prescriptions of morality must refer for their authority" (1990, 31). Inasmuch as they represent human or anthropomorphic (inter)action, consciousness, and attitudes, literary works display elements that belong to morality and offer them for ethical reflection: values, norms, preferences, and choice; the relation between self and other; self-fashioning; responsibility; and the like. In this essay, I limit the discussion to the novel, as is often the case, but not necessarily so, in ethical criticism.

Most contributions to ethical criticism share at least two convictions: that literature has a special relation to ethics, or more narrowly to morality, and that criticism should express a personal engagement with a specific work, instead of striving for objectifiable knowledge about a text or about texts in general, as in structuralist times. But beyond this basic agreement, divergence reigns: for instance, on the notion of ethics itself and its relation to morality, and on how literature is related to both: what *is* or *ought* to be ethical or moral in literature and art? Essential differences appear as to the conception of language. Moreover, what literary roles and relations are under consideration: the author and his or her responsibility, the reader, the texts, or even literary teachers, scholars, critics, or publishers? And although some "ethical" themes seem fairly constant—for instance, literature as the experience of, and attitude toward, alterity—views on these questions vary dramatically. Quite divergent too is the attention given to the specifically aesthetic dimension of literature: for some, the literary form does in itself some ethical work, as in Bakhtin's concept of the fundamentally polyphonic structure of the novel (see Bakhtin 2001) or in Greimas' notion of plot as the display, through time and characters, of a value-conflict (see Greimas 1973); for others, the attention goes rather to ethical themes, or to the moral development and experiences of fictional characters regarded as human beings (as in Palmer 1992).

Literature and Moral Philosophy

The ethical turn in literary criticism came partly from the sideline. Ironically, in the same period that literary criticism tended to evacuate ethical issues, moral philosophers such as Martha Nussbaum (1986 and 1990), Alisdair McIntyre (1981), Charles Taylor (1989), or Richard Rorty (1989) attributed precisely to literature a crucial moral role. Meanwhile, from within literary studies, Marxist approaches since the 1970s engendered much research into the ideological or "sociocritical" dimension of texts, with strong moral(istic) overtones and an ethical concern with the representation of "otherness." Ethics as such, however, could not but be suspect in a Marxist view, considering its focus on the individual instead of collective perspective. Since then, cultural studies in general, and feminist, postcolonial, gender, and queer criticism in particular, have voiced their suspicion of any "universalistic" ethics, considered as a cover for domination by a Western white patriarchal elite; this critique of course paved the road for alternative—feminist, gay, etcetera—ethics.[5] But the need to reflect on ideological and ethical aspects of writing, reading, and mediating literature has become widely recognized. It would be interesting to investigate how and when the slide from ideological concerns to more "personal" ethical ones took place, but that falls outside the scope of this essay.

A strong call for a moral approach to literature has come from Martha Nussbaum, whose works, *The Fragility of Goodness* and *Love's Knowledge. Essays on Philosophy and Literature*, received a wide audience. Nussbaum handles notions such as the human, subject, dialogue, moral elevation, and reason as if deconstruction and its "masters of suspicion" had been no more than ripples in the pool, although it is clearly against such "undermining" approaches that she provocatively revives ancient thinking on morality. Her approach claims to be anti-foundationalist, pluralistic, and pragmatic. Taking as her starting point Aristotle's notion of practical wisdom, *phronesis*, rather than a strict deontological morality, Nussbaum argues that literature is an indispensable complement to moral philosophy: the latter is condemned to abstract language, concerned with universals and generality, whereas moral disposition and action require imagination and the flexibility to adapt to concrete situations. By engaging us in situations of value-conflicts, literature exercises our practical moral sense, allowing for a kind of "experiential learning."

Ethical criticism, according to Nussbaum, does not just discuss the moral standpoints that a work explicitly thematizes, but also carefully traces the more implicit messages of form: here she comes close to the kind of rhetorical analysis developed by Booth (see Booth 1988). The alliance of literary theory to moral philosophy leads not (only) to "scientific understanding," but to "practical wisdom" (Nussbaum 1990, 55). Ethical criticism studies novels for the way they lead to a deeper awareness of moral issues, and ultimately, for showing "how to live a good life"—that is, for the moral guidance they provide. Reading literature can contribute to the moral and civic education of readers, a crucial function according to Nussbaum. Like Booth, she stresses the ethically clarifying function of the conversation between readers, which Booth calls "coduction."

Obviously, such moral impact does not hold for all kinds of literature. Most rewarding, in Nussbaum's view, are the works of Henry James, Proust, and the like, "deliberative" novels which combine "attention to particulars" and "richness of feeling" (103). Nussbaum deals much less easily with experimental writing or with anonymous, shifting voices and characters, and formless (non-)plots. Not unexpectedly, in spite of her admiration of Proust and Beckett, she finally rejects their works: Beckett's novels are too nihilistic and engage in a socially unproductive, though deeply religious, search for silence. The absence of human agency in his work, she finds, does not correspond to real experience in the development of individuals nor to society's needs (308–309). Even Proust's world, however admirably complex, is too solipsistic, whereas a novelist such as Ann Beattie shows us how to overcome Proustian scepticism and solitude by loving and sharing. On one occasion, in *Love's Knowledge*, Nussbaum admits that some novels (in this case James' *The Ambassadors*) "gesture[s] toward the limits of ethical consciousness, making us aware of the deep elements in our ethical life that in their violence or intensity lead us outside of the ethical attitude altogether, outside of the quest for balanced vision and perfect rightness" (190). This is a fundamental insight, bearing on the cognitive and ethical relevance of representations that challenge morality and confront the reader with an unassimilable otherness, with the *other* of morality. But on the whole, it is a "balanced vision" and understanding she looks for in literature, and not the radically unsettling experience of otherness, nor does she seem sensitive to the fascination of the moral abyss. This clearly stands out in her comment on *difference*, on which, *postmodernisme oblige*, she has to take position:

> The Aristotelian procedure tells us to be respectful of difference; but it also instructs us to look for a *consistent and sharable answer to the "how to live" question*, one that will capture what is deepest and most basic, even though it will, of necessity, to achieve that aim, have to give up certain other things. To this extent its flexibility is qualified by a deep commitment to *getting somewhere* (28, my italics).

This moralism is easy to criticize: it leads to a rather naive ranking of writers on a moral scale (Beattie better than Proust), the aesthetic being made subservient to the moral. Nussbaum hardly problematizes literary representation itself, where ambiguity often remains unsolved. Good literature for her relies upon an "immediate" recognition of daily life situations, it is ultimately social and constructive, and teaches love and compassion. One could argue on the contrary that literature is also the institutionally defined place where the forbidding strangeness of the world and of the other can be represented, as well as the conflict between personal desires and needs and an often coercive society or community: who will tell where the right values and the good life lie? Besides, many "immoral" texts do excellent ethical work by triggering vigorous discussions on fundamental issues. And who constitute the "we" so evidently sharing values? Minority criticisms recently have voiced a strong scepticism toward such "evident" communities. From yet another angle, psychology and deconstructive philosophy (not to speak about history itself) have demonstrated the illusory nature of a rational, coherent human agency, which Nussbaum presupposes.

However, to shove aside the moral perspective itself as a "lower" apprehension of literature, lacking the more sophisticated aesthetic detachment, appears to me as reductive as the criticized moralism itself. Many readers—and writers, for that matter—have attested that at crucial moments, reading literature did offer them a precious clarification of values and norms, moral guidance, or consolation. Literature can have different functions for individuals, groups, cultures, and societies, and research into these different functions should be part of literary studies, without normative exclusions. The argument I raise against Nussbaum is not so much that she concentrates on the moral function of literature, which is her legitimate focus as a moral philosopher; it is rather that she does not investigate other ethically and morally relevant workings of literature beyond its immediately constructive function, and does not problematize the literary or aesthetic mediation itself.

Postmodern Ethics and the Novel

Andrew Gibson's *Postmodernity, Ethics and the Novel: From Leavis to Levinas* shares with Nussbaum the wish to make criticism an encounter, an "event," in Levinas' terms, which engages the critic's own basic convictions. But here the cleft widens. Gibson's ethics and conception of literature and language are strongly influenced by Levinas and by postmodern philosophers such as Derrida and Lyotard, by the "theory" in short which Nussbaum deemed responsible for emptying literary studies of their vitality.[6] I do not try to summarize all the issues Gibson broaches, but only highlight a few themes characteristic of postmodern ethical criticism.

From the start, Gibson distinguishes ethics from morality, with reference to Geoffrey Harpham (1992), Drucilla Cornell (1991 and 1992), and Bernard Williams (1985). Morality is on the side of deontology, whereas ethics "operates a kind of play within morality, holds it open, hopes to restrain it from violence or the will to domination, subjects it to a kind of autodeconstruction" (Gibson 1999, 15). Although he agrees with Harpham and Cornell that we should not "shrug off the ordinary, difficult world of moral choices for the lofty, high-minded indeterminacies of ethics," the more interesting issue for him is obviously the latter. Morality, in the subsequent analyses, appears always in the role of that which must be subverted. As he rather dismissively puts it, ethics—what he is after in literature—has nothing to do with "virtues to be practised" (85), nor even with its traditional definition as a critical reflection on values: it refrains by principle from any positive statement, and remains a radical and endless questioning, haunting all processes of meaning and value-giving. Of this radical questioning, literature offers the privileged experience (like many ethical critics, Gibson tends to limit himself to the novel). The ethical significance of the novel lies in its "function, as form which . . . dissolves any given set of cognitive horizons" (91). Ethical criticism reads the text as "a mobile and subtle complex of relations, as always caught up in a play of composition and fission. . . . Such an attitude would posit the experience of plurality, surprise, radical inter-ruption of given horizons as a characteristic feature of our experience of a fictional text."

Defined significantly as a "set of epistemological procedures," ethical criticism questions basic assumptions about literary texts and reading, about representation, the cognitive value and "content" of literature, or the appropriation of the text in reading.

Referring to Lyotard and Blanchot,[7] Gibson argues that literature does not represent the real, but "puts forward the unrepresentable in presentation itself" (70). Echoing Blanchot, he describes literature as "le vide même [qui hante le monde des choses]" ("the emptiness itself that haunts the world of things," 192). Just like avant-garde art in Lyotard's view, the task of ethical reading is "tending the empty centre" (76). This negative, resisting conception of representation is extended to a distrust of the possessiveness displayed by any quest for knowledge. Ethical criticism should instead investigate how knowledge is distributed and conveyed in and through literature: who claims to possess knowledge about whom, and how is the reader made to know? Gibson's preference goes to works that problematize this quest for knowledge/possession of the other. Thus, he shows in his reading of *A Heart of Darkness* that Marlowe's search for truth does not lead to clear insight, into the distinc-tion between right and wrong for instance, or into the "essence" of Kurtz, but to the experience of infinite and radical alterity.

Related to the Levinasian rejection of knowing is the notion of the ethical primacy of the act of *saying* over its result, the *Said*. In *Otherwise than Being*, Levinas describes the *said* as a freezing of time, a concession to generality; therefore only the moment and the act of *saying* can be ethical, as they imply the face-to-face relation between the other and me. For literature, as Gibson recognizes, this is problematic, as there is no direct face to face in reading a written literary work. Gibson countervenes this difficulty by showing, via Lyotard, how modern literature, as in Beckett's work, stages and problematizes the act of saying, the origin and destination of speech, inviting the reader to join in the "event" of saying, which can thus become an ethical experience.

In the same deconstructive vein, reading is conceived not as an appropriation of a work of art experienced as a totality, a coherent whole offered to the intellectual grasp, as an "oeuvre" (work), but as a "désoeuvrement" (a word in which resound together both its regular meaning, idleness, and the unusual literal meaning, the "un-doing" of the work). According to Levinas, this kind of reading manifests an "irreducible, ethical resistance to the 'Je peux' [I can] of enlightened knowledge" (Quoted in Gibson 1999, 190). And instead of reflecting back to the reader the unity and uniqueness of one's self, modern art offers the experience of the dissemination and the weakness of the self (88). Against Booth or Nussbaum, for instance, who define reading as a conversation or friendship between an (implied) author and a reader, presupposing distinct personalities on each side, Gibson argues that the selves constructed in literary texts (characters) and through them (readers) are multiple and evanescent.[8] To read is, as Levinas writes, to submit oneself to the call of the other, an "incessant dégrisement du même enivré de soi" (an "unceasing sobering up of the self drunken with itself," 25).[9]

Not surprisingly, where Nussbaum's canon consisted of realist and modernist writers, besides Greek tragedy, Gibson cherishes works performing the dissolution of the novel, the epistemological problematization of representation. He shares Proust and Beckett with Nussbaum, but values precisely what she regrets: the experience of the fundamental strangeness of the other and of the self, memory as dissemination instead of totalization.

The "epistemological procedures" of this postmodern hermeneutics amount to an "ethics of the negative," of questioning, a "dissolution of the sphere of the common."[10] Like many postmodernist thinkers, heirs to romanticism, Gibson crowns this negative ethics with a celebration of exile and marginality, which, his text suggests, are in themselves more ethical than any belonging to a place or centre—in which, it is implied, morality, static, and limited, is grounded.[11] However, the negativity of this ethics is contained by a deep commitment to the Other, and to quote Levinas, by "the incessant event of subjection to everything" (Quoted in Gibson 1999, 165). The openness toward the other that

Gibson pursues in reading is defined, according to him, in Levinas' notion of "sensibility," Lyotard's notion of "passibilité," as well as in the feminist "ethics of affect" (161–185). So the ethical contribution of the reading experience is not just, as for Nussbaum, a greater awareness or compassion, feelings of empathy in which the ego is consolidated, but more radically, the readiness to loose the self, vulnerability. Gibson's ethical eclecticism may leave the reader puzzled. I do not, however, comment in detail on his argumentation, but only raise some interrogations and reservations about salient features of a postmodern ethics of literature, as exemplified by his work.

First, to define ethics as this radical command of undecidability and literature as the locus of this experience seems at the same time crucial and one-sided. Crucial, because literature thus is defined as a place where morality itself can be exposed to reflection and to the disruptive power of imagination and ambivalence. This notion belongs to the critical and utopian function of literature, which has been defended by German romanticism, Adorno, up to Derrida. From this perspective, the deconstructive notion of the undecidability of reading as fundamentally ethical appears not as a failing to take a moral stand, but as respect for alterity, as a way of resisting the widely shared desire for totality and closure. But it is one-sided too, because in reducing ethics to the suspension of judgment, one misses other dimensions of ethics and of literature, which are just as relevant in this respect: the less radical but very familiar grappling with dilemmas and choices, the identification offered to readers with respect to value positions and cultural representations— the common stuff of morality and ideology. A general reflection on ethics, in my view, needs to address precisely the whole span and the tension between the realm of morality (how the do's and don'ts are expressed and maintained, how they are experienced by individuals), and the radical questioning of a deconstructive ethics. To reduce ethical criticism to the latter, is like limiting the Bible to the Ecclesiastic.

Second, Gibson's rejection of the idea, or ideal, of self-possession, which he shares with many postmodern thinkers, needs qualifying. He insists rightly, I think, on the experience of self-loss in reading, as a necessary corrective to the contrary image of reading as an appropriation of the text by a conscious and articulate self (however, more phenomenological and empirical research would be welcome on this point). But is the awareness of the multiplicity of the self, and the surrender to "the other," always an evident good in itself? Is it not naive and dangerous, as has been objected earlier to Levinas, to cultivate such uncritical submission to the text as other, such abstention to qualify the different effects and guises of this alterity? Is submission to any text-as-other always *in itself* ethical? Or only because some kind of ethical work is done in the negotiation between this porous self, exposed to rapture, and some moment where this self says "Here I stand"—expressing a response-ability "for everything and everyone," which Levinas also considers of fundamental importance?

It would be interesting to confront Gibson's elaboration on Levinas with Ricoeur's careful argument in *Soi-même comme un autre* (Oneself as another), where he tries to formulate an alternative to relativistic philosophies of the subject and a basis for ethics. In opposition to Rorty or Lyotard, who define the subject by its plurality of roles or "games" without envisaging a unifying moment, Ricoeur strives to both maintain this plural conception of the self and recognize a responsible, which is moral, self. The aesthetic experience for him fulfils a crucial function, as it is intimately linked to ethics in a "fruitful tension": in reading, the reader exposes her "narrative identity" to the text, and experiences the loss of self in the identification either with a multitude of different points of view, or with the empty characters abounding in contemporary literature. However, this volatile or multiple "Moi-ipse" is, according to Ricoeur, complemented by a moral self, which at a certain point steps out of this multitude to state "here I am." He agrees that this gesture, through which the person recognizes herself as a responsible subject, means freezing the "errance" (drifting) of the narrative subject; but this erring narrative imagination, which threatens to "paralyse the capacity of firm commitment," has its own ethical function. By impeding the self to petrify into a "raide constance à soi" (a rigid fidelity to oneself), it introduces in the heart of the self the necessary awareness of its fragility, its "dépossession" and thus opens it toward the other (see Ricoeur 1990, 197–199).[12] The understanding of what reading does to the reader's sense of self is evidently bound up with normative views on what selves should be. However, like books, selves may serve different functions, which a general theory of ethics and an ethical criticism of literature would have to carefully distinguish.

The third point has to do with the status and objective of ethical criticism. "In their own manner novels perform an ethical work," writes Gibson, "or *can be made to*, and it is *worth trying to enable that work to take place*" (emphasis mine). This sentence itself calls for deconstruction. Is it the novel itself which "performs" the ethical work, as the first part of the sentence states? Should this apply to all novels, on the basis of what kind of features? Or is it the intervention of the critic through which novels "can be made to" perform ethical work? Interestingly, this intervention is almost effaced by the passive formulation, as if the critic is only help-ing in the maïeutical process of ethical truth being born, a process of which the "worth" is already given, in a supra-personal way. This effacement is somewhat curious, as Gibson clearly indicated, from the beginning, that ethical criticism for him is a personal, hence subjective, engagement with the text. What seems at stake here is the need to find a guarantee for the truth and the "worth" of the insight, which lies out-side the critic himself and thus saves the approach from "subjectivity."

This leads to the more general issue of validity and method in (ethi-cal) criticism and literary studies. Structuralist and semiotic approaches have been criticized for their naive belief in the objectivity of their description and analysis of texts. Ethical criticism, in Nussbaum's style as well as in Gibson's, quite to the contrary argues for a personal response to texts, grounding the truth and worth of their analysis in the force of their ethical beliefs themselves. Only those who share these beliefs, or are persuaded into sharing them, will agree on the worth of the analysis: Nussbaum indeeds counts on an evident "commonality" of insight, as ultimately does Gibson, albeit an insight of a different kind. I think that in our current multicultural societies, ethics, or more concretely: norms, values, ways of life, need to be presented in such a way that the found-ing principles can be discussed, and are not taken for granted. This gives a somewhat different outline to ethical criticism.

Toward a Narratological-Rhetorical Approach
of Ethics in Narrative

Indeed, the concern for the ethical dimension of literature, I would argue, has only gained more urgency in contemporary culture, but it has more, or something else, to achieve than either life-lessons or the radical subversion of morality. On a general level, a study of literature has to describe—not to prescribe—the various functions literature fulfils in a culture at a given historical moment. The rapport between its ethical, aesthetic, and ideological functions is to be carefully investigated. Literature indeed has many functions, and can as well consolidate values, norms, and attitudes, or ideologies, as problematize and "subvert" them. On the level of individual works, one is entitled to expect from an ethical approach to literature on the one hand a systematic (model for the) investigation of textual structures and devices that carry moral/ethical weight, and may trigger ethical reflection; and on the other hand, the development of empirical research into the actual moral or ethical effect of literature on (various groups of) readers. For the former, although repeatedly declared dead and buried, narratology offers a useful approach, combined with rhetorical and historical analysis: if one drops the high-strung pretensions of objectivity, such an approach goes as far as possible toward an intersubjective analysis of texts, trying to make explicit the textual evidence for interpretive moves.[13] This methodological and argumentational explicitness appears to me indispensable as it provides explicit grounds for discussions and (dis)agreement, instead of counting on shared beliefs.

Certain narrative structures and devices seem particularly relevant with respect to ethics: the representation of *action*, to start with, as the motivation and evaluation of action involve values and norms. The analysis of dilemmas and choices belong to this sphere, and can be described as conflicting value systems between which a subject is caught. Second, the representation of *speech* and *perception*, as expressions of ways of being in the world, and of negotiating the rapport between self and other. Third, the textual *rhetoric*, which influences the reader's adhesion to the represented values and attitudes. What pattern of desire, what contact and contract with the reader does a text establish, through pathos, reliability, irony, ambivalence, authority, or self-reflexivity? This kind of narratological-rhetorical analysis does not lead to the determination of "the" ethics or ideology of a text, but to an insight in what values and dilemmas are thematized, and into ambivalence and polysemy, which can be differently actualized by different readers, in accordance with their own values and beliefs. Obviously, a critic can use this kind of analysis as a basis for her own interpretation, from a distinct ethical frame. I tend however to believe, with Ricoeur (1986, 110), that *distancing* through a more systematic procedure of textual analysis offers some corrective against a too eager and too easy appropriation of the work.

Conclusion

The ethical turn, of which only a small sample has been discussed here, has done a lot to put the existential dimension of literature back on the agenda. Literature is argued not only to represent conflicting values and meanings, but also to constitute the locus where these are offered up to reflection, debate, and held against counterfactual imagination. After the structuralist and poststructuralist approaches, which left many readers bewildered and wondering where their beloved books had gone, studies like Nussbaum's or Booth's seem written with much common sense: any cultivated reader can read them, and the moral concerns they tackle are close to those readers know from daily life. This is their strength, and their weakness. Deconstructive ethics, though desiring to set literature in the midst of real existential experience, questions precisely that "common" sense and the illusory immediacy of representation, and has as such an important critical role to play. But as with Nussbaum, with Gibson one wonders what literary works still can contribute to his preexisting moral or ethical insights, except illustrations. The danger of reductionism looms large in both cases. Any approach indeed is reductive, which, in defining the ethical dimension of literature, privileges either language as simply transitive and literature as offering a familiarization of the strange and clear moral guidance; or which, on the other hand, views language as radically intransitive, and literature as the experience of strangeness, of the absence of meaning, and of the evanescence of the self. Perhaps the only protection against reductiveness lies in a more principled openness to the *various* potential ethical functions and meanings of literary texts.

If we take literature's critical, utopian function seriously, if it is not to be reduced to convictions already held beforehand, then the importance of two practices cannot be underrated: the practice of debate—within oneself, and between readers—about represented ways of world-making; and the acquisition of the *aesthetic competence* needed for this debate. To end on an appropriately normative note, as no criticism in this field can escape its own normativeness: schools and universities as well as literary critics have an important task in exercising readers' aesthetic sense and analytical skills, indispensable for any ethical reading. Experience in the "careful teasing out of warring forces," as Barbara Johnson (1980, 5) aptly described it, is needed precisely in order to allow a critical assessment of literature as *Morallaboratorium*.[14]

Notes

1. In the Anglo-American context alone, see Alasdair McIntyre, *After Virtue—A Study in Moral Theory* (Notre-Dame: University of Notre-Dame Press, 1981); Martha Nussbaum, *The Fragility of Goodness. Luck and Ethics in Greek Tragedy and Philosophy* (Cambridge/New York: Cambridge University Press, 1986) and *Love's Knowledge. Essays on Philosophy and Literature* (New York/Oxford: Oxford University Press, 1990); John Hillis Miller, *The Ethics of Reading. Kant, De Man, Eliot, Trollope, James, and Benjamin* (New York: Columbia University Press, 1987); Wayne Booth, *The Company We Keep. An Ethics of Fiction* (Berkeley/Los Angeles/London: University of California Press, 1988); or Richard Rorty, *Contingency, Irony, and Solidarity* (Cambridge/New York: Cambridge University Press, 1989). A useful early survey is to be found in Tobin Siebers, *The Ethics of Criticism* (Ithaca/London: Cornell University Press, 1988).

2. See among others Simon Critchley, *The Ethics of Deconstruction. Derrida and Levinas* (Oxford, UK/Cambridge, USA: Blackwell, 1992); Jacques Derrida, *Acts of Lliterature*

(New York/London: Routledge, 1992); Robert Eaglestone, *Ethical Criticism*. *Reading after Levinas* (Edinburgh: Edinburgh University Press, 1997); Shoshana Felman and Dori Laub, *Testimony*. *Crises of Witnessing in Lliterature, Psychoanalysis, and History* (New York/London: Routledge, 1992); Andrew Gibson, *Postmodernity, Ethics, and the Novel*. *From Leavis to Levinas* (London/New York: Routledge, 1999); and Jerrold Levinson, ed., *Aesthetics and Ethics*. *Essays at the Intersection* (Cambridge: Cambridge University Press, 1998). See also note 4 about feminist ethics and literary criticism.

3. In continental Europe, the aestheticizing and political or historical approaches to literature seem to hold the ground, and the ethical appears much less an explicit concern. In France, though, it shows up in the philosophical reflection on literature of, for instance, Ricoeur, Blanchot, Levinas, Todorov, Irigaray, or Cixous (in these last two cases, from a feminist angle).

4. See for the notion of clarificationism, Noël Carroll, "Art, Narrative and moral Understanding," in *Aesthetics and Ethics: Essays at the Intersection*, ed. Jerrold Levinson (Cambridge: Cambridge University Press, 1998), 126–160. For a previous discussion of the ethical turn, focused also on Wayne Booth's and some deconstructivist approaches (Hillis Miller, Felman), see Liesbeth Korthals Altes, "Le tournant éthique dans la théorie littéraire: Impasse ou ouverture?" *Ethique et Littérature*, special issue of *Etudes Littéraires*, 31.3 (1999): 39–56 and *Le Salut par la fiction? Sens, valeurs et narrativité dans Le roi des aulnes de Michel Tournier* (Amsterdam: Rodopi, 1992).

5. For feminist ethical readings, see, for instance, Isobel Armstrong, "Writing from the Broken Middle: The Post-Aesthetic," *Women: A Cultural Review*, 9.1 (Spring 1998): 62–96; Seyla Benhabib, *Situating the Self: Gender, Community and Postmodernism in Contemporary Ethics* (New York: Routledge, 1992); or Luce Irigaray, *An Ethics of Sexual Difference*, trans. Carolyn Burke and Gillian C. Gill (Ithaca: Cornell University Press, 1993); or from a postcolonial perspective, Homi Bhabha, *The Location of Culture* (London: Routledge, 1994).

6. Gibson refers to a wide range of works by Emmanuel Levinas. Seminal however are *Totality and Infinity: An Essay on Exteriority*, trans. Alphonso Lingis (Pittsburgh: Duquesne University Press, 1992), *Otherwise than Being, or, Beyond Essence*, trans. Alphonso Lingis (Pittsburgh: Duquesne University Press, 1998 [1974]), or *Sur Maurice Blanchot* (Montpellier: Fata Morgana, 1975).

7. For Jean-Françoise Lyotard, Gibson refers mainly to *La condition postmoderne* (Paris: Minuit, 1979) *Moralités postmodernes* (Paris: Editions Galilée, 1993), and *Leçons sur l'analytique du sublime* (Paris: Galilée, 1991) as for Blanchot, among the many works he refers to, *The Unavowable Community*, trans. Pierre Joris (New York: Station Hill Press, 1988) plays an important role.

8. In his earlier *Towards a Postmodern Theory of Narrative* (Eidenburgh: Eidenburgh University, 1996) chapter 4, he already criticized the notions of voice, character, and reading subject for suggesting illusory coherence and unity.

9. From yet another—postcolonial—angle, Gibson argues in accordance with Homi Bhabha that literature gives us the experience of belonging to different spaces at the same time. It thus constructs "split-space identities," discovering to us our own intimate alterity.

10. Harpham's comment on the ethics of reading advocated by Hillis Miller, would be shared by Gibson: "the value of the text lies in its power to disabuse the reader precisely of all forms of edification and instruction that Murdoch, Nussbaum, MacIntyre prize so highly. The text as represented by Miller does not teach its readers . . . and certainly entails no appeal to community, but rather works to dissolve such notions as the conscious, freely willing, socialized ego," Geoffrey Galt Harpham, *Getting it Right: Language, Literature and Ethics* (Chicago/London: University of Chicago Press 1992, 49).

11. The images are significant: for Nussbaum literature and criticism contribute to making the world a "home," where individuals need "sharable answers."

12. See Thomasset's excellent study of Ricoeur's position in this respect in Alain Thomasset, *Paul Ricoeur. Une poétique de la morale. Aux fondements d'une éthique herméneutique et narrative dans une perspective chrétienne* (Louvain: Presses universitaires de Louvain, 1996).

13. See, for instance, Harpham, *Getting it Right* or Kearns (Lincoln: University of Necraska Press, 1999).

14. This notion was coined by the Austrian writer, a master of ambivalence and ethical reflection, Robert Musil, *Gesammelte Werke* (Hamburg: Rowohlt, 1978), VIII: 1351.

Works Cited

Armstrong, Isobel. "Writing from the Broken Middle: The Post-Aesthetic." *Women: A Cultural Review* 9.1 (Spring 1998): 62–96.

Bakhtin, Mikhail. *The Dialogic Imagination: Four Essays*. Trans. Caryl Emerson. Ed. M. Holquist. Austin, TX: University of Texas Press, 2001.

Bataille, Georges. *La littérature et le mal*. Paris: Gallimard, 1957.

Benhabib, Seyla. *Situating the Self: Gender, Community and Postmodernism in Contemporary Ethics*. New York: Routledge, 1992.

Bhabha, Homi. *The Location of Culture*. London: Routledge, 1994.

Booth, Wayne. *The Company We Keep. An Ethics of Fiction*. Berkeley/Los Angeles/London: University of California Press, 1988.

Bourdieu, Pierre. *The Field of Cultural Production: Essays on Art and Literature*. Cambridge: Polity Press, 1993.

Carroll, Noël. "Art, Narrative and Moral Understanding." In *Aesthetics and Ethics: Essays at the Intersection*. Ed. Jerrold Levinson. Cambridge: Cambridge University Press, 1998.

Cornell, Drucilla. *Beyond Accommodation: Ethical Feminism, Deconstruction and the Law*. London: Routledge, 1991.

———. *The Philosophy of the Limit*. London: Routledge, 1992.

Critchley, Simon. *The Ethics of Deconstruction. Derrida and Levinas*. Oxford, UK/Cambridge, USA: Blackwell, 1992.

Derrida, Jacques. "Violence et métaphysique. Essai sur la pensée d'Emmanuel Levinas." In *L'écriture et la différence*. Paris: Seuil, 1967.

———. *Acts of literature*. New York/London: Routledge, 1992.

Eaglestone, Robert. *Ethical Criticism. Reading after Levinas*. Edinburgh: Edinburgh University Press, 1997.

Felman, Shoshana, and Dori Laub. *Testimony. Crises of witnessing in Lliterature, Psychoanalysis, and History*. New York/London: Routledge, 1992.

Gibson, Andrew. *Towards a Postmodern Theory of Narrative*. Edinburgh: Edinburgh University Press, 1996.

———. *Postmodernity, Ethics, and The Novel. From Leavis to Levinas*. London/New York: Routledge, 1999.

Greimas, A.J. "Un problème de sémiotique narrative: les objets de valeur." *Langages* 31 (1973): 13–35.

Harpham, Geoffrey Galt. "Ethics." In *Critical Terms for Literary Study*. Ed. Frank Lentricchia. Chicago/London: University of Chicago Press, 1990.

———. *Getting it Right: Language, Literature and Ethics*. Chicago/London: University of Chicago Press, 1992.

———. *Shadows of Ethics. Criticism and the Just Society*. Durham/London: Duke University Press, 1999.

Hillis Miller, J. *The Ethics of Reading. Kant, De Man, Eliot, Trollope, James, and Benjamin*. New York: Columbia University Press, 1987.

Irigaray, Luce. *An Ethics of Sexual Difference*. Trans. Carolyn Burke and Gillian C. Gill. Ithaca: Cornell University Press, 1993.

Johnson, Barbara. *The Critical Difference: Essays in the Contemporary Rhetoric of Reading*. Baltimore: Johns Hopkins University Press, 1980.

Korthals Altes, Liesbeth. *Le Salut par la fiction? Sens, valeurs et narrativité dans Le roi des aulnes de Michel Tournier.* Amsterdam: Rodopi, 1992.

———. "Le tournant éthique dans la théorie littéraire: Impasse ou ouverture?" *Ethique et Littérature.* Special issue of *Etudes Littéraires* 31.3 (1999): 39–56.

Levinas, Emmanuel. *Sur Maurice Blanchot.* Montpellier: Fata Morgana, 1975.

———. *Otherwise than being, or, Beyond Essence.* Trans. Alphonso Lingis. Pittsburgh: Duquesne University Press, 1998.

———. *Totality and Infinity: An Essay on Exteriority.* Trans. Alphonso Lingis. Pittsburgh: Duquesne University Press, 1992.

Levinson, Jerrold. Ed. *Aesthetics and Ethics. Essays at the Intersection.* Cambridge: Cambridge University Press, 1998.

Lyotard, Jean-François. *Moralités postmodernes.* Paris: Editions Galilée, 1993.

McIntyre, Alisdair. *After Virtue—A Study in Moral Theory.* Notre-Dame: University of Notre-Dame Press, 1981.

Nussbaum, Martha. *The Fragility of Goodness. Luck and Ethics in Greek Tragedy and Philosophy.* Cambridge/New York: Cambridge University Press, 1986.

———. *Love's Knowledge. Essays on Philosophy and Literature.* New York/Oxford: Oxford University Press, 1990.

Palmer, Frank. *Literary and Moral Understanding: A Philosophical Essay on Ethics, Aesthetics, Education and Culture.* Oxford: Clarendon Press, 1992.

Ricoeur, Paul. *Du texte à l'action. Essais d'herméneutique, II.* Paris: Seuil, 1986.

———. *Soi-même comme un autre.* Paris: Seuil, 1990.

Rorty, Richard. *Contingency, Irony, and Solidarity.* Cambridge/New York: Cambridge University Press, 1989.

Siebers, Tobin. *The Ethics of Criticism.* Ithaca/London: Cornell University Press, 1988.

Suleiman, Susan R. *Le roman à thèse, ou l'autorité fictive.* Paris: Presses universitaires de France, 1983.

Taylor, Charles. *Sources of the Self: the Making of the Modern Identity.* Cambridge, MA: Harvard University Press, 1989.

Thomasset, Alain. *Paul Ricoeur. Une poétique de la morale. Aux fondements d'une éthique herméneutique et narrative dans une perspective chrétienne.* Louvain: Presses universitaires de Louvain, 1996.

Todorov, Tzvetan. *Critique de la critique: Un roman d'apprentissage.* Paris: Seuil, 1984.

Williams, Bernard. *Ethics and the Limits of Philosophy.* London: TS: Fontana/Collins, 1985.

PART 2

Reading and the Biblical

CHAPTER TWO

Only Irresponsible People would go into the Desert for Forty Days: Jim Crace's Quarantine Or the Diary of another Madman

DAVID JASPER

Introduction

Jim Crace's novel *Quarantine* (1997) revisits the story of the temptations of Jesus in the wilderness. It does not adhere closely to the gospel narratives, yet it has uncanny resonances with Scripture, with the stories of the fourth-century Desert Fathers and Mothers, and with modern texts and films concerned with the theme of the desert. The experience of desert brings the variety of this literature into a degree of coherence. Crace is not a theologian, nor is he directly interested in the traditions of Christian desert spirituality or theology. Yet his fiction echoes patterns familiar in those traditions and provides a new, sometimes uncomfortable starting place for religious thought and reflection, from within universal experience of what it is to be human in encounters with those outsiders "by whom the world is kept in being."

Key Words

Desert, Jesus, Desert Fathers, Scripture, fiction.

*   *   *

Within this essay[1] there resides a certain degree of irresponsibility at a
number of levels. Its subject is irresponsible acts, and its method is to
approach theological discourse and questions through the medium of
fiction. It was initially conceived as an element in a larger project with
the title "Theological Humanism" being pursued by scholars in the
United States and the United Kingdom, and part of its purpose is to
revisit issues of "truth" in fiction as well as the truth to be found in irresponsibility and its necessary importance for revealing the insanity of our
conventional categories of sanity and normality. For this reason I do not
expect it to please people in general, and it is not really intended to. You
don't go out from the normal and everyday to do something that cannot
be measured by its standards and expect people to be happy about it.
They will probably say you have lost it, or worse. But I do not want to
be melodramatic and I am not writing about me, or making excuses for
anything. My point is that sometimes you have to do crazy things in
order to make sense of the world. Jim Crace remarked in a lecture given
in the University of Iowa in 2003 that as a novelist his task is to make
things up, to work from his imagination and not simply from the data of
history, authoritative texts, or science.

In his fiction we boldly go where no one has gone before, and that
may involve strange encounters which we can find recounted in such
various places as the Bible, or the *Lives of the Desert Fathers*, or a modern
novel. Before the beginning of his ministry, Jesus went out alone into
the desert, we are told in the Gospels, and wrestled with Satan. In the
third-century CE, St. Antony of Egypt, according to the *Vita Antonii*,
reputedly written by St. Athanasius, gave away all his possessions, disappeared into the desert, and like many after him in Egypt, fought with
devils in the arid sands which were both inside him and outside. The
modern literature of the desert is enormous, and continues to tell the
same, bizarre story. I mean precisely the *desert* and not the *wasteland*. For
in the desert nothing is wasted, and all the literature of the desert of all
ages and traditions insists on its purity and its extremes which effectively
disintegrate categories of human measurement and normality. People
who go there must be mad, because you do not live in the desert—
deserts are for passing through and meeting other people, and demons,

on the way. They are, by definition, deserted and without inhabitants. But, perhaps for this reason they are clean, unlike wastelands, which are places of waste and human detritus. You might be in the desert for forty years or forty days, but you "come back" to the world of people in the end. Jesus of old came back and was baptized, cleansed, and ready for action and ministry. A modern American desert traveller, the irascible Edward Abbey, goes out "to meet God or Medusa face to face, even if it means risking everything human in myself. I dream [he says] of a hard and brutal mysticism. . . ." (Abbey 1992, 6) Another hard-bitten wanderer, the English explorer Sir Wilfred Thesiger, also wandered into the desert realm where theology might be the only resource left, writing how "hour after hour, day after day, we moved forward and nothing changed; the desert met the empty sky always the same distance ahead of us. Time and space were one. Round us was a silence in which only the winds played, and a cleanness which was infinitely remote from the world of men" (Thesiger 1991, 32). And what does this desert mean for the novelist, the armchair traveller who has never set foot, physically, on sand or stone? Read Gustav Flaubert's *The Temptation of St. Anthony* (1874), Cormac McCarthy's *Blood Meridian* (1985), or read Jim Crace's remarkable novel *Quarantine* (1997), which is a sort of revisiting of the story of Jesus' temptations, only it is not really Christian and in the end—well, in the end we are not sure what actually *happens*, its last sentence a mystery at once in and out of time: "Nor could he contemplate the endless movements on the trading road, the floods, the rifts, the troops, the ever-caravans, the evening peace that's brokered not by a god but by the rocks and clays themselves, *shalom, salaam,* the one-time, all-time truces of the land"(Crace 1998, 243).

"Quarantine," by the definition of the *Oxford English Dictionary*, is the period of time, originally forty days, during which persons who might spread a contagious disease (especially travellers) are kept apart and isolated. In Crace's novel four individuals, one woman and three men, go out into the desert to fast and pray that they might find and recover themselves. They are variously afflicted by infertility, cancer, and madness. A merchant, Musa, with his pathetic wife Miri, have been left in the desert by the caravan of traders, struggling with a terrible fever. And there is a fifth pilgrim, an idealistic youth from Galilee called Jesus, who had come to "encounter god or die, that was the nose and tail of it. That's why he'd come. To talk directly to his god. To let his god provide the water and the food. Or let the devil do its work. It would be a test for all three of them." (Crace 1998, 22). Crace prefaces his novel with a "scientific" observation that would seem to dismiss the claims of the gospel narratives that Jesus "fasted for forty days and forty nights, and afterwards he was famished." (Matthew 4:2. New Revised Standard Version):

> An ordinary man of average weight and fitness embarking on a total fast—that is, a fast during which he refuses both his food and drink—could not expect to live for more than thirty days, not to be conscious for more than twenty-five. For him, the forty days of fasting described in religious texts would not be achievable—except with divine help, of course. History, however, does not record an intervention of that kind, and medicine opposes it. (Winward and Soule 1993; Crace 1998, Preface)

The Jesus of Crace's novel is, in one sense, such an ordinary man—but one who defies nature's limitations, and is defeated. Or is he? He works miracles of healing—but then there are always miracles in the desert, which suspends normal categories of human experience. It is recorded that the Desert Fathers of Egypt in the fourth century all worked miracles, just as the Jesus of the Gospels worked miracles of healing, for that is what happens in the desert. It is quite usual. And in Crace's fiction there is no god and no real devil—only Musa, the merchant—a sadist, rapist, manipulator of lives lived in caves on the very edge of existence, where a drink of water is worth a fortune. And this is not the Jesus we know from the Gospels of Mark or Matthew, for this Jesus dies in his cave, as one would expect after such a rigorous fast. He is not like the Desert Fathers who lived for years on nothing, or St. Antony, who for twenty years lived in solitude, fed only twice a year with loaves and yet emerged from his prison like Lazarus from his tomb so that those who saw him "wondered at the sight for he had the same habit of body as before, and was neither fat, like a man without exercise, nor lean from fasting and striving with the demons, but he was just the same as they had known him before his retirement" (Athanasius 1991, 14). But this Jesus, this fictional Jesus, this page of Scripture:

> He was all surface, no inside. His leaf had fallen finally. He was a dry, discarded page of scripture now. . . . This was his final blasphemy. He begged the devil to fly up and save him from the wind. He'd almost welcome the devil more than god. For the devil can be traded with, and exorcized. But god is ruthless and unstable. No one can cast out god. It was too late. Jesus was already standing at the threshold to the trembling world which he had sought, where he would spend his forty everlasting days. So this was death. So this was pain made powerless. So this was fruit turned back into its seed.

Jesus was a voyager, at last, between the heavens and the earth. (Crace 1998, 193)

Crace's novel, like the desert itself, confuses the sense of what is interior and what is exterior. What is it about—a parable of the soul, or a narrative of seven crazy, human lives fighting for survival, for forgiveness, and for power? Is it a religious book, a book about religion, and an intertext of the gospel narratives, with which it plays? It is, perhaps all of these things. What is remarkable, given this background as a self-confessed work of fiction by Crace, is the book's capacity to evoke in the mind, and inside the mind, of the reader the harsh place of the desert, a real place of scrubland, and heat and unforgiving rocks, which is at the same time a place of retreat from the "real" world. The desert in this novel is a place to be entered into, an interior where battles are fought with the self against real devils and there is nothing, for all is a negation—even, and especially, its pitiless God. The book is remarkable for its unity with the great tradition of desert literature, from the scriptural Pentateuch, to the records of the lives of the Desert Fathers, the *Historia Monachorum in Aegypto* of the fourth-century CE, to (leaping the millennia) T.E. Lawrence's *Seven Pillars of Wisdom* (1935). They are all, in their different ways, stories of crazy people. When Crace's Jesus dies there is "no god, no gardens, just the wind." Lawrence also felt that same wind. In a famous passage early in *The Seven Pillars* he is led to a ruin in North Syria, dating from Roman times, where, at an opening in the wall he and his companions

drank with open mouths of the effortless, empty, eddyless wind of the desert, throbbing past. That slow breath had been born somewhere beyond the distant Euphrates and had dragged its way across many days and nights of dead grass, to its first obstacle, the man-made walls of our broken palace. About them it seemed to fret and linger, murmuring its baby-speech. "This," they told me, "is the best: it has no taste." (Lawrence 1935, 38)

The wind, or in Hebrew *ruach*, spirit: it carries nothing and is nothing, the biblical still small voice. And for Lawrence, at once despised and admired by the critic Edward Said as an extreme form of the decentred life, the desert provokes in all its dwellers an extreme form of the religious life (Said 2001, 32). Lawrence wrote of his Arab companions with characteristic lack of restraint:

His [the Arab's] sterile experience robbed him of compassion and perverted his human kindness to the image of the waste in which he hid. Accordingly he hurt himself, not merely to be free, but to please himself. There followed a delight in pain, a cruelty which was more to him than goods. The desert Arab found no joy like the joy of voluntarily holding back. He found luxury in abnegation, renunciation, self-restraint. He saved his own soul, perhaps, and without danger, but in a hard selfishness. (Lawrence 1935, 39–40)

This is a description of desert religion (it does not matter *which* religious tradition it is—it probably never does) which echoes frequently in the lives of the Desert Fathers and Mothers—those weird men and women of the fourth century of the Christian era who wandered off into the Egyptian, Syrian, and Judean deserts and fought their demons in extremes of asceticism and self-denial. How can this be said—that these saintly people are to be likened to Lawrence's cruel desert Arab? Was not St. Antony a friend of the great Bishop St. Athanasius, the scourge of the Arian heretics? Was not Evagrius a pupil of the great Christian scholar Origen and did not John Cassian bring monasticism out of the Eastern desert into France and the West? In the Prologue to the *Historia Monachorum in Aegypto* it is said of the monks that they are indeed "true servants of God [and] while dwelling on earth . . . they live as true citizens of heaven," and that "it is clear to all who dwell there that through them the world is kept in being, and that through them too human life is preserved and honoured by God" (Russell 1981, 50). What at the same time is clear, however, is that the records and narratives we have of the early desert monks and hermits, although contemporary with their subjects, are highly tempered, romanticized, and theologized writings. These saintly fathers and mothers were rough and could sometimes be cruel. Indeed, it has been said that the quest for the historical lives of these men and women through these early literary records is as problematic as the quest for the historical Jesus through the gospel traditions—and for much the same reasons. What we have are lives filtered through the traditions of Christian theology, spirituality, and ethics, and in particular, through the life of the Church, so that their desert becomes a place of community, or in Derwas Chitty's phrase drawn from the *Vita Antonii*, Chapter 14, the desert a city. In a sense this was the opposite of the apostolic move out of and beyond the city (Acts 1:8) into a world where the Christian has no abiding city (Sheldrake 2001, 33 ff.). And in all other literature of the desert it is also almost always a place for solitaries, for wanderers who seek not to abide, or for eccentrics, or people seeking cleanness or escape from the social world of cities. And so, I regard such works as the *Historia Monachorum* as essentially "fiction," though fiction which became translated into a way of life (like the Gospels themselves) as people gathered together and invented desert communities and the desert became precisely what its earliest monkish inhabitants had fled from—"home" and a place of cities.

So, what I am suggesting as I begin to work back toward Jim Crace's novel *Quarantine*, is a curious kind of reversal. Early accounts of the Desert Fathers in works like the *Vita Antonii*, the *Historia Monachorum*, or Palladius' *Lausiac History* (*c.* 419 CE) are narratives of historical fiction interpreted through Christian theology (though undoubtedly some of these early monks themselves did engage in theological debate, even on an international scale), and literary illustrations of Christian experience indicated, as in the gospels and the books of the New Testament canon, through miracle, parabolic sayings, and apocalyptic vision. On the miracle stories of the desert, one modern commentator, Sister Benedicta Ward, in her Introduction to *The Lives of the Desert Fathers*, makes my point quite clearly:

> It is . . . possible and very profitable to examine these miracles *in their literary form*, in order to see what they are intended to say and to form some idea of the approach to such matters in the minds of both the writers and of the participants of these events. . . . They illustrate the *virtus* of the monks, and place them directly in the line of the biblical revelation of the power of God. (Russell 1981, 39, emphases added)

In other words, these exotic narratives of the desert are constructed as interpretations of the lives of these strange exiles, from the tradition and perspective of their biblical antecedents. These Fathers, we are told, "raised the dead and walk on the water like *Peter*." The holy man Apollo and his companions are visited by an angel in prison, an incident described almost exactly like the visitation of an angel to Peter in prison in Acts 12:7–10 (71). The sun stood still for Father Patermuthius, as it did for Gideon (84). The rough lives of these Fathers and Mothers come to us, I would argue, in the literary form which Douglas Templeton in his book *The New Testament as True Fiction* has used to describe the gospels themselves, as "true fiction." This is not to dispute their "truth," but it does raise the question, what does it mean for fiction to be true, and might a different fiction, different typologies, different metaphors, reveal a different yet still coherent and valid truth which does not contradict difference?

For these literary lives of the Desert Fathers of the Christian Church participate not only in literary traditions of Scripture itself, but also in the

larger and wider traditions of desert literature. These, also, are traditions of
miracle and of deep religiosity born of lives lived on the edge of bodily
possibility between flesh and spirit, of mirage and vision, of loneliness and
community, of harshness and necessary kindness, of a yearning for pure
water springs and verdant gardens, of wandering and meeting, of *praxis*
and *theoria*. Such things link the fathers Antony, Evagrius, Macarius, and
Patermuthius with Jim Crace's strange fictional group of travellers and
mystics, who are also obsessed with sex, water, and purity. But the difference is that the one group is, one might argue, a necessary fiction which
somehow validates the desert through the abiding consolations of
Christian theology and belief, while the other, in a modern novel, delicately deconstructs such consolations, blurring their definitions and clarity
in the heat haze of a different vision which just might, but certainly does
not inevitably, invalidate what has gone before. For in the desert nothing
is ever lost—its dry heat and sand are the best of preservatives—yet to gaze
into its sun is not to see but to be blinded to our world, like Saul as he was
blinded on the road to Damascus, only to see more clearly as a result.

At the beginning of *Quarantine* the reader (never forget, dear reader,
that as you read this is a purely literary experience; the heat you feel is
pure fiction, entirely inside your head) is introduced to the vile merchant
Musa and his dutiful wife Miri after they have been abandoned in the
desert by their caravan fearful of his fever. For

> a devil had slipped into his open mouth at night and built a fire
> beneath the rafters of his ribs. Devils were like anybody else; they had
> to find what warmth they could or perish in the desert cold. Now
> Musa had provided lodging for the devil's fever. (Crace 1998, 2)

The devil of sickness is inside Musa, or perhaps Musa *is* the devil. Or is
he merely a grasping, unscrupulous merchant and desert brigand who
will exercise his power over any helpless victim who falls into his path—
a pure monster of greed and sexual appetite? When the film maker Pier
Paolo Pasolini realized the narrative of Matthew 4:1–11 in his film *Il
Vangelo secondo Matteo* (1964), he portrayed Satan as this Musa, a grubby,
ordinary man who catches people foolish enough to travel into the des-
olation at their weakest and most dependent. The demons of the
Christian Fathers would come to their victims taunting and tempting
them with succulent food and cool drink, while they sought ascetic
purity. So does Musa to his victims, for, he says, "there's nothing like a
desert water-hole for making good, brief neighbours out of animals that
have nothing much in common other than a thirst" (49). But neighbors
soon quarrel and become jealous, and Musa is an expert in the policy of

divide and rule. Only the strange, idealistic Galilean Jesus (with all the crazy idealism of youth) keeps himself apart, a stubborn child who neither drinks nor sleeps the more thirsty and tired he becomes. (Like another selfish, selfless, decentered prophetic figure, Lawrence of Arabia, he could be best described as "different." It is the word used by the character of Lawrence in David Lean's 1962 film *Lawrence of Arabia* to describe himself to his Arab guide). Jesus miraculously heals Musa by his touch, for Crace, like Pasolini in his film, neither avoids nor explains the miraculous in the desert. By the end of the story, this Jesus has followed to the letter the ascetic discipline of the Desert Fathers.

> His fast had made him ready. Perhaps he had served his thirty days just to be equipped for the wind. Quarantine had been the perfect preparation for his death. His body was quiescent and reduced; dry, sapless, transparent almost, ready to detach itself from life without complaint. A wind this strong could pluck him like a leaf, and sweep him upwards to the palaces and gardens that angels tended in the stars. (Crace 1998, 191)

He was ready to be another rider in the chariot, to fly to the garden paradise that all desert dwellers dream of. And in the end does he die pointlessly in the cave, while the other travellers, more sensible, have fought their battles with Musa and returned to their homes and normality, a little wiser and perhaps more human at the end of their quarantine of forty days? It is Musa, the defeated devil, though a survivor in this world, who sees the final vision, after Jesus has been buried, dead and done with.

> Musa looked towards the distant scree again. He told himself this was no merchant fantasy. His Gally was no longer thin and watery, diluted by the mirage heat, distorted by the ripples in the air. He made his slow, painstaking way, naked and bare-footed, down the scree, his feet blood-red from wounds, and as he came closer to the valley floor his outline hardened and his body put on flesh.
> Musa raised his arm in greeting, but there was no response. (Crace 1998, 243)

Like St. Antony, like Lazarus, like another Jesus from another text, Jesus here seems to emerge miraculously from his tomb in bodily splendour, though with the marks of wounds on his feet. Or is this just a mirage upon mirage—a double miracle of desert seeing? Certainly this young lunatic had somehow effected a justice, god knows how, for the travellers are shriven and the devil is defeated, though he, of course, survives, unrepentant, to fight another day.

Quarantine is fiction. Like all literature, it plays with other texts and fictions that have influenced it, consciously or unconsciously. It is part of the literature of the desert, neither outside nor inside, and it tells a story which is another rewrite of an ancient story. As a fiction it delicately unpicks and even deconstructs the interpreted lives of the desert saints, who themselves followed the believed-in fictions of the gospels, and find their way to us in the West through the writings and practice of John Cassian, St. Benedict, and the long story of Western monasticism. But, since this is a novel, we are not asked to believe this story except in the literary sense, and yet its effect is strangely familiar to those of us accustomed to the Christian narratives of repentance, temptation, asceticism, resurrection, forgiveness. We perhaps continue to waste our time reading in the make-believe world of this fiction because it is again the old story of one "by whom the world is kept in being," who acts irresponsibly for no possible good purpose or reason. It is a story of the mysterious work of grace.

Note

1. An earlier and shorter version of this essay was published in the author's book *The Sacred Desert: Religion, Literature, Art, and Culture* (Oxford: Blackwell, 2004).

Works Cited

Abbey, Edward. *Desert Solitaire: A Season in the Wilderness*. London: Robin Clark, 1992.

Athanasius, St. Vita Antonii (c. 360). "A Select Library of Nicene and Post-Nicene Fathers of the Christian Church." Vol. IV. *Selected Works and Letters*. Ed. Philip Schaff and Henry Wace. Edinburgh: T & T Clark, 1991.

Chitty, Derwas. *The Desert a City: An Introduction to the Study of Egyptian and Palestinian Monasticism under the Christian Empire*. New York: St. Vladimir's Seminary Press, 1999.

Crace, Jim. *Quarantine*. London: Penguin Books, 1998.

Flaubert, Gustave. *The Temptations of St. Anthony*. Trans. Lafcadio Hearn. New York: Modern Library, 2001.

Lawrence, T.E. *The Seven Pillars of Wisdom*. Vol. 1. London: World Books, 1935.

Mc Carthy, Cormac. *Blood Meridian: Or, The Evening Redness in the West*. London: Picador, 1989.

Russell, Norman (translated). *The Lives of the Desert Fathers (Historia Monachorum)*. Kalamazoo: Cistercian Publications, 1981.

Said, Edward. *Reflections on Exile and Other Literary and Cultural Essays*. London: Granta Books, 2001.

Sheldrake, Philip. *Spaces for the Sacred: Place, Memory and Identity*. London: SCM Press, 2001.

Templeton, Douglas. *The New Testament as True Fiction: Literature, Literary Criticism, Aesthetics*. Sheffield: Sheffield Academic Press, 1999.

Thesiger, Edward. *Arabian Sands*. London: Penguin Books, 1991.

Winward, Ellis, and Professor Michael Soule. *The Limits of Mortality*. New Jersey: Eco Press, 1993.

CHAPTER THREE

The Ethics of Biblical Interpretation: Rhetoricizing the Foundations

ROBERT J. HURLEY

Introduction

Historically, biblical ethics dealt with the question of what the Bible has to say about right living and moral decision making. Given that the same texts yield a variety of ethical stances, the basis upon which ethical conclusions are specifiable has come into question. Text-centred interpretive paradigms understand meaning to be predetermined; the task of interpreters being to recover *the* meaning embedded in the text. More recently, exegetes have begun to look to the culture, economics, and politics of readers as keys to understanding the ethical dimensions involved in the interpretive act itself. Attention has shifted from the past to the present, from the context of production to the contexts of reception. Scholars have also begun to consider the effects that a given reading may produce, from an ethical perspective, on the historical situation into which it is received. This essay examines the contribution of a few scholars working in the area, paying particular attention to the work of Elizabeth Schüssler Fiorenza. While Schüssler Fiorenza's conclusions are sound and insightful, I believe she ultimately undercuts her own argument by refusing to complete the move away from essentialist hermeneutics. She incorrectly categorizes all postmodern thinkers into a homogenous group bent on the "relativizing proliferation of meaning"; a charge, which if true, might indeed be at odds with the goals of political activism. My response to this charge is inspired by the anti-foundationalist rhetoric of Stanley Fish who argues forcefully in favor of political activism.

Key Words

Ethics Interpretive paradigms, reader-centred versus text-centred criticism, social location, politics, Elizabeth Schüssler Fiorenza, rhetoric, neo-Pragmatism, Stanley Fish, androcentrism, foundationalism, anti-foundationalism.

★   ★   ★

Until recently, research dealing with biblical ethics has dealt almost exclusively with the question of what the Bible has to say about right living and moral decision making.[1] Since the same texts have yielded a variety of ethical stances depending upon the historical circumstances in which they are interpreted, the question has arisen as to the basis upon which ethical conclusions are specifiable. From divine inspiration to the canons of "unbiased" scientific description, the assumption of most paradigms for interpreting Holy Writ is that the ethics under investigation are in some sense an attribute of the biblical text itself, and as such, have already been determined at the time the text was written. Interpreters, by whatever method of extraction, need only busy themselves with recovering the deposited meaning.

Exegetes now look to culture, economics, and politics as keys to understanding the ways in which meaning in general and ethics in particular are construed during the interpretive act. Attention has shifted from the context of production to the contexts of reception, as scholars consider the influences exerted by the social, cultural, and political location of the reader. Language in these models of analysis is understood, either tacitly or explicitly, as a form of power. In addition to drawing attention to factors that constrain biblical interpretation prior to the interpretive act, a call has been heard to consider the effects that a given reading may produce, from an ethical perspective, on the historical situation into which it is received.

In what follows, I examine the contribution of a few scholars working in the area, paying particular attention to the work of Elizabeth Schüssler Fiorenza. While I agree with the inspiration of Schüssler Fiorenza's work and with most of her conclusions, I believe that in the end she undercuts her own argument by refusing to follow the argument for a rhetorical stance to its persuasive conclusion. Motivated by her desire to stand in solidarity with those struggling against the poisoned legacy of a colonial past, She refuses to make the move away from essentialist hermeneutics; a decision that prevents her from fully embracing a hermeneutics of persuasion and faith.

Changing Paradigms

E. Schüssler Fiorenza recently examined the ethical stance of four interpretive models operating in the field of biblical studies.[2] The paradigms examined include; the following: (1) the doctrinal-fundamentalist; (2) the scientific-positivist; (3) the (postmodern cultural); and (4) the rhetorical-emancipatory. Some years earlier, Fernando Segovia had already charted the use of four similar paradigms, albeit using a different nomenclature.[3] Each of these models are discussed as I situate my own contribution to the debate surrounding the ethics of biblical interpretation.

Neoconservative Christians from a variety of fundamentalist movements subscribe to the doctrinal-fundamentalist paradigm, which insists on a literalist reading of Scripture understood both as factual truth and will of God. These readers tend to depoliticize the biblical message and spiritualize the current global crisis of injustice in which the necessities of life and happiness are denied to the majority of the world's population. Rejecting religious tolerance and pluralism and insisting on the subordination of women as natural and ordained by God, fundamentalists promise religious security, a certainty of faith, and a clear-cut identity in an ever-changing and conflictive world.[4]

The scientific-positivist paradigm of historical exegesis was established by scholars seeking to free themselves from doctrinal prejudices in biblical interpretation. This approach emerged against the backdrop of several heresy trials, a legacy which explains its continued rejection of all overt religious, sociopolitical, and theological engagement as unscientific.[5] Seeking to establish historical study of the Bible as an academic discipline capable of establishing the single true meaning of the text, these biblical critics tended and tend to perceive the biblical era as fundamentally alien to modern people and assert a deep chasm between the past and the present. One of the overarching assumptions in the positivistic paradigm of historical biblical scholarship is the notion that the work of exegesis consists of a recovery of the thoughts of the author and therefore with a flow of ideas from the past to the present.

Many newer forms of formalist (text-centred) criticism fit the scientific-positivist paradigm as well in that they do little more than shift the foundations of epistemological surety from the empirical data of history to the seemingly objective forms and structures of the text. As with the historical model of exegesis, information in the formalist model flows from text to reader with little or no recognition of the reader's essential contribution to the production of meaning in the reading event. In both the author and text-centered paradigms, influences from the world of the exegete are frowned upon as unscientific contamination, as impairing the emotional, intellectual, and political detachment required for obtaining results that are objective, reliable, and "repeatable."

Even a cursory examination of the results of biblical scholarship last century, however, reveals the remarkable degree to which scientific exegesis has proved inescapably value-laden. Daniel Patte characterizes the so-called neutral practices of the scientific model as both Eurocentric and *androcentric*[6] while Schüssler Fiorenza impugns positivist theory as *scientistic*. Her neologism intends to expose the supposedly value-neutral and objective discourse of science as simply a form of rhetoric behind which positivistic methods hide as they legitimate the existing structures of oppression.[7] Inquiry which is unaware of its own presuppositions and oblivious to the impact its results will have in the context in which they are released is not genuinely scientific at all.

Positivist paradigms of both the historical and formalist variety have come under attack over the last decade by theoreticians who have effectively undermined the very foundations not only of biblical criticism but of all scientific description. A growing number of theorists and practitioners have taken the *linguistic turn* and recognize that all scientific observation and interpretation is subject to the conventional and therefore provisional character of language. This theoretical position undercuts claims to a possible truth of correspondence between linguistic constructions and a world once thought to be knowable independent of those linguistic constructions.[8] Knowledge of the world or, for that matter, of ourselves seems to be ineluctably tied up with language; and in one sense, one might even say that the world comes into existence, becomes an object of knowledge, at the moment we begin to speak about it.

Since words do not refer directly to objects that exist in the world but rather to a linguistic system,[9] the notion that description of any sort can be entirely accurate, in the sense that it would be grounded in the object itself, comes undone. Mikhail Bakhtin expresses a similar idea in *Discourse in the Novel*:

> The direct word, as traditional stylistics understands it, encounters in its orientation toward the object only the resistance of the object

itself . . . but it does not encounter in its path toward the object the fundamental and richly varied opposition of another's word. No one hinders it, no one argues with it. But no living word relates to its object in a *singular* way: between the word and its object, between the word and the speaking subject, there exists an elastic environment of other alien words about the same object, the same theme . . . Indeed, any concrete discourse (utterance) finds the object at which it was directed already as it were overlain with qualifications, open to dispute, charged with value, already enveloped in an obscuring mist—or, on to the contrary, by the "light" of alien words that have already been spoken about it. It is entangled, shot through with shared thoughts, points of view, alien value judgments and accents.[10]

Methods such as reader–response criticism, poststructuralist literary analyses, and semiotics understand that texts, far from being univocal, can produce a plurality of readings. Certain versions of these methods proceed upon an anti-foundationalist tack as they accept the argument that scientific inquiry cannot ground its claims to objectivity either on the independence of observational data (so T. Kuhn, M. Heidegger) or on the existence of a scientific language (so S. Fish), either of which might allow scientists to communicate their results in a value-free way. Exegesis takes place within a methodological framework and, like all inquiry, remains always and unavoidably theory-laden and limited in perspective; and this remains true whether the exegete is aware of the epistemological underpinnings of his or her work or not.[11] Within this paradigm, feminist theologians and liberation theologians have been particularly deft in pointing out just how the social, cultural, political, and economic location of male researchers from affluent societies have determined the kinds of questions we ask of the biblical text as well as the kinds of prejudice we bring to the text.[12]

The Power of Language

For theologians and exegetes who make no effort to hide the "interested" character of their research, there is a danger that we get bogged down in a quagmire of epistemological foundations, unable to move forward or backward to the question of the effects produced by language. By "effects," I mean the rhetorical power of language to move people to change old habits of thought and action.

If language is a closed system cut off from direct contact with a world outside language, we may, with Jacques Derrida, be tempted to see all linguistic interaction as a series of games that refer to nothing but themselves.[13] If the power of language to produce effects is not taken seriously, justice in areas of food distribution, work, education, and health care, and freedom from sexual, racial, ethnic, and academic discrimination may be examined chiefly as linguistic phenomena. *Hunger*, as a word, may indeed refer first to the English language, but most of us understand that the effects of hunger even on nonlanguage-bearing animals produce effects every bit as devastating as those experienced by starving humans. When we suffer, we will of course want to move beyond the idea of language as our only way of reflecting upon our situation, if indeed we have the luxury of reflecting long on anything except the misery in which we find ourselves. We will naturally seek out that particular use of language that will allow us to put an end to our distress.

While the very genius of postmodern thought is tied up with an unavoidable anti-foundationalist reflection, intellectuals risk losing touch with the power of language to shape the physical, social, and economic worlds in which we live and thus of losing sight of the real effects our discourse produces on those who languish at the margins of the global economy and who have no voice in decision making. It is interesting to note that the term "Gospel" was originally part of the rhetoric of a succession of Roman Caesars who announced the *good news* of imperial salvation to those who managed to survive their imperial conquest.[14] This word and several other political terms (for example *faith, justice, peace, parousia,* and *apantesis*) were co-opted by subversive writers like Paul who were trying to direct a word of liberation and hope at the despised underclasses whose very status was essential to the functioning of the pyramidal social structure of the Roman system.[15] Politically interested exegesis remains interested in the question of an *euangelion* for the victims of empire, the central question being how to put exegesis at the service of the liberation of the modern-day counterparts of those whom Paul refers to as the weak.

Neo-pragmatism may offer a way of avoiding an impasse in anti-foundationalist reflection. Thinkers such as Stanley Fish and Richard Rorty do not look to the past for essentialist clues to the meaning of discourse, but direct their attention to the future and to the effects produced by language as a way of determining meaning. I return to the neo-pragmatists a little later but for now I introduce the fourth and final interpretive paradigm which Schüssler Fiorenza describes as still in the process of emerging.

The rhetorical-emancipatory paradigm "inaugurates not just a hermeneutic-scientific but an ethical-political turn."[16] Other names considered for the model were the pastoral-theological, the liberationist-cultural, the rhetorical-ethical, and the rhetorical-political.[17] Whatever its name,

> this fourth paradigm seeks to redefine the self-understanding of biblical scholarship in ethical, rhetorical, political, cultural, emancipatory terms and to understand the scholar in religion as a public, "transformative," connected, or integrated intellectual who is able to communicate with a variegated public with the goal of personal, social and religious transformation for justice and well-being [for everyone].[18]

My own position fits well into the rhetorical-emancipatory paradigm thus described and I highly recommend Schüssler Fiorenza's book *Rhetoric and Ethic: The Politics of Biblical Studies* for its lively and creative introduction to the most important issues currently being discussed in the ethics of biblical interpretation. Like hers, my position

1. proceeds from a politically and theologically inspired perspective;[19]
2. is "energized and compelled by marginalized discourses and minority theories";
3. renounces claims to positivistic objectivity and neutrality of the sort claimed by biblical scholars whose main interest proves antiquarian;
4. seeks to elucidate the ethical consequences and political functions of biblical texts and their interpretations,[20] identifying not only contemporary structures of domination but also those inscribed in biblical texts;[21]
5. reads with the victims of poverty, of sexism and misogyny, racism, religious exclusion, heterosexism, and colonialism in mind;[22]
6. believes that biblical studies should be advanced as a form of public discourse,[23] which makes the public character and political responsibility an integral part of its contemporary readings and historical reconstructions.[24]

Schüssler Fiorenza offers a brilliant list of elements which biblical studies, as a public discourse should attempt to do:[25]

- Explicitly reflect on its sociopolitical religious location and ideological functions;
- Understand biblical discourses as inscriptions of struggle and reconstruct them as public debates of the *ekklesia*;

- Identify the languages of hate and the death-dealing ideologies inscribed in the Scriptures;
- Identify biblical visions and values that would contribute to a radical democratic understanding of society and religion;
- Explore cultural practices such as film, music, or art and their use of the Bible;
- Foster an understanding of biblical authority that allows for the questioning of the text in a critical practice of the discernment of the Spirit;
- Create public discourses and debates that could intervene in the discourses of the religious right and other antidemocratic groups;
- Refashion biblical education in such a way that it engenders scholars and religious leaders who are critical public intellectuals.

The Promise of Neo-Pragmatism

Despite these wide areas of agreement, however, some notable differences distinguish our positions. While Schüssler Fiorenza describes her position as "conversant with postmodernism" even though "it does not derive its inspiration from post-modern debates,"[26] my own position understands the anti-foundationalist challenge to the ontological stability of author, text, and reader to be central to a discussion of the ethics of interpretation. All three elements in this triad have been variously deconstructed in recent years. The very need for a "rhetorical" model, it seems to me, is a consequence of the destabilization of metaphysical dualism which provided the philosophical grounding for the idea that the knowing subject could assume a critical distance from the object of knowledge. That all knowledge is necessarily personal knowledge and that it is subject to the historical limits of the knower and the constraints of language as a conventional means of communication is now a widely accepted interpretive principle. In anti-foundationalism, the distance separating the knower and the object, imagined possible in the Enlightenment, has collapsed. Knowledge is always linked to people of a particular time and place and, short of death, it remains an illusion to imagine we can separate ourselves from the objects of our study in such a way as to provide a value-free, perspective-free description of them.

Schüssler Fiorenza's radical solidarity with those at the political and social margins of the world leads her to an à la carte approach to the postmodern.

In contrast to post-modern criticism, the voices from the margins of biblical studies insist that the colonialized others cannot afford to abandon the notion of the subject and the possibility of knowing the world differently. Rather, they insist that the subordinated others must engage in a political and theoretical process of constituting themselves as subjects of knowledge and history.[27]

I believe it would be a mistake to lump all postmodern thinkers into a group of defeatists who oppose political activism. In fact, it is a mistake to maintain that anti-foundationalists claim that there are no truths that hold across cultures that would allow for such activism. In his book *Doing What Comes Naturally*, Stanley Fish, an American neo-pragmatist, contends that this kind of argument proceeds from false premises:

> it mistakes the nature of the anti-foundationalist claim, which is not that there are no foundations, but that whatever foundations there are (and there are always some) have been established by persuasion, that is, in the course of argument and counter-argument on the basis of examples and evidence that are themselves cultural and contextual. Anti-foundationalism, then, is a thesis about how foundations emerge, and in contradistinction to the assumptions that foundations do not emerge but simply *are*, anchoring the universe and thought from a point above history and culture, it says that foundations are local and temporal phenomena and are always vulnerable to challenges from other localities and times. This vulnerability also extends, of course, to the anti-foundationalist thesis itself, and that is why its assertion does not involve a contradiction, as it would if what was being asserted was the impossibility of foundational assertion; . . . anti-foundationalism can without contradiction include itself under its own scope and await the objections one might make to it; and so long as those objections are successfully met and turned back by those who preach anti-foundationalism (a preaching and a turning back I am performing at this moment), anti-foundationalism can be asserted as absolutely true since (at least for the time being) there is no argument that holds the field against it.[28]

In *Is There a Text in This Class?*, Fish had already explained that his goal was not to rule out the possibility of a true reading.

> The business of criticism, in other words, was not to decide between interpretations by subjecting them to the test of disinterested evidence but to establish by political and persuasive

means . . . the set of interpretive assumptions from the vantage of which the evidence . . . will hereafter be specifiable.[29]

Fish preserves the possibility of arriving at truth in language by rhetoricizing it. In the absence of a single truth, communities and their agents will have to enter the *polis*, the *ekklesia*, and seek to have their voices heard. This position assumes, of course, that all have access to the *ekklesia*.

Beyond her rejection of the deconstructed self, Schüssler Fiorenza rejects other concepts commonly associated with postmodern criticism. Even as she welcomes a plurality of readings, she introduces such notions as "legitimate" interpretation and finds a basis for evaluating the legitimacy of a particular reading either in the historical context of the text's production or in the form and structures of the text. "Texts have a surplus of meaning that can never be fully mined," she affirms at one point.[30] In other words, meaning is an attribute of the text. I, on the other hand, would argue that neither authorial intent nor formal features but rather the reader in his or her particular historical circumstances is the source of the surplus of meaning that has normally been associated with the text. Different communities produce similar but different texts when confronted with an identical arrangement of ink on paper. *Text* should be understood in this context not as a static object but as a dynamic, meaning-forging event.

Elsewhere Schüssler Fiorenza writes:

> An ethics of critical reading changes the task of interpretation from finding out "what the text meant" to the question of what kind of readings can do justice to the text in its historical context. Although such an ethics is aware of the plurality of historical- and literary-critical methods as well as the plurality of interpretations appropriate to the text, it nevertheless insists that the number of interpretations that can legitimately be given to a text are limited.[31]

Again the notion of legitimate interpretation assumes that the criteria for judging legitimacy preexist the reading of the text in a community. Now legitimacy, in the form of objectivity, is precisely what positivist exegesis is concerned with bestowing, using the canons of historical or formalist interpretation as a yardstick. It seems to me that Schüssler Fiorenza cannot have it both ways. Thanks to the way in which anti-foundationalists have undermined the foundations of the self—of both author and reader—and of the text, the truth and legitimacy of any and all interpretation issuing from even the most rigorous method are debatable.

Schüssler Fiorenza attacks scientism and *kyriarchy*[32] (a broader, less gender-based notion than patriarchy) by attacking the truth-of-correspondence theory upon which their claims to scientific objectivity and power are based. One cannot rationally destroy the truth-of-correspondence theory for language in general and then proceed as if the "self" existed independently of language. Because the self is constantly emerging from a language, which is not its property but upon which it is dependent for its flickering presence, it cannot be bracketed in epistemological arguments under the claim that it is somehow a special case. This lapse of logic unnecessarily imperils Schüssler Fiorenza's otherwise convincing argument.

Legitimacy, like meaning, is a function of reception rather than one of correlation with some preexisting standard, be it authorial intent or formal features. With Fish, I would argue that meaning is held neither within the text nor with the author who put ink to paper, but with the reader in the world where the text-event occurs. Textual meaning is construed during an event which emerges as a result of the poïetic activity of the reader with ink and paper that has been arranged in a predictable manner using recognizable linguistic and literary conventions at many different levels. In this sense the flow of meaning during the reading event is not from author to reader or text to reader but from reader to text. The reader is in this sense writing the text as she reads it.

If the reader does not know the language well (Hebrew, Greek, Aramaic, etc.), if he or she is unaware of certain literary conventions (e.g., chiasm or apocalypse), of hints of the presence of irony, of the play of intertextuality, of the levels of story and discourse and so forth, the reader will have a different experience from the exegete who has a long experience with ancient texts and has developed competencies in the appropriate areas. Only if the conventions that produced the text are still in effect (that is to say *known*) in the tradition into which the text is received, will the reader be able to assume convincingly the place of the author in the creation of the text-event.

An example may prove useful here. Genre is one such literary convention that governs both the composition and interpretation of texts. Frank Kermode describes it as a state of expectation, "an internal probability system" that helps one comprehend a sentence, book, or life.[33] E.D. Hirsch understands it to be a sort of *contract* or agreement, often unspoken if not unconscious, between an author and a reader, which allows the author to write according to a set of expectations and conventions and the reader to interpret what was written according to those same conventions, thereby giving the reader a way of predicting what is likely to come up next in a given type of text.[34]

Beyond a mastery of techniques and conventions, reading is more than a way of organizing material. When a method helps readers pay attention to what is happening to them throughout the reading experience, reading can then become a way of transforming minds.[35] This is precisely what the affective stylistics of Stanley Fish attempt to do.

Although the notion of objectivity has been set aside in the paradigm of neo-pragmatism, the subjectivity which emerges is far from a solipsistic individualism. On Fish's understanding, which I share, readers do not construe meaning in an arbitrary manner but act as the agents of the interpretive communities from which they emerge. Language is not simply a mechanical system for encoding and decoding information, it is shot through with values and perspectives that represent the interests of the community which uses it. Interpretive communities are of course as unstable and evolving as the subjects of which they are comprised.

The reader is thus constrained in many more ways than by requirements related to grammar, language, literary devices, and the like. Not only will the reader not pay attention to a literary form or stylistic convention he does not know before reading a text (we can only recognize what we know in advance), neither will he pay attention to elements in the text that his socioeconomic situation, political beliefs, and gender-based assumptions preclude him from seeing. Social location is not simply one more element among several in the construal of textual meaning. Beyond the grammatical and stylistic decoding that must go on, it plays a central role in the production of meaning during the reading event. Interpretations will appear to the reader to be legitimate if they conform to the values currently in force within the community of which he or she is a member. Communities often have a history of reading that forms a recognizable tradition; tradition being that set of presuppositions that guide the reader in the correct construal of the text. Fundamentalists, for example, legitimate readings which reinforce the values they espouse as a community: apolitical, literalist readings which see female submission, and often wealth and poverty as predestined by the Creator. Readers from the feminist community focus attention on elements of the text which reveal structures of oppression and paths to liberation, either as they affect women specifically or, more commonly, in solidarity with all oppressed people.

Ian McDonald's book, *Biblical Interpretation and Christian Ethics*, may be read as an anthology of the way in which agents of various theological communities have approached the question of the ethics of interpretation during the twentieth century.[36] Exegetes and theologians have inquired about the ethics that the Bible itself (usually the Christian Bible) advances. The assumption in force in the academic community where such projects were carried out was, of course, that the biblical position or positions on ethics could be described in an objective way, given that rigorous scientific methods were available for studying them. If one undermines the notion of value-neutral description, no access to the biblical witness independent of theory or communitarian interests could ever be established. The reader attempting to specify what the text says will always be doing so against the backdrop of the values and perspectives in force in that community. Fish states the position well when he says:

> I now believe that interpretation is the source of texts, facts, authors and intentions. Or to put it another way, the entities that were once seen as competing for the right to constrain interpretation (text, reader, author) are now all seen to be *products* of interpretation. A polemic that was mounted [by Fish] in the name of the reader and against the text has ended in the subsuming of both the text and the reader under the larger category of interpretation.

This is not to say that a community can convincingly place any meaning it wishes on a text, since grammatical rules and other conventions of reading normally provide certain safeguards for anyone looking for even a modest degree of acceptance by an audience. Since recourse to an objective standard is impossible, and given the enclosed nature of all language, what options are left?

For Stanley Fish, a sense of the limits of language and human knowledge leads to the conclusion that a plurality of perspectives exists, each representing a community of interests, or to borrow a phrase from Northrop Frye, a myth of concern.[37] Fish argues in favour of public discourse and debate. Without the ability to specify "truth" in any absolute sense, thinkers must enter the *ekklesia* and make themselves heard, identifying their community and its particular interests. The community, the community's agent, and its dialogue partners are transformed by this action: debate is redefined, voices are heard, and change may take place. All of this of course assumes that access to public speech and influence is readily available to all comers in a democracy—this notion is, of course, patently ridiculous. Those at the margins of society are so described precisely because they normally remain voiceless and powerless in the political arena. People at the margins of society are not always equipped to take part in direct political activism; neither are they often convinced that anything good can come of it. Writing "letters to the editor" in local newspapers, giving interviews on radio or television are difficult tasks for people who are not always capable of formulating the case for change in a persuasive manner. Theologians, exegetes, church representatives, and all manner of advocates with progressive views can choose to stand in solidarity with the disenfranchised, helping them to have their voices heard. Those interested in justice will need to network in support of the disenfranchised; time and effort are required on the part of those with skills in these areas if change is to occur. Despite the difficulties strewn upon the path of those at the margin who would enter the *ekklesia*, I see no alternative to encouraging them to enter the debate, identifying their community and its interests and trying to persuade others of the justness of their cause.

To the extent that we understand the other, we agree with them, maintains Fish. Since complete disagreement remains impossible,[38] even groups with conflicting values and material interests share some ground. Any who would have their voice heard and their interests respected need to gain enough support from those who exercize power over them to do something about it and to do this they must, if dialogue is possible, seek out common ground with their oppressors. Barring this, peaceful resistance of the sort practiced by Gandhi and by many of the protestors currently opposed to the policies of globalization proposed by the G-7 group of countries may be the only other viable solution. If unambiguous truth remains inaccessible and war is to be avoided, the only option is faith in the power of political rhetoric to transform the world. For religious people, this political rhetoric will, of course, be formulated within an overall theological perspective, even if the language in which it is expressed remains secular.

Although the constraints of this essay prevent me from pursuing the question here, it is obvious that individual conversion will not be enough to change the structures of oppression. If conservatives seek to preserve the status quo, and liberals are content to tinker with what they see as a perfectible system, radicals seek no less than a reconceptualization and a restructuring of economic, social, and sexual relationships based on domination.

Foundationalist hermeneutics have been used by those who seek and exercise power over others. Their political rhetoric, which disguises itself as common sense, must be deconstructed as the process of liberation moves forward. Giving priority to the supposedly embedded meaning found in texts, over and against the discovery of meaning as it emerges from the lives of "flesh and blood" readers, is one way in which foundationalist hermeneutics (the hermeneutics of recovery) fosters intellectual, cultural, and political imperialism. This manoeuvre effectively ensures that the "victims of interpretation" will continue to languish at the margins of society, often unaware that they have internalized the ideology of an oppressor whose interests are served by the maintenance of the status quo. Giving priority to readers over texts in the production of meaning is an ethical requirement within the interpretive process and is a necessary condition for liberation.

Conclusion

The debate around the ethics of biblical interpretation has begun to shift from issues of authorial intent and the context of production to a consideration of how the social, economic, and political location of readers determines what they are able to see and understand in the biblical text. Elizabeth Schüssler Fiorenza has called for a consideration of the effects that a given reading will produce in the context into which it is likely to be received.

Without repeating the many positive features set out in Schüssler Fiorenza's programme, suffice it to say that she argues convincingly in favor of a position which is both theologically and politically interested. She stands eloquently in solidarity with those many people, especially women, who have been marginalized by myriad forms of colonizing imperialism. Despite overwhelming agreement with Schüssler Fiorenza's conclusions, her notions of the "self" and of "legitimate" interpretation must be rejected by the very force of the argument which she puts forward in favour of a rhetorical-emancipatory approach.

In the absence of an unambiguous truth, which rallies the support of all those taking part in public debate, rhetoric and persuasion are all that are left. Colonized others, oppressed others will have to find persuasive ways of convincing their dialogue partners to stop the oppression. To attempt to constitute the self as an island of stability in the interpretive act, as Schüssler Fiorenza recommends, is to dismiss the notion that the "self" is a linguistic construct which is subject to the force of rhetorical persuasion in its attempts at self-assertion. Although this sort of change has as much to do with conversion of the heart as it does with simple cognitive assent to a set of objective principles, it cannot stop there. The conversion required for the deconstruction and reconceptualization of systemic oppression involves seeing the world from the perspective of its victims. Wherever this perspectival shift occurs, truth is no longer understood to be a property of a text or a preexisting authoritative stance. It emerges rather from dialogue with the victims of oppression; and only this "lived" truth is of any use in the service of liberation.

Notes

1. This essay is published with the permission of *ARC: The Journal of the Faculty of Religious Studies*, McGill University. See Robert Hurley, "The Ethics of Biblical Interpretation: Rhetoricizing the Foundations," ARC: The Journal of the Faculty of Religious Studies, McGill University (Montreal, Canada). "Essays in Honour of Frederik Wisse: Scholar, Churchman, and Mentor" (Supplement Issue to volume 33, 2005), 386–403. 2006.

2. Elisabeth Schüssler Fiorenza, *Rhetoric and Ethic: The Politics of Biblical Studies* (Minneapolis: Fortress, 1999). Whereas, these paradigms clearly interact with one another on the level of method, their theoretical frameworks, as Schüssler Fiorenza maintains, are nevertheless mutually exclusive.

3. Fernando F. Segovia, "Introduction: 'And They Began to Speak in Other Tongues': Competing Modes of Discourse in Contemporary Biblical Criticism," in *Reading from this Place: Social Location and Biblical Interpretation in Global Perspective*, ed. Fernando F. Segovia and Mary Ann Tolbert (Minneapolis: Augsburg/Fortress, 1995), 1–32.

4. Schüssler Fiorenza, *Rhetoric and Ethic*, 39.

5. Ibid., 41.

6. This androcentrism often takes the form of patriarchy according to Patte. See Daniel Patte, *Ethics of Biblical Interpretation: A Re-evaluation* (Louisville: Westminster John Knox Press, 1995), 25.

7. Schüssler Fiorenza, *Rhetoric and Ethic*, ix.

8. Ibid., 43.

9. For example the word "tea" does not refer *first* to a reddish potable liquid usually drunk hot but rather to the English language where its meaning is established by contrasting it to all the other signifiers in the system.

10. Mikhail Bakhtin, "Except from *Discourse in the Novel*," in *Critical Theory Since 1965*, ed. Hazard Adams and Leroy Searle (Tallahassee: Florida State University Press, 1986).

11. Thomas Kuhn, the physicist become philosopher, concluded that even in the pure sciences researchers opting for one theory over another inevitably make subjective choices that depend not only on shared criteria but also on idiosyncratic factors arising from individual biography and personality. What appears at first glance to be an entirely logical and scientific process proves to be shot through with subjective values. See Thomas Kuhn's *The Structure of Scientific Revolutions* (Chicago: University of Chicago Press, 1970), especially the chapter on theory choice and value judgment.

12. That women and other oppressed majorities who remained voiceless for much of the history of positivist and fundamentalist exegeses likely has something to do with the fact that white men from affluent countries have not been quick to ask questions of the sort that would require them to share power and influence. See the critique offered by thinkers such as E. Schüssler Fiorenza, M. Bal, R.R. Ruther, J.L. Segundo, L. Boff, and so on. See Segovia's *Reading from this Placee*, quoted earlier, and J.L. Segundo's *The Liberation of Theology* (Maryknoll: Orbis Books, 1976), 13–25. For examples of male [*mis-*] readings of biblical texts, I would recommend Mieke Bal's meta-critique of the work of male exegetes on the David and Bathsheba episode: see Mieke Bal, *Lethal Love: Feminist Literary Readings of Biblical Love Stories* (Bloomington: Indiana University Press, 1987).

13. On the self-reflexive character of language, see especially pages 122–125 of Jacques Derrida's "Différance," available in translation in *Critical Theory Since 1965*, ed. Hazard Adams and Leroy Searle (Tallahassee: Florida State University Press, 1986).

14. See S.R.F. Pierce, "Rituals and Power," in *Paul and Empire: Religion and Power in Roman Imperial Society*, ed. R. Horsley (Harrisburg, PA: Trinity Press International, 1997), 48.
15. Horsley, *Paul and Empire*, 140.
16. Schüssler Fiorenza, *Rhetoric and Ethic*, 44.
17. Fernanda Segovia refers to this model as the paradigm of cultural studies. See Fernando F. Segovia, "Cultural Studies and Contemporary Biblical Criticism: Ideology Criticism as a Mode of Discourse," in *Reading from this Place*, 1–17.
18. Schüssler Fiorenza, *Rhetoric and Ethic*, 44.
19. Ibid., 28.
20. Ibid., 28.
21. Ibid., 50.
22. Ibid., 5–6. Schüssler Fiorenza coins new words and uses old ones in most innovative ways, thereby calling the reader's attention again and again to the scars left by misogyny and other forms of oppression on the shape of the English language. Her use of the nouns "wo/men," "kyriocentrism," and of the adjective "*scientistic*" are but three examples of how she raises the readers consciousness in such a sustained way that the experience of reading her work becomes not only an invitation to acquire new information but also an invitation to a critical conversion.
23. Ibid., 11. That is, as a service to the *ekklesia*, where *ekklesia* is understood both as a Greek political term denoting the decision-making assembly of full citizens and as the NT term for Church.
24. Ibid., 45.
25. Ibid., 10.
26. Ibid., 1.
27. Ibid., 46.
28. Stanley Fish, *Doing What Comes Naturally: Change, Rhetoric, and the Practice of Theory in Literary and Legal Studies* (Durham, NC: Duke University Press, 1989), 29–30.
29. Stanley Fish, *Is There a Text in this Class?: The Authority of Interpretative Communities* (Cambridge/London: Harvard University Press, 1980), 16.
30. Schüssler Fiorenza, *Rhetoric and Ethic*, 43.
31. Ibid., 27.
32. Ibid., ix coins this word from the Greek term for lord, underscoring the idea that domination is not simply a matter of patriarchal, gender-based dualism but of more comprehensive, interlocking, hierarchically ordered structures of domination, evident in a variety of oppressions, such as racism, poverty, heterosexism, and colonialism.
33. Frank Kermode, *The Genesis of Secrecy: On the Interpretation of Narrative* (Cambridge: Harvard University Press, 1979), 162–163, note 20.
34. See E.D. Hirsch, *Validity in Interpretation* (New Haven: Yale University Press, 1967) 83.
35. Fish, *Is There a Text in this Class?*, 66.
36. J.I.H. McDonald, *Biblical Interpretation and Christian Ethics* (Cambridge: Cambridge University Press, 1993).
37. Northrop Frye, "From *The Critical Path*," in *Critical Theory Since 1965*, ed. Hazard Adams and Leroy Searle (Tallahassee: Florida State University Press, 1986), 253 ff.
38. See Philipp J. Donnelly, *Rhetorical Faith: The Literary Hermeneutics of Stanley Fish* (Victoria, BC: University of Victoria, 2000), 30–31.

Works Cited

Bakhtin, Mikhail. "Except from *Discourse in the Novel*." In *Critical Theory Since 1965*. Ed. Hazard Adams and Leroy Searle. Tallahassee: Florida State University Press, 1986. 664–678.

Derrida, Jacques. "Différance." In *Critical Theory Since 1965*. Ed. Hazard Adams and Leroy Searle. Tallahassee: Florida State University Press, 1986. 120–136.

Donnelly, Phillip J.*Rhetorical Faith: The Literary Hermeneutics of Stanley Fish*. Victoria, BC: University of Victoria, 2000.

Fish, Stanley. *Doing What Comes Naturally: Change, Rhetoric, and the Practice of Theory in Literary and Legal Studies*. Durham, NC: Duke University Press, 1989.

———. *Is There a Text in this Class?: The Authority of Interpretative Communities*. Cambridge/London: Harvard University Press, 1980.

Frye, Northrop. "From *The Critical Path*." In *Critical Theory Since 1965*. Ed. Hazard Adams and Leroy Searle. Tallahassee: Florida State University Press, 1986. 252–264.

Hirsch, E.D. *Validity in Interpretation*. New Haven: Yale University Press, 1967.

Horsley, Richard. "Paul's Counter-Imperial Gospel." In *Paul and Empire: Religion and Power in Roman Imperial Society*. Ed. R. Horsley. Harrisburg, PA: Trinity Press International, 1997. 140–147.

Kermode, Frank. *The Genesis of Secrecy: On the Interpretation of Narrative*. Cambridge: Harvard University Press, 1979.

Kuhn, Thomas. *The Structure of Scientific Revolutions*. Chicago: University of Chicago Press, 1970.

McDonald, J.I.H. *Biblical Interpretation and Christian Ethics*. Cambridge: Cambridge University Press, 1993.

Patte, Daniel. *Ethics of Biblical Interpretation: A Reevaluation*. Louisville: Westminster John Knox Press, 1995.

Pierce, S.R.F. "Rituals and Power." In *Paul and Empire: Religion and Power in Roman Imperial Society*. Ed. R. Horsley. Harrisburg, PA: Trinity Press International, 1997. 45–71.

Schüssler Fiorenza, Elisabeth. *Rhetoric and Ethic: The Politics of Biblical Studies*. Minneapolis: Fortress, 1999.

Segovia, Fernando F. *Reading from this Place: Social Location and Biblical Interpretation in Global Perspective*. Ed. Fernando F. Segovia and Mary Ann Tolbert. Minneapolis: Augsburg/Fortress, 1995. 1–32.

CHAPTER FOUR

Samuel Beckett's Use of the Bible and the Responsibility of the Reader

SPYRIDOULA ATHANASOPOULOU-KYPRIOU

Introduction

Samuel Beckett's use of the Bible might seem quite inconsistent, ambiguous, and irresponsible, especially when seen from a Christian point of view, for the plethora of allusions and direct references to the Bible and to some Christian understandings of the concept of God along with his emphasis on nothingness and "mystical" silence are followed by parody and a tendency to reduce God, the divine, and religion in general to the level of the ludicrous. The fact that, on the one hand, Beckett uses the Bible and the Christian religious beliefs with which he is familiar and, on the other, he ridicules them, has caused much confusion among those critics who attempt to analyze his stance toward Christianity. Thus, on the one hand, there are critics who stress Beckett's negative attitude toward Christianity and, on the other, critics who actually believe that he has a positive attitude toward the Christian tradition. In this essay, I distance myself from the debate about Beckett's attitude toward the Bible and Christianity in general. My main argument is that Beckett's positivist use of language and his effort to eliminate the possible connotations that certain words have are suggestive of his attempt to demonstrate the role and the responsibility of the readers when interpreting a text and when ascribing meaning to various biblical allusions and references.

Key Words

Reader responsibility, denotation, literalism, positivism.

★ ★ ★

Attempting to write about Samuel Beckett and his use of the Bible is tantamount to trying to make sense of an ambiguity, for Beckett's ambiguous attitude toward the Bible and Christianity in general is well rooted in his biography. Beckett was born at Cooldrinagh in Foxrock, County Dublin, on Friday, April 13, 1906, that is to say, the Good Friday of that year. Although the coincidence of his own birth with Good Friday, the thirteenth, was not created by him, as it has been claimed, it was assimilated by him into a view of life which sees birth as connected with suffering and death and which sees life as a painful road to be trod.[1] Under the supervision of his mother he was brought up in the strict Protestantism that seems to thrive in Ireland alongside a general Catholicism and a "distressed" Anglicanism (Butler 1992, 169). Without a doubt and as his work gives evidence, he received along with a Protestant upbringing a thorough grounding in the Bible as a child and added to it, as Irishmen must, a close knowledge of Catholic doctrine and belief. This double heritage, Christianity in two forms, constitutes the mythology with which he has declared himself perfectly familiar.[2]

Yet, when Beckett went to Trinity College in 1923 to study for an Arts degree, he distanced himself from his Christian heritage under the influence of one of his teachers, Rudmose-Brown. Rudmose-Brown, who was rabidly anticlerical, irreligious, and a staunch believer in individual freedom, not only influenced Beckett so far as his anticlericalism is concerned, but also affected his attitude to life. "Every one of us must strive, unflinchingly, to be himself," he said. (quoted in Knowlson 1997, 51) Beckett's entire oeuvre could be regarded as an illustration of that particular principle.

Trying to be himself, Beckett would question and doubt his religious heritage while at the same time this would not stop him from being thoroughly acquainted with classic theological thought. There is a good deal of evidence available nowadays, particularly through Charles Juliet's *Rencontre avec Samuel Beckett* (Juliet 1986, 48–51) and from *Beckett's Dream Notebook 1931/32 (1998)*, recently edited by John Pilling, that throughout his life Beckett was a consistent reader of theological writings. Marius Buning records that John Calder, Beckett's English publisher, remarked in a private communication to Buning that he found Beckett immersed in Eckhart only half a year before his death in 1989. When asked, Beckett expressed his great attachment to Eckhart's work (Buning 2000, 49).

The fact that, on the one hand, Beckett is familiar with and uses the Christian tradition, and, on the other, he is highly suspicious of his religious heritage, is reflected in his writings. Thus, the plethora of allusions and direct references to the Bible and to various understandings of the concept of God along with his emphasis on nothingness and "mystical" silence are followed by parody and a tendency to reduce God, the divine, and religion in general to the level of the ludicrous. The fact that, on the one hand, Beckett uses the Bible and the Christian religious beliefs with which he is familiar and, on the other, he ridicules them, has caused much confusion among those critics who attempt to analyze his stance toward the Bible and Christianity in general. Thus, on the one hand, there are critics who stress Beckett's negative attitude toward the Bible and Christianity and, on the other, critics who actually believe that Beckett has a positive attitude toward the Christian tradition.

Among the critics who stress Beckett's positive or at least responsible attitude toward the Bible and the concept of God, we find the names of Günther Anders, Gabriel Vahanian, Richard Coe, Jean Onimus, Eugene Combs, Hélène Baldwin, Shira Wolosky, and Marius Buning. An indication of the way these critics view Beckett's attitude toward the Christian tradition and in particular toward the Bible is Francis Nichols' exploration of the parallels between *Ecclesiastes* and Beckett's play *Waiting for Godot*. In terms of Nichols, Beckett, like *Ecclesiastes*, makes the assertion about the vanity of all things and illumines dimensions of the experience of faith. This is a faith that remains a step beyond reason and is an act of trust (Nichols 1984; 14–16, 20–21). Similarly, Samuel Terrien looks at *Waiting for Godot* from a theological point of view and argues that "Beckett proposed a sardonic satire of what may be called 'real-estate Christianity' and at the same time made a subtle plea for a faith that fully respects the transcendence of God" (Terrien 1989, 140).

Among the critics who emphasize Beckett's negative attitude toward the Bible and Christianity in general, there is Friedrich Hansen-Löve, John Fletcher, Martin Esslin, and, more recently, Laura Barge. Hersh Zeifman, analyzing the religious imagery in the plays of Beckett, emphasizes Beckett's negative attitude toward the Bible and says: "Instead of providing support for a Christian interpretation, the presence of biblical imagery in the plays serves rather to undermine such an interpretation through ironic counterpoint" (Zeifman 1975, 93). In 1998, Mary Bryden published an exhaustive study entitled *Samuel Beckett and the Idea of God* where she attempts to identify the original sources of Beckett's religious allusions and where she implies that Beckett is not a pious or religious person. As she puts it: "if Beckett uses both the Old and the New Testament extensively within his own early writing, it is usually not to enshrine or venerate them, but rather to wring ironic or deviant readings out of them. This is not to say that he consistently undermines or parodies them, for Beckett is too alive to the strength and poetry of many elements within that complex of literatures which constitute the Bible to target them simplistically or homogenously. It does mean, however, that (in contrast to à Kempris's exploitation of the same sources), his use of biblical phrases must not necessarily be seen as signifying his assent to their inspirations" (Bryden 1998, 35).

Taking exception to the previous accounts of Beckett's attitude toward the Bible that stress either his negative or his positive attitude toward this holy book, I want to argue that the way Beckett uses the biblical phrases or the biblical allusions is closely associated with his general tendency to pure denotation. Instead of arguing for either Beckett's responsible or irresponsible attitude toward the Christian tradition and the Bible, I want to suggest that his positivist use of language and effort to eliminate the possible connotations that certain words or expressions have are indications of his attempt to shift the responsibility from the author to the reader. In what follows, I elaborate further on how Beckett's tendency to denotation makes the reader responsible for the meaning he or she ascribes to various biblical allusions and direct references to both the Old and the New Testament.

It was Stanley Cavell who, in an early essay on Beckett's *Endgame*, first spoke of Beckett's tendency to pure denotation. Cavell wrote that "Beckett (along with other philosophers recognizable as existentialist) shares with positivism its wish to escape connotation, rhetoric, the noncognitive, the irrationality and awkward memories of ordinary language, in favor of the directly verifiable, the isolated and perfected present. Only Beckett sees how infinitely difficult this escape will be. Positivism said that statements about God are meaningless; Beckett shows that they mean too damned much" (Cavell 1976, 120). Cavell argues that in his effort to escape connotations, Beckett employs grammar and language in such a way that a "hidden literality" is what describes best Beckett's art. Sometimes it is hard to make sense of what Beckett says in his novels or plays simply because the meaning of the most incomprehensible expressions is so utterly bare. As Cavell puts it: "The words strew obscurities across our path and seem to thwart comprehension; and then time after time we discover that their meaning has been missed only because it was so utterly bare—totally, therefore unnoticeably, in view. Such a discovery has the effect of showing us that is *we* who had been uncomprehending, misleading ourselves in demanding further, or other, meaning where the meaning was nearest" (119).

A very good example of Beckett's tendency to pure denotation and of his "hidden literality" is given by Cavell himself. Cavell points out that the name of God appears in *Endgame* typically in a form of words, which conventionally expresses a curse. However, it is not used (by the character, Clov, of course) to curse, but rather in perfect literalness. Clov asks: "What in God's name could there be on the horizon?" (Beckett 1990, 107). In context, this question shows Clov really asking whether anything on the horizon is appearing in God's name, as his sign or at his bidding. One of the Christian's special curses is that we can use the name of God naturally only to curse, take it only in vain. Beckett, however, removes this curse by converting the rhetoric of cursing and by turning its formulas into declarative utterances, ones of pure denotation. To move beyond the context of the play where Clov simply asks if there is anything on the horizon that appears in God's name and argue that Clov is actually cursing means that it is the reader who sees something more in the utterance. This does not mean of course that we cannot read Clov's question as a curse; it only means that we must acknowledge that it is our reading, as it is of course our reading to interpret it as a declarative utterance.

Similarly, later on in the play, Hamm decides to pray to God. He thus adopts an attitude of prayer but when there is no response from God, he exclaims: "The bastard! He doesn't exist!" (Beckett 1990, 119). This declaration seems at first as an atheistic statement that is also profoundly blasphemous. To call God "a bastard" does not indicate piety. Yet, if we take it literally, God is a bastard since God is considered ingenerate, having thus no legitimate parents. Analogously, to claim that God does not exist is not an atheistic statement especially if we take this claim literally. God does not exist in the way that we, human beings, understand existence. If God existed in the same way that we do, then God would not be a transcendent God. The utterance: "The bastard! He doesn't exist!" can be interpreted in both an atheistic and a theological way, depending on the reader's approach.

Thus, it can be said that Beckett turns away from the connotations of certain words and expressions and, with his extended exercises in reduction, he also turns away from figures. Taking this last point further, Shira Wolosky argues for the "figural evasions" in Beckett's later works. To explain what she means by figural evasions, she takes the text of "Fizzles" that is governed by a denotative or positivist use of language and says: "The action of 'Fizzles' is comprised of this and only this activity [a protagonist makes his way through what seems an underground labyrinth of walks and turns and sudden sheer falls]; its plot, that is, becomes exactly plotting a course through space: 'He halts, for the first time since he knows he's under way, one foot before the other, the higher flat, the lower on its toes, and waits for a decision. Then he moves on.' Temporal succession is in turn entirely defined within the space the protagonist traverses, step by step: 'But see how now, having turned right for example, instead of turning left a little further on he turns right again. And see how now again, yet a little further on, instead of turning left at last he turns right yet again. And so on until, instead of turning right yet again, as he expected, he turns left at last' " (Wolosky 1989, 165–166). For Wolosky, words of temporal measure, like "now," "again," "yet," "until," "at last," in the text of *Fizzles*, mediate spatial progression. As for the protagonist, his very life too becomes a compilation of the space he crosses. In this way "little by little his history takes shape, with if not yet exactly its good days and bad, at least studded with occasions, passing rightly or wrongly for outstanding, such as the straightest narrow, the loudest fall, the most lingering collapse, the steepest descent, the greatest number of successive turns the same way, the greatest fatigue, the longest rest, the longest—aside from the sound of the body on its way—silence . . . In a word all the summits" (Beckett 1995, 227–228).

For Wolosky, in the aforesaid passage what occurs is "the sustained elimination of any sense not confined within the spatial motion that it alone admits. Indeed, there seems a radical de-figuration of a whole tradition of literary journeys in which progress is presented physically in order to re-present progress of a moral, emotional, religious, or psychological kind. Terms of judgment such as 'good' and 'bad' are assimilated into the term 'outstanding,' which emerges in its physically determined sense" (Wolosky 1989, 166). In an analogous way, words such as "the straightest narrow," "fall," or "descent" that open into metaphysical or theological meanings lose any sense but that of the physical dimension and direction. If one were to give a metaphysical reading of that passage, one would have to acknowledge that he or she buys into the connotations of the language used. Interestingly, then, in his effort to eliminate the connotations of language, Beckett points also to the figurative or metaphysical and religious meanings that language might otherwise convey; yet, it is the reader who takes responsibility for actually ascribing such a figurative meaning to language, for Beckett delimits the sense of his words to an unmitigated literalism.

In terms of J.L. Austin's distinction between constative and performative utterances, Beckett seems to favor constative utterances in so far as he abstracts from both the illocutionary and the perlocutionary aspects of the speech-act and concentrates on the locutionary.[3] Beckett's heroes and narrators describe, report, and constate something. By being part of a literary work, the constative utterances of Beckett's heroes do not correspond to reality. Yet they do something to the reader, thus turning into performative utterances: they seek to entertain the responsibility of the reader. In his works, it is as if Beckett was saying: "I use words that open to metaphysical meanings but I use them literally. If you, the readers, wish to buy into their metaphysical connotations then you should take full responsibility for doing so."

Given Beckett's tendency to pure denotation and his delimiting of the sense of language to an unmitigated literalism, the references to the Bible and the comments on the Scripture must be taken in their literalness. For example, in his play for radio, *All that Fall*, Mrs. Rooney informs her husband that the preacher's text for the following Sunday is to be: "The Lord upholdeth all that fall and raiseth up all those that be bowed down" (Psalm 145, 14). Then, they join in wild laugher (Beckett 1990, 198). For Mary Bryden, this reference to the Bible does not signify Beckett's assent to its inspirations. But why not? For her, the quotation occurs close to the end of a play, which has been riddled with near-falls and with straining locomotion. Thus, the wild laughter of the couple is an ironic response to the Bible since there is a mismatch between the assured sentiments of the psalm and the couple's experience of its unfulfilled promise. Unlike Bryden, I think that we can take the biblical reference as a declarative utterance and the couple's laughter as a positive and trusting response. "Lord upholds all that fall and raises up all those that be bowed down" is what we might take to be the case in the play. Literally speaking, no one up to the point the psalm is quoted has fallen. Thus, the laughter can equally mean that these two people trust God and are happy to recognize divine providence. Beckett refers to the Bible and writes about a couple who breaks into laughter. It is left to the readers to link these two things together and ascribe meaning.

On one occasion, Beckett's heroes comment on the role of the reader's response to a text, and not just any text but the biblical text. In *Waiting for Godot*, Vladimir speaks of the Gospels and maintains that "of the four Evangelists only one speaks of a thief being saved." "Of the other three two don't mention any thieves at all and the third says that both of them abused him [Jesus]" (14). At this point what is interesting is not the accuracy of Vladimir's observation but his challenging question to Estragon: "But all four were there. And only one speaks of a thief being saved. Why believe him rather than the others?" Estragon replies with a question: "Who believes him?" "Everybody. It's the only version they know," says Vladimir. Estragon, then, concludes: "People are bloody ignorant apes" (15). That incident is suggestive of what we as readers can do with a text. *We* take responsibility for believing the one Evangelist, it is a choice that *we* make. There is always a different reading, but *we* decide to overlook it. It is the same with Beckett's use of the Bible. He provides the readers with the allusions and the references to the Bible but it is the readers who are going to concede meaning.[4]

Conclusion

Acknowledging Beckett's tendency to pure denotation and his effort to escape the connotations of the language used (be they theistic or atheistic) is tantamount to shifting the responsibility from the author to the reader who is the one to ascribe theological or nontheological meaning to the language of a text. Thus, Beckett seems to be interested in the real reader and her actual response to his works. Beckett does not write for the ideal reader who is anyway a fictional being who is employed in order to close the gaps that constantly appear in any analysis of literary effects and responses. By focusing on the literal meaning of the words, Beckett challenges also the concept of the informed reader who is able to understand and interpret all the sophisticated figures of speech and connotations of language. Using Wolfgang Iser's concept of the implied reader that denotes the role of the reader of Beckett's works, I propose that Beckett's implied reader is the real and responsible reader that faces literalism and pure denotation and tries to make sense of it.[5]

Notes

1. There has been a lot of debate as to whether Friday April 13 was or was not the true date of his birth. His birth certificate records the date as May 13, not April. And his father registered the event on June 14, a month later, it is argued, than he would have done if the birth had been in April. So it has been claimed that Beckett deliberately created the myth that he was born on a Good Friday. As Knowlson reveals, the truth is much less dramatic. "A mistake was clearly made. Everyone who knew Beckett as a child thought of his birthday as being on 13 April. This never changed" (James Knowlson, *Damned to Fame: The Life of Samuel Beckett*. [London: Bloomsbury, 1997], 1).
2. When Colin Duckworth asked Beckett whether a Christian interpretation of *Waiting for Godot* was justified, he replied: "Yes. Christianity is a mythology with which I am perfectly familiar. So naturally I use it" (Colin Duckworth, *Angels of Darkness* [London: Allen and Unwin, 1972], 18).

3. According to Austin, the three types of verbal "acts" are: the "locutionary," the "illocutionary," and the "perlocutionary." The "locutionary" act "is roughly equivalent to uttering a certain sentence with a certain sense and reference," and again "is roughly equivalent to 'meaning' in the traditional sense." The "illocutionary" acts "such as informing, ordering, warning, undertaking, &c.," are "utterances which have a certain (conventional) force." The focus here is on the force such utterances seek to apply to their discursive situation. The "perlocutionary" acts mean "what we bring about or achieve by saying something, such as convincing, persuading, deterring, and even, say, surprising or misleading." The focus here is not on what the utterance is doing, but what it seeks to bring about in a hearer (J.L. Austin, *How to Do Things with Words: The William James Lectures delivered at Harvard University in 1955.* 2nd ed, ed. J.O. Urmson and Marina Sbisà [Oxford, NY: Oxford University Press, 1990], 109).

4. By arguing that the readers are going to concede meaning to the allusions and the references to the Bible, I do not overlook the author and his intention. However, an author should never be granted ownership of the definitive interpretation of his/her work for two main reasons. First, the authorial intention is too interconnected with external factors (linguistic context, historico-political situation) to be fully controlled or even recognized by the author. Second, our cultural products, including literary ones, always exceed our reach because they are again too interconnected in necessary exchanges for them to be conceded univocal meaning. Having said that, I do not imply that an author should have no say in the interpretation of her or his work. What I am suggesting here is that the author is just another reader of his or her own work and his/her interpretation is one among many possible others.

5. For Wolfgang Iser, "the concept of the implied reader is a transcendental model which makes it possible for the structured effects of literary texts to be described. It denotes the role of the reader, which is definable in terms of textual structure and structured acts. By bringing about a standpoint for the reader, the textual structure follows a basic rule of human perception, as our views of the world are always of a perspective nature" (Wolfgang Iser, *The Act of Reading: A Theory of Aesthetic* Response [London/Henley: Routledge and Kegan Paul, 1978], 38).

Works Cited

Anders, Günther. "Being Without Time: On Beckett's Play *Waiting for Godot.*" In *Samuel Beckett: A Collection of Critical Essays.* Ed. Martin Esslin. Englewood Cliffs, NJ: Prentice-Hall, 1965. 140–151.

Austin, J.L. *How to Do Things with Words: The William James Lectures Delivered at Harvard University in 1955.* 2nd ed. Ed. J.O.Urmson and Marina Sbisà. Oxford, NY: Oxford University Press, 1990.

Baldwin, Hélène. "The Theme of the Pilgrim in the Works of Samuel Beckett." *Christian Scholar's Review* 8.3 (1978): 217–228.

———. *Samuel Beckett's Real Silence.* University Park/London: Pennsylvania State University Press, 1981.

Barge, Laura. "Light in a Dark Place." *Christianity Today* 18.21 (1973): 13–16.

———. *God, the Quest, the Hero: Thematic Structures in Beckett's Fiction.* Chapel Hill: University of North Carolina Press, 1988.

———. "Beckett's Metaphysics and Christian thought: a comparison." *Christian Scholar's Review* 20.1 (1990): 33–44.

Beckett, Samuel. *The Complete Dramatic Works.* London: Faber and Faber, 1990.

———. *The Complete Short Prose (1929–1989).* New York: Grove Press, 1995.

———. *Beckett's Dream Notebook 1931/1932.* Ed. J. Pilling. Reading: Beckett International Foundation, 1998.

Bryden, Mary. *Samuel Beckett and the Idea of God.* London: Macmillan Press, 1998.

Buning, Marius. "Samuel Beckett's negative way: intimations of the *via negativae* in his late plays." In *European Literature and Theology in the Twentieth Century: Ends of Time*. Ed. David Jasper and Colin Crowder. London: Macmillan, 1990. 129–142.

———. " 'The Via Negativa' and its first stirrings in *Eleutheria*." In *Samuel Beckett Today/Aujourd'hui 9*. Ed. Marius Buning et al. Amsterdam, Atlanta: Rodopi, 2000. 43–54.

Butler, Lance St. John. " 'A mythology with which I am perfectly familiar': Samuel Beckett and the absence of God." In *Irish Writers and Religion*. Ed. Robert Welch. Buckinghamshire: Colin Smythe, 1992. 169–184 and 229–231.

Cavell, Stanley. "Ending the Waiting Game." In *Must We Mean What We Say?: A Book of Essays*. Cambridge: Cambridge University Press, 1976. 117–137.

Coe, Richard N. "Le Dieu de Samuel Beckett." *Cahiers Renaud-Barrault* 44 (1963): 6–36.

Combs, Eugene. "Impotency and ignorance: A parody of prerogatives in Samuel Beckett." *Studies in Religion/Sciences Religieuses* 2.2 (1972): 114–130.

Duckworth, Colin. *Angels of Darkness*. London: Allen and Unwin, 1972.

Esslin, Martin. *The Theatre of the Absurd*. London: Penguin Books, 1991.

Fletcher, John. *Samuel Beckett's Art* London: Chatto and Windus, 1971.

Hansen-Löve, Friedrich. "Samuel Beckett oder die Einübung ins Nichts." *Hochland* 50.1 (1957): 36–46.

Iser, Wolfgang. *The Act of Reading: A Theory of Aesthetic Response*. London/Henley: Routledge and Kegan Paul, 1978.

Juliet, Charles. *Rencontre avec Samuel Beckett*. Paris: Editions Fata Morgana, 1986.

Knowlson, James. *Damned to Fame: The Life of Samuel Beckett*. London: Bloomsbury, 1997.

Nichols, Francis W. "Samuel Beckett and Ecclesiastes on the borders of belief." *Encounters* 45 (1984): 11–22.

Onimus, Jean. *Beckett. Les écrivain devant Dieu*. Paris: Déclée de Brouwer, 1968.

Terrien, Samuel. "A theological look at *Waiting for Godot*." *Theology Today* 46 (1989): 139–153.

Vahanian, Gabriel. *The Death of God: The Culture of Our Post-Christian Era*. New York: George Braziller, 1961.

Wolosky, Shira. "Samuel Beckett's Figural Evasions." In *Languages of the Unsayable: The Play of Negativity in Literature and Literary Theory*. Ed. Sanford Budick and Wolfgang Iser. New York, Oxford: Columbia University Press, 1989. 165–186.

———. *Language and Mysticism: The Negative Way of Language in Eliot, Beckett, and Celan*. Stanford: Stanford University Press, 1995.

Zeifman, Hersh. "Religious imagery in the Plays of Samuel Backett." In *Samuel Beckett: A Collection of Criticism*. Ed. Ruby Cohn. New York: McGraw-Hill, 1975. 85–94.

CHAPTER FIVE

On Trial: Mikhail Bakhtin and Abram Tertz's Address to "God"

LEWIS OWENS

Introduction

The literary work of Mikhail Bakhtin and Andrey Sinyavsky (also known as Abram Tertz) can be fully understood in the light of their critical responses to the Soviet doctrine of socialist realism, which was officially introduced in 1932. This doctrine advocated that all art should be realistic, optimistic, and heroic, and conversely all forms of degenerate and pessimistic experimentalism should be denounced as anti-Soviet. Both Bakhtin and Sinyavsky offer their own original responses to the static and preordained dictates of socialist realism: for Bakhtin, this led to prioritizing open-ended dialogue and "otherness" within a text, whilst for Sinyavksy it led to an emphasis on the fantastic and grotesque, reminiscent of nineteenth-century Russian literature, most notably Gogol. Nevertheless Bakhtin, by proclaiming the existence of a "superaddressee" or "God" who ultimately stands outside of history and "judges" the text, remains essentially modern in his thought, whereas Sinyavsky refuses the existence of a meta-historical and eschatological "Judge" and argues instead that any ultimate purpose or "God" must remain relative to the current historical era. The thought of Sinyavky, therefore, has more relevance and importance to any contemporary discussion on the meaning and use of the word "God."

Key Words

Mikhail Bakhtin, Andrey Sinyavsky (also known as Abram Tertz), superaddressee, socialist realism, ultimate purpose, eschatological "Judge."

★ ★ ★

The literary work of both Mikhail Bakhtin and Abram Tertz (Andrei Sinyavsky) can be fully understood only in the light of their critical response to the Soviet doctrine of socialist realism. This doctrine was officially introduced at the First Congress of the Writers' Union in 1934, although the origins of the term can be traced back to a series of discussions held in Spring 1932 that included Stalin, Bukharin, Gorki, and Zhdanov.[1]

According to this doctrine, all art should be optimistic and heroic, and conversely all forms of degenerate and pessimistic experimentalism were denounced as anti-Soviet. The congress asserted that the job of literature is to provide an optimistic outlook on life, and a truthful, historical portrayal of socialism's revolutionary component. The responsibility and duty placed on Soviet authors was paramount—Zhdanov famously declared:

> Comrade Stalin has called our writers "engineers of the human soul." What does this mean? What *obligation* does such an appellation put upon you? . . . It means, in the first place, that you must know life to be able to depict it truthfully in artistic creations, to depict it neither "scholastically" nor lifelessly, nor simply as "objective reality," but rather as reality in its revolutionary development. The truthfulness and historical exactitude of the artistic image must be linked with the task of ideological transformation, of the education of the working people in the spirit of socialism. This method in fiction and literary criticism is what we call the method of socialist realism. Zhdanov 1969, 694–695 (My emphasis)

This was the atmosphere from which Bakhtin and Tertz constructed their own alternatives to the methodology of socialist realism, which consequently forced them both into exile.

Bakhtin

From the late 1920s to the 1940s, during which time he suffered exile to Kazakhstan, Bakhtin championed communication with multiple actors or participants and saw the modern European novel as the mode of intersubjectivity and communicative experience par excellence. In his 1929 book *The Problems of Dostoevsky's Poetics*, Bakhtin argues that the writings of Dostoevsky exhibit a tendency of "polyphony," that is, writing in which several contesting voices, representing a variety of ideological positions, can engage equally in dialogue, free from authorial judgment or constraint. He saw in Dostoevsky's work, *"plurality of independent and unmerged voices and consciousnesses, a genuine polyphony of fully valid voices . . . with equal rights and each with its own world"* (Bakhtin, 1984, 6). The author is democratically positioned "alongside" the speeches of the characters so that no single point of view is privileged. In a sense, therefore one cannot even be certain at times who is speaking.[2]

For Bakhtin, therefore, language has an essentially social function and social "truth." By its very nature, dialogue is fluid, open-ended, and its course is not predetermined but created by the participants, who must agree on the meaning of the words used within the particular narrative. There is an inherent incompleteness lying within the polyphonic novel, where, unlike a monologic novel, the idea placed in the mouth of the hero does not consist of a fixed, final meaning (79). More broadly: the *I* cannot stand alone—it needs to recognize, adopt, and incorporate the voice of the *other*.[3] Without such agreement and mutual interaction dialogue is impossible.

Whereas the doctrine of socialist realism championed the positive hero who overcomes all trials and tribulations in his struggle to define the glorious Soviet future, Bakhtin raises doubts about the legitimacy of such characters. His stress on the interweaving of various conflicting voices marks a stark contrast from the precision and clarity sought by socialist realism. In his work "Discourse in the Novel" he asserts that there can be no such person as a "hero without faults" (Bakhtin 1996, 259–422; Clark and Holquist 1984, 273–274). Likewise, in his 1941 work *Epic and Novel*, Bakhtin opposes the open, dynamic world of the novel, unable to be characterized in any formal way, to the closed and supposedly perfectly complete world of the epic (Bakhtin 1996, 3–40). For Bakhtin, the genre of the epic, which mythologized an ideal, perfected past, was comparable to the closed, static, and unrealizable world desired by socialist realism. This "authoritative" word organizes other types of speech around it, but does not merge with them; it remains apart, separate, dominant, and unwilling to enter into dialogue with new voices.

Nevertheless, Bakhtin remains essentially *modern* in this thought: he cannot forsake ultimate value and meta-historical Truth. He proclaimed the existence of a mysterious and rather perplexing "superaddressee" who is addressed *beyond* the immediate audience. This "superaddressee," existing in some distant metaphysical or historical realm, does not participate in the dialogue, but is presumed to *understand* the dialogue and hence becomes a "third party" or "Judge." Bakhtin writes:

[T]he author of the utterance, with a greater or lesser awareness, presupposes a higher *superaddressee* (third), whose absolutely just responsive understanding is presumed, either in some metaphysical distance or in distant historical time (the loophole addressee). (Bakhtin 1986, 126)

Bakhtin claims that the author of any utterance or word has "faith" in the existence of this superaddressee, who never arrives but judges only at the end of history, and is believed to understand the speaker or writer perfectly: "Not faith (in the sense of a specific faith in orthodoxy, in progress, in man, in revolution, *et cetera*) but a *sense of faith*, that is, an integral attitude (by means of the whole person) toward a higher and ultimate value." (Bakhtin 1984, 237–238). In differing ages, with different understandings of the world, this superaddressee has assumed various ideological expressions: "God, absolute truth, the court of dispassionate human conscience, the people, the court of history, science and so forth" (Bakhtin 1986, 126).

This judge, according to Bakhtin, gives a person confidence to risk speaking or writing without the fear of being misunderstood. There is nothing worse for the word (as for a person) than a *lack of response*. Therefore, each dialogue "takes place as if against the background of the responsive understanding of an invisibly present third party who stands above all the participants in the dialogue (partners)" (126).

Tertz

The similarities between Bahktin and Tertz are significant. Tertz read Bakhtin's *Problems of Dostoevsky's Poetics* and met the author after his release from the prison camps.[4] He sees the method of socialist realism as akin to the precise and static classicism of eighteenth-century Russian literature, and advocates instead a form of fantastic realism, a "phantasmagoric art" dominated by the grotesque and absurd (Tertz 1982, 218). Like Bakhtin, he claims that there are an infinite number of competing centers of interpretation when reading a text. Words are no longer inherently authoritative, but open to the manifold interpretative capacity of the reader. Also like Bakhtin, he seeks a move away from locating "truth" in the realm of self-obsessive egotism: it is rather constituted by dialogic relations or "conversations." Any attempt for each separate "point of view" to establish priority leads to a failure of dialogue and consequent authoritarianism. Dialogue is open-ended; the argument never reaches a definite conclusion. This inevitably involves an element of *risk* on the part of the individual who, like Bakhtin, must accept "no alibi in being" (Hirschop 1999, 229–230) and forsake all previously accepted ontological, epistemological, and ethical security whilst entering into an ever-changing narrative.

Yet Tertz also proclaims the existence of a "third party" or "judge" but his thought remains essentially historical, unlike the implicit meta-historicism of Bakhtin. He claims that "God" is synonymous with humanity's highest "Purpose" that continually and dialectically changes as it exhausts itself (Tertz 1982, 152). It has previously been seen as Christianity, humanistic individualism, and communism. However, due to communism's lack of dialogue, and Stalin's refusal to recognize and adopt the perspective of the *other*, hence leading to a static, non-dynamic and sterile world view, communism served only as a repressive totalitarian authority, with Stalin becoming the judge or "God" of all "conversation." This is poignantly portrayed in Tertz's work *The Trial Begins*, to which I now briefly turn.

The Trial Begins

The title of the novel is itself indicative of the atmosphere of judgment that hovers over the plot and the characters. As early as the Prologue we are presented with a judge with all the characteristics of Bahktin's "superaddressee." He addresses the author thus:

> "Mortal, arise. Behold the hand of God. Wherever you may steal away and hide, it will reach and find you, merciful and chastising. Behold!"
>
> Do you recognise him, writer? The divine voice murmured in my ear. "He is the hero of your tale: Vladimir, my beloved and faithful servant. Follow him, dog his footsteps, defend him with your life. Exalt him!"
>
> "Be my prophet. Let the light prevail and may the enemy tremble at your word." (Tertz 1970, 9)

This "God" is of course Stalin. The "beloved and faithful servant" is Vladimir Globov, the public prosecutor loyal to the Party line who feels very strongly: "God is with us!" (11). Loyal to the 1948 Zhdanov decree which condemned, amongst other musicians, Shostakovich, Prokofiev, and Khatachurian for "formalism" or anti-Soviet music, Globov's thoughts whilst attending a concert are indicative: " 'What music!' exclaimed Globov. 'That's not Prokofiev or Khachaturian for you. That's real classical stuff'. . . What struck him was that the flowing music wasn't left to its own devices, it was controlled by the conductor" (20).

In the Epilogue to the novel, the narrator asserts that, after the death of this "conductor," that is, Stalin: "The town seemed as empty as a desert. You felt like sitting on your haunches, lifting up your head and howling like a homeless dog . . . Dogs who have lost their masters stray about the earth and sniff the air in anguish. They never bark, they only growl. They keep their tail between their legs, or if they do wag them, they look as if they were crying . . . They wait, they are for ever waiting, gazing, longing: 'Come! Come and feed me! Come and kick me! Beat me as much as you like (but not too hard) if you please. Only come!'. . . I don't want freedom. I want a Master" (86–87). Tertz therefore realizes the desire to embrace a new "Purpose" whilst not negating the responsibility that this freedom demands on each individual.

Dialogism and Religious Thought

What can we draw from all this? As Jean-Luc Marion famously asserted, "postmodernity" began when the metaphysical God was called into question and ultimately undermined. God, as a metaphysical Being, is dead.[5] Nevertheless, God, as that which gives meaning and purpose to one's existence, is still alive and accessible. Tertz writes:

> However man may have originated, his appearance and purpose are inseparable from God—that is, the highest idea of purpose which is accessible to us, if not through our understanding, then through our wish that there should be such a purpose. (Tertz 1982, 152)

If dialogue is to be a cornerstone for twenty-first century religious thought, as the work of both Bakhtin and Tertz imply, then it must be remembered that any closed, inflexible conclusion can lead only to stagnation and sterility. As Tertz claims through the character Rabinovich in *The Trial Begins*, "Every decent end consumes itself. You kill yourself trying to reach it and by the time you get there it has been turned inside out . . ." (Tertz 1970, 56). Should we be concerned that this open-ended dialogue will lead to an all-out scrap in the name of relativism? By examining the methodology similar to Bakhtin and Tertz we may be able to chart a course for contemporary religious thought which embraces the postmodern subjective, hermeneutical, and psychological emphases, whilst retaining a modern stress on unity and meaning, that is, purpose.[6] Like an analysis of Shostakovich's Eighth Symphony, (ignorantly) condemned as "formalist" by Zhdanov in 1948, this approach is uncomfortable, disarming, challenging, but is of the utmost importance requiring intense concentration and commitment. It is ultimately to be understood as a comprehensible conversation of different, conflicting voices. This dialogue, nevertheless, may mark the very *locus* of "God" and subsequently formulate meaning and value for the individual life. Thinking about "God" never occurs in a vacuum—the concepts we use are not our individual possessions, but are formulated or merely "borrowed" from our social and historical environment. We are "thrown" into a "symphony" that is already in progress. "God" is not located in a timeless meta-history, therefore, but is a historically conditioned, open-ended concept that is constantly revised in dialogue with other religious beliefs, political, and moral commitments.

Religious thought must never claim it has arrived at a completed end. Like Bahktin we may choose to claim a "redemption" at the very end of history (and must ask whether such a quasi-Christian eschatological position is to the detriment of an authentic dialogic philosophy), or like Tertz we can resist any meta-historical arbitration yet find a purpose— "God"—necessary for our own historical era. What we cannot reject is that history marches on, and with it, all thought about God. Even if there is a "judge" this judge is clearly residing in chambers. Tertz's following comment, made in the 1960s, is directed essentially toward us and our contemporary responsible duty:

Today's children will scarcely be able to produce a new God, capable of inspiring humanity into the next historical cycle. Maybe He will have to be supplemented by other stakes of the Inquisition, by further "personality cults" and by new terrestrial labours, so that after many centuries a new Purpose will rise above the world. But today no one yet knows its name. (Tertz 1982, 127)

Notes

1. For more details on the specifics of Socialist Realism, see Kh. Gyunter and E. Dobrenko, eds., *Sotsrealisticheskii kanon* (St. Petersburg: Akademicheskii proekt, 2000); H. Ermolaev, *Soviet Literary Theories 1917–1934* (Berkeley/Los Angeles: University of California Press, 1963); C.V. James, ed., *Socialist Realism in Art and Literature* (Moscow: Progress Press, 1971); C.V. James, *Soviet Socialist Realism: Origins and Theory* (London: MacMillan, 1973); T. Lahausen and E. Dobrenko, eds., *Socialist Realism without Shores* (*South Atlantic Quarterly*, 1995, 94); and R. Robin, *Socialist Realism: An Impossible Aesthetic* (Stanford: Stanford University Press, 1992).

2. This interplay of narrators is also evident in Tertz's short story "You and I" where the reader is addressed with an interchanging of the first, second, and third person. See Abram Tertz, *Fantastic Stories* (Evanston, IL: Northwestern University Press, 1963), 3–32.

3. "Just as the body is formed initially in the mother's womb (body), a person's consciousness awakens wrapped in another's consciousness." Mikhail Bahktin, "From Notes Made in 1970–71," in *Speech Genres and Other Late Essays*, trans. Vern W. McGee., ed. Caryl Emerson and Michael Holquist (Austin: University of Texas Press, 1986), 138.

4. See Caterine Theimer Nepomnyashchy, *Abram Tertz and the Poetics of Crime* (Yale University Press, 1995), 331, note 67.

5. "The aforementioned third party is not any mystical or metaphysical being (although, given a certain understanding of the world, he can be expressed as such)." Mikhail Bakhtin, "The Problem of the Text in Linguistics, Philology and the Human Sciences: A Experiment in Philosophical Analysis," in *Speech Genres and Other Late Essays* (Austin: University of Texas Press, 1996), 126.

6. The work of George Pattison is a fine example of such a course. See George Pattison, *The End of Theology and the Task of Thinking about God* (London: SCM Press, 1998).

Works Cited

Bakhtin, Mikhail. *Problems of Dostoevsky's Poetics.* Ed. and Trans. Caryl Emerson. Introduction by Wayne C. Booth. Theory and History of Literature Series, Vol. 8. Manchester: Manchester University Press, 1984.

——. "From Notes Made in 1970–71." In *Speech Genres and Other Late Essays.* Trans. Vern W. McGee. Ed. Caryl Emerson and Michael Holquist. Austin: University of Texas, 1986.

——. "The Problem of the Text in Linguistics, Philology and the Human Sciences: An Experiment in Philosophical Analysis." In *Speech Genres and Other Late Essays.* Austin: University of Texas, 1986.

——. "Discourse in the Novel." In *The Dialogic Imagination.* Trans. Caryl Emerson and Michael Holquist. Ed. Michael Holquist. Austin: University of Texas Press, 1996.

——. "Epic and the Novel: Towards a Methodology for the Study of the Novel." In *The Dialogic Imagination.* Trans. Caryl Emerson and Michael Holquist. Ed. Michael Holquist. Austin: University of Texas Press, 1996.

Clark, Katerina, and Michael Holquist. *Mikhail Bakhtin.* Cambridge, MA: Harvard University Press, 1984.

Hirschkop, Ken. *Mikhail Bakhtin: An Aesthetic for Democracy.* Oxford: Oxford University Press, 1999.

Nepomnyaschy, Caterine Theimer. *Abram Tertz and the Poetics of Crime.* New Haven, CT: Yale University Press, 1995.

Tertz, Abram. *Fantastic Stories.* Evanston, IL: Northwestern University Press, 1963.

——. *The Trial Begins.* Trans. Max Hayword. Fontana: Collins, 1970.

——. *On Socialist Realism.* Trans. George Dennis. Berkley: University of California Press, 1982.

CHAPTER SIX

Bible and Ethics: Moral Formation and Analogical Imagination

Johannes Nissen

Introduction

The use of the Bible in ethics is comparable with the way in which literature and film are used in ethics.[1] Every great work of literature, film, or drama invites us into an alternative reality where new possibilities are disclosed for our lives. In a similar way, the New Testament presents a different way of living. Yet, it seems that the parallel to other great literature also has its limits, in so far as the Bible is considered to have a specific authority. In the New Testament the new possibilities for living are described as "life in Christ," "discipleship," "living the Truth," and so on. Since appropriation means making my own what is genuinely "different" or "other," there must first be some critical distance from the texts to know that their world is not my world. Sandra Schneiders-rightly notes that the biblical "text must maintain its identity, its 'strangeness,' which both gifts and challenges the reader. It must be allowed to say what is says, regardless of whether this is comfortable or assimilable by the reader" (Schneiders 1991, 171).

In order to appreciate a classic text—whether it is a biblical text or a text from Shakespeare (for example, *Hamlet*)—a critical distance is necessary. If, however, we keep our distance to the biblical text in critical consciousness, it would be like studying Shakespeare's text but never enjoying a performance of it. The truth of Hamlet would not come home to us in a transformative way because our imagination, emotions, and personal identities would not be engaged. We need to move beyond to what Ricoeur has named "the second naiveté" where we can appreciate that the new world disclosed in the encounter can transform our lives (Spohn 1995, 11).

Key words

Moral formation, analogical imagination, correlation, reader-response, reader-resistance.

★ ★ ★

Text and Reader: Bible Reading as a
Transformative Act

How do we read the biblical text? This is a crucial question that is answered in different ways. Traditional hermeneutics argues that we read in order to understand, that is, we read in order to grasp the author's meaning. Another possibility is presented by reader-response criticism according to which meaning is related to the ways in which texts are received by readers. There are, however, at least two different ways of perceiving reader-response criticism.[2]

First, there is a more moderate form of reader-response criticism ("Reader-Reception"). This approach highlights the importance of the reader "realizing" textual meaning. The text is inert until reactivated by the reader. As Paul Ricoeur puts it, "reading is like the execution of a musical score; it marks the realization, the enactment, of the semantic possibilities of the text" (Ricoeur 1981, 159). But this is not to say that all reading is arbitrary. Paul Ricoeur sees the reading as a balancing act between, on the one hand, believing that each text has only one correct interpretation, and, on the other, projecting us into the text, although, ultimately, he privileges the world of the text over the reader.[3] The texts are occasions to understand ourselves in a new light. The reader is active, but the reader's activity is oriented to receiving the text.

The second approach is a more radical form of reader-response criticism ("Reader-Resistance"). It is known in different forms (e.g., post-structuralism, neo-pragmatism). A common idea is that the reader has to resist any claim—either textual or interpretive—that pretends to be authoritative, exclusive, and absolute. To find and fix "the meaning" of texts are seen as covert attempts to impose an authoritarian rule on the reader. So, for instance, Stanley Fish who claims that the authority belongs to the "interpretive community." Thus, meaning is a function of the reading strategy brought to the text.[4]

My own position is in line with the more moderate form. In accordance with Kevin Vanhoozer I would claim that readers should seek to ascertain the nature of the text's communicative intent (its genre and sense) before seeking to use and evaluate it. "To treat a text justly is to respect it for the kind of thing it is, that is, to entertain its perspective and to heed its voice" (Vanhoozer 1995, 315). "If meaning were not in some sense 'there' in the text, how could texts ever challenge, inform, or transform their readers? How could texts ever criticize a dominant ideology?" (317)

The relation between text and reader can be seen as a fusion between two horizons, between the world of the text and the world of the reader. In the fusion of the reader's world with the world of the text both the reader and the text are transformed. When the readers enter the world of the text it transforms them by providing a new way of seeing and being, it offers them new possibilities. When the world of the reader is brought to the text it transforms the text by allowing a plurality of possible meanings not perceived in the past to be appropriated in the present by the reader; it offers the text a new way of speaking (West 1999, 44). Further, by the very fact that we react to the text, we are transformed by the text. This is particularly clear in the case of a positive response to the text. We are informed, instructed, or taught by it. This is also clear when we are angered or infuriated by the text (Patte 1995, 97).

Any reading of the Bible will start with some specific questions. We cannot, after all, jump to some privileged place of neutrality or complete objectivity; it is from within our "life-worlds" that we engage in the reading task. This, however, raises some questions (Green 1995, 415). If our own life-worlds are the starting point for reading the Bible, will we not find in its pages only that for which we are looking? Can we as readers be open to the challenge of the biblical text? Any use of Scripture must face the risk that the text just becomes just a mirror reflecting back what we want it to say. Therefore, some reading must be used which allows the text to speak its piece, and to function as a window through which we see something besides our own thoughts.[5]

The dialogue between text and interpretation demands a twofold critical reading (West 1999, 23 and 76). The first step is a critical reading of the Bible; the second step is a critical appropriation and "reading" of our own context. This means that there is no simple correspondence between the Bible and our context. We cannot simply move from our biblical reading to a present application. The move from text to context is a critical, complex, and cautious exercise. The conversation between the biblical text and our experiences must have the form of a mutual critical correlation (Schillebeeckx 1980, 94).

Different Ways of Using the Bible in Ethics

Just as there are many ways of understanding the interaction between text and reader, there are many ways of relating the Bible to ethics. To begin with, it might be useful with a brief survey of the most important ways. I suggest that the various approaches can be classified in four major groups.[6]

The first category covers those theories according to which the moral teaching of Scripture is of no (or very little) relevance for ethics. A few examples must suffice. The first theory is the interim ethics (e.g., Albert Schweitzer). According to this theory, Jesus taught a heroic and rigorous obedience applicable only to the brief time before the cosmic crisis associated with the dawn of the apocalyptic kingdom. Two other theories are existential ethics (e.g., Rudolf Bultmann) and situations ethics (e.g., Joseph Fletcher). According to these theories Jesus taught no ethics at all in the sense of offering guidance about what actions ought to be done. What he taught is reduced to the love command in a formal shape.

The second category consists of *prescriptive* approaches. Here the focus is on individual biblical "commands." The Bible is seen as moral recipes. Examples of this approach are biblicism, and casuistry.[7]

The third category suggests that the Bible offers basic criteria, perspectives, or paradigms. One example is the *moral law model* that takes Scripture to be the revelation of a moral law of certain rules and principles to be obeyed. The *moral ideal model* takes Scripture to be the source of moral ideals, of certain goals to be striven for (e.g., love of neighbor; the kingdom, justice; freedom, the imitation of Jesus). The *analogical model* takes Scripture to be the source of moral precedents. One can discern God's judgment for a contemporary situation in the precedent provided by his recorded judgment in some similar biblical situations.

The fourth category emphasizes *theo*-logy as source of moral action. These are theories which focus on the *indicative* (what the Bible tells us God is like and about how God acts) and take that as a point of departure for recommending how the Christian, in freedom and responsibility before God, should best respond to God in the present situation (the basic ethical *imperative*). Examples of this category are various models such as "ethics as response to God's action"; "narrativity and ethics," "moral formation of the identity," and "paradigmatic patterns."

The first two categories cover positions that are problematic.[8] On the one hand are biblicists or fundamentalists who see the Bible as a repository of divine commands. This approach reduces the moral life to Christian legalism. Especially in the matter of the Bible's diversity the advocates of this position are faced with great difficulties. On the other extreme is the work of Jack Sanders, whose recommendation for the continuing use of the New Testament candidly demands a selection of those concepts and teachings that the modern and moral person can accept, so that we are "freed from bondage to that tradition" (130).

Instead of this I would suggest a multidimensional approach based on the third and fourth categories. Following James Gustafson we might speak of the *great variety model*. This model takes Scripture to be a witness to a great variety of values and norms through a great variety of literary forms. It refuses to reduce the forms of moral instruction in the Bible to a single form or the moral themes in the Bible to a single theme. The Bible "informs" the agent or "illuminates" the situation, but it is not sufficient to authorize any particular judgment.

The use of the Bible in ethics needs to guard against two forms of reductionism. The first form might be called "*genre reductionism*" (Birch and Rasmussen 1976, 109). This is the effective selection, whether deliberate or not, of only certain kinds of biblical materials as the materials pertinent to ethics. Thus the wisdom sayings, moral teachings, and prophetic injunctions are used, and the devotional materials, apocalyptic visions, and miracle stories are not. The second form can be characterized as "*norm reductionism*." It is methodologically erroneous to proceed with the assumption of a single biblical norm for Christian ethics. This means that norm reductionism should be avoided as well as genre reductionism (115).

One of the most interesting models is that of the Bible shaping the moral identity of the Christians and of the Church. This model belongs to the fourth category. In what follows I go into more detail with the model and relate it to one of the other models: the model of analogy (the third category).

The Formative Role of Scripture

What is meant by "formation"? *Moral formation* is a nurturing process in which a certain sense of identity, a certain recognition of community, and a certain pattern of motivation evolve. Any community of which we are members "forms" us in the sense of orienting us to the world in a certain way, encouraging certain kinds of behavior, and discouraging others (Best and Robra 1997, 55). The Bible plays a significant role in the formation of the character of the ethical decision maker. Bruce C. Birch and Larry L. Rasmussen suggest that the role of the Scriptures in the nurturing of a basic orientation and in the generating of particular attitudes and intentions is a central one. Furthermore, they argue that "our 'being' shapes our 'seeing' and the way we see things gives us a particular outlook and orientation toward life" (Birch and Rasmussen 1976, 89). "*Who we are* and are becoming as a result of faith we hold determines in large part *what we see*" (88).

It is beyond dispute that the story of Jesus is the most important text for moral formation of the Christians. This story shapes Christian action which conforms to, corresponds to, or embodies aspects of his life. All these verbs express the activity of *patterning*, of extending to new material the shape that was inherent in an original. The response is guided by the original. The original serves as paradigm, prototype, and precedent to guide the actions and dispositions of Christians in new circumstances: "Because biblical patterns combine a stable core with an indeterminate, open-ended dimension, the moral response can be both creative and faithful. We extend a pattern by analogy since we move from the recognizable shape in the first instance to new situations within certain limitations" (Spohn 1995, 100).

As a paradigmatic figure Jesus was for his followers and for later Christians a chief source for their way of looking at the world and responding to it. This shaping of the moral identity is characteristic of various literary genres (Birch and Rasmussen 1976, 106–107). It includes the healing and feeding narratives, the parables (e.g., the story about the Good Samaritan and the stories about the lost sheep, coin, and son); the teachings on the mountain; Jesus' announcement of his ministry in Luke 4:16–30; and the events of Passion Week. It is worth noticing that many biblical stories are "counter-stories," in which things happen or are said which hearers would not naturally expect. Often there are sudden twists, reversals, and amazing conclusions, as in most parables of Jesus (Weber 1995, 4).

Analogical Imagination

The analogical approach has played a significant role in the use of Bible in ethics. However, there are some deficits which must be faced. One might, for instance, propose that Christians are to imitate the virtuous deeds of biblical characters and to reenact the biblical story or stories in their own line. There is a suggestion of this possibility when Karl Barth says: "We are not only invited to be contemporaneous and like-minded with the biblical men. We are not only exhorted to hear the command as they hear it . . . The command given to them and heard by them becomes directly the command given to us and to be heard by us. Their task becomes our task" (Barth 1957, 706). However, this use of Scripture is problematic (Nelson 1987, 105). In the first place, it is difficult to see how the analogies between biblical situations and our own are to be controlled. Second, what is to be done when no biblical analogy is apparent? Are Christians bereft of guidance in the face of radically new moral challenges? Third, this approach seems to disrespect the autonomy and freedom of the moral agent.

To avoid the risks of a simple analogical model one must argue that patterns and paradigms exercise a normative role through the analogical imagination, which seeks to act in new situations in ways that are faithful to the original pattern. William Spohn rightly notes that in order to be both free and faithful, modern believers reason by analogy from the earlier interaction which is witnessed in the biblical text to a similar response to the challenges of their own time. Analogical thinking relies on imagination and on the ability to discern similarities and differences between one situation and another.[9] Richard Hays, in a similar way, says: "The use of the New Testament in normative ethics requires *an integrative act of the imagination*, a discernment about how our lives, despite their historical dissimilarity to the lives narrated in the New Testament, might fitly answer to that narration and participate in the truth it tells" (Hays 1997, 298; emphasis in original). Two historical situations are never totally analogous. However, one might speak of a "dynamic analogy" between the text and the contemporary situation (Long 1989, 128). This means that no historical situation is repeated exactly, but a dynamic analogy results when we identify in some ways with characteristics or circumstances in the text and thus participate in the tensions and resolutions of the text.

Analogical imagination presupposes a creative transfer because like the exodus and the exile, the gospel events and teachings are *historical prototypes* rather than *mythical archetypes* (Fiorenza 1984, 14). The new response harmonizes with the prototype but in order to be responsive to the actual needs of the day, it cannot copy the original as if it were a completely determined archetype.

New Testament Examples of Analogical
Imagination

When we read New Testament texts our perceptions are reoriented. We are challenged to see things in a new way and to act in radically different ways. We are moved to reimagine our lives in the light of the texts. A few examples might illustrate this.

1. *The parable of the Good Samaritan* (Luke 10:25–37) is the first example to illustrate what it means that the imagination moves from the pattern of Jesus' story to discover how to act faithfully in a new situation. The parable does not answer the original question of the lawyer because it was the wrong question. "Who is my neighbor?" (10:29) poses the question in insider/outsider terms. It tries to establish the boundaries of love. But in Jesus' answer "neighbor" shifts from the object of love to the subject who shows love: "Which of these three, do you think, was a neighbor to the man . . . ?" (10:36). The original question is turned around in a way that cancel boundaries "To whom can I show love?"

The final statement is "Go and do likewise" (Luke 10:37). The mandate is not "Go and do exactly the same" as the Samaritan. It is decidedly not: "Go and do whatever you want". The term "likewise" implies that Christians should be faithful to the story of Jesus yet creative in applying it to their context. The image of the Good Samaritan, if internalized as a major image, might evoke a general perspective that sees all humankind as a single family under God, and it might evoke the specific intention of helping to break down the barriers that in fact still separate "Jew" and "Samaritan," male and female, bond and free (Birch and Rasmussen 1976, 107).

Jesus does not tell the lawyer what to do as an active outgoing neighbor. Instead the Samaritan is presented as an exemplar to be followed. In doing so Jesus is challenging the expectations of the Jewish audience.[10] They probably would have been shocked by his use of a Samaritan as an exemplar, while discrediting the respected priest and the Levite. Today a similar reversal of expectations might occur if we speak of "The Good Muslim" or "The Good Homosexual." That is, if we combine the notion of compassion with the notion of a foreigner or another person we dislike.

2. *The account of the footwashing* (John 13:1–17). In John 13:15 Jesus says: "For I have set you an example that you also should do as I have done to you." This is not an appeal to a mere repetition of what Jesus has done. There is a reversal of expectations in the story just as the reversal in the parable of the Good Samaritan. The disciples are really shocked

by this event. By acting like a slave their master is turning the world upside down.

After the meal, Jesus articulates the "new commandment" (John 13:34–35) thereby telling his disciples they should use their imagination and think analogically. It is the move from "*as* I have loved you" to "*so* you ought to love one another" (Spohn 1999, 52). The pattern of Jesus' love for them should guide and empower them to love others in analogous ways. The statement "as I have loved you . . ." emphasizes that Jesus is the source of the Christian's love for one another. At the same time it refers to Jesus as the standard of Christian love (cf. 13:15).

It is well known that the account in John 13 has inspired a number of Holy Thursday rituals to remember and reenact the washing of feet. It is often done in a very literal way, and one has the impression that this is not very imaginative. The character of reversal that was so fundamental to the original story has not really come into its own.

3. *The hymn in Philippians 2:6–11* has the form of a poetic description of the Christ-event. This hymn is used in a context of moral exhortations. In 2:1–4 Paul specifies particular forms of behaviors that the Christians should practice. The force of these ethical demands is that if they are to walk in a manner "worthy of the Gospel of Christ" (1:27) in the face of opponents seeking their destruction, then they must remain steadfast in their faith, united in selfless love and concern for one another. These ethical demands are based on the poetic description of Christ's activity in the hymn. Stephen E. Fowl and L. Gregory Jones are probably right when arguing that Paul and the Philippians would have realized that no human could perfectly imitate this story about Christ. "There cannot be a one-to-one relationship between the Christ-event narrated in 2:6–11 and the Philippians' situation. If the Philippians are to let the events presented in 2:6–11 guide their common life, they will have to draw an analogy from those events to their own situation."[11] They will have to embody the text (the Jesus story) in their particular social context. They must learn to become people of character.

In this connection it should be noticed that the most important discontinuities between the story of Jesus and the story of Philippians (and our story) might not be historical but moral and theological (Fowl and Jones-1991, 61). That is, the discontinuities between Scripture and our contemporary settings are more likely found within us, specifically in our inability and unwillingness to provide and *embody* wise readings of the texts, than in gaps of historical time.

4. *The account of the early community in Jerusalem* in Acts 2:41–47 and 4:32–37. An important question is—Did Luke consider the community

in Jerusalem as a model to be imitated? Or was his theological thinking marked by a delay in the coming of the "parousia" so that his own audience was perhaps unable to adopt the pattern of the first believers (interim ethics)? As far as I can see, Luke's portrait of the primitive community at Jerusalem served as a model for his own readership. This situation is not unlike the situation described in 1 Corinthians 11:17–34. In both these passages we have a conflict between "eschatological egalitarianism" (the social utopia) and division in the community (Nissen 1999, 59).

This means that the descriptions in Acts 2:41–47 and 4:32–37 provide a positive paradigm for the Church. However, it should be noticed that in these texts we are given neither rules for the community life nor economic principles; instead we are given a story that calls us to consider how in our own communities we might live analogously (Hays 1997, 302).

Parables as Visions of the Good Life

The parables in a particular way reveal how the moral identity is shaped by telling stories. An investigation of the synoptic tradition indicates that the "the church used the tradition of Jesus' parables and adapted it creatively so that the living Lord himself could form and inform his community" (Verhey 1984, 48).

The parables of Jesus have four characteristics: realistic, metaphorical, paradoxical or surprising, and open-ended. While myths establish a world, parables subvert our ordinary expectations. The reader can become caught by listening attentively to a parable. When this engagement occurs, we do not interpret parables so much as they interpret us (Spohn 1995, 88). Because parables are open-ended, they do not allow the hearer to remain inactive. They do not tell us what to do because, "as religious language they present not simply a series of ethical paradigms or exhortations, though they are often so interpreted, but a *vision of reality which becomes a presupposition to ethics*" (Donahue 1988, 17).

John Donhaue shows how the parables of Jesus work to shape the morality of the audience. He disagrees with literary critics who locate the transformative power of the parables in the metaphorical process itself. Instead he sees the parables as narratives in metaphoric form which refers to another realm beyond themselves. Those who seem to imagine that "salvation comes from metaphor alone" ignore the one who is speaking these metaphors.[12]

The element of reversal is an important aspect of many parables. So, for instance, in the parable of the workers in the vineyard (Matt. 20:1–16) there is a collision between two worlds, between two sets of experiences, namely life as fairness versus life as grace. A similar collision can be detected in the parable of the prodigal son (Luke 15:11–32). To understand such parables is to be changed by them. It is to have our vision of the world reshaped by them. "To 'understand' them is to enter the process of reflecting about how our lives ought to change in response to the gospel—a gospel that unsettles what we 'know' about responsibility and ethics" (Hays 1997, 301).

The Performance of the Text

In the past, New Testament hermeneutics has been occupied predominantly with how texts serve to pass on *information*. Today the focus has shifted to the question of how texts might have a *transformative* role (Green 1995, 413). A similar shift has taken place in the understanding of the relationship between the Bible and ethics. New Testament ethics has often been understood as the attempt to extrapolate norms and principles from a biblical narrative, for example, the texts from the early chapters of Acts about "community of goods." Stephen Barton points out that this attempt to "translate Luke's testimony into 'norms and principles' is a strategy, not so much for appropriating the text, as for *neutralizing* it. If New Testament ethics as a whole is interpreted in this way, one must ask the hard question: Is it a strategy for endlessly postponing the (excruciating) business of allowing ourselves *to be changed*?" (Barton 1999, 203–204).

An alternative way would be to understand New Testament interpretation as performance. According to Nicholas Lash, among the closest analogies to biblical interpretation is the interpretation of a Beethoven score or a Shakespearean tragedy (although he also appeals to other analogies, including the interpretation of legal texts and written constitutions). The central act of the interpretation of a Beethoven score is the performance, which has to be a matter of more than technical accuracy. Instead it is a kind of *creative fidelity* that allows the musical score to come alive again in the present moment. Important also is the recognition that this is a social or communal activity involving not just conductor and orchestra, but an audience of listeners and critics as well. These analogies help establish Lash's main point that there are at least some texts that only begin to deliver their meaning in so far as they are "brought into play" through interpretative performance. The Bible is one such text. The fundamental form of the Christian interpretation of Scripture is the life, activity, and organization of the believing community (Lash 1986, 42).

It is not simply the question of the Christian communities reading the Scriptures, but of actually performing them (Fowl and Jones 1991, 62–63). Such performances require the development of well-formed character. We read and perform Scripture in the hope that our own lives will be transformed into the likeness of Christ. Such transformation takes place in and through the formation of a community of disciples.

The New Testament itself insists on the necessity of the embodiment of the Gospel. The sequence of the verbs in Romans 12:1–2 is interesting: "*Present* your bodies as a living sacrifice . . . Be *transformed* . . . that you may *discern* what is the will of God, what is good and acceptable and perfect." This text indicates that the knowledge of the will of God *follows* the transformation of the Christian community. Why? Because, until we see the embodiment of the text, we cannot begin to conceive what it means. The most crucial hermeneutical task is the formation of communities seeking to live under the Word (Hays 1997, 306).

Liturgy and Moral Formation

The heart of Christian moral formation lies in worship, through which the story of salvation is reenacted in the modes of prayer, proclamation, and sacrament (Best and Robra 1997, 66; Mudge 1998, 81). In worship we receive identity; we are formed morally. By encountering God we learn how to be disciples. We learn to love by being loved; we learn to forgive by being forgiven; we learn generosity by being treated generously (Forrester 1997, 56). The two liturgical acts, baptism and the Lord's Supper, both had an important formative role in the first communities (e.g., Romans 6; 1 Cor. 11:17–34). Most important, however, was the Lord's Supper, because it was celebrated more frequently than baptism.[13] As at Jesus' table there was an open invitation to overcome suspicions, divisions, and hostilities, so at the Eucharistic table Jew and Gentile, rich and poor, weak and strong come together and experience a new and challenging depth of community (Forrester 1997, 54). The Eucharistic liturgy ties memory and hope specifically to our participation in the story of Jesus. This participation gives us new eyes to see the world and new energy to bear witness in it. Liturgy is thus not something added to the moral but its nourishing ground.

Sometimes, however, there is a collision between the new era (the Lord's Supper as unity) and the daily reality, between Paul's theological vision and the social consequences drawn from that vision (Nissen 1984, 112–113). An example of this is the celebration of the Eucharist in Corinthians. Paul's statements in 1 Corinthians 11:17–34 indicate that he had expected the Christians to act according to the vision with analogical imagination. The Corinthians should have acted faithfully to the tradition and creatively to the new situation. However, the rich members of the community disregarded the needs of the poor members, and so the sacrament became invalid: "It is not the Lord's supper that you eat" (1 Cor. 11:20).

Paul recorded the institution of the Lord's Supper in order to remind the Christians of the *significance* of the death of Jesus. By saying, "you proclaim the Lord's death," Paul tells his readers that to celebrate the Eucharist is on every occasion to renew one's acceptance of a love that serves.

Formation and Malformation

Christians are not only formed by the Jesus story and by the sacraments, they are also formed by the powers of the world. And this might result in malformation (Mudge 1998, 72 and 91). This is what Paul criticizes in 1 Corinthians 11:17–34. The congregation's liturgical, moral formation may turn out to be *mal*formation. We might call this an irresponsible answer to the Gospels.

Both formation and malformation can be the result of the encounter of the churches with the public world. As the ecumenical document "Costly Obedience" states: "Instead of being agents of just social transformation, churches too often uncritically conform to unjust social and economic patterns within their cultural and national contexts. The result is moral malformation of the membership of the churches" (Best and Robra 1997, 62).

The church does not practice formation in abstraction from its history. The memory of past experience, including the experience of moral failure in the face of challenges such as those of nationalism, ethnicity, racism, and violence, needs to be taken into our consciousness. A church not positioned where the Gospel demands it to be amid social forces and events will *mal*form its members.[14]

The Hermeneutics of Correspondence—the Method of Correlation

The reflections on formation and malformation lead to some methodological reflections on analogical thinking and the method of correlation.

Correlation or "correspondence of relationships" between the horizon of our world and those of the text is a key factor in interpretation. Imperfect correlation is almost bound to be tendentious: as in "modernizing" Jesus and the "domestication" of the Bible. A proper correlation is dependent on "distantiation," the differentiation of the worlds so that each of them is treated with integrity; but it also involves participation of the reader in the dynamics of the text, and theological reflection on issues arising from it. If carelessly correlated to the modern situation, a text might be morally objectionable: for example, if it were used to stir up prejudice, racism, or sexism, to justify violence or war, or to further human greed and power (McDonald 1993, 244).

Clodovis Boff has made a helpful distinction between a "correspondence of terms" and a "correspondence of relationships."[15] A correspondence of terms approach is a very simple one. On the basis of a simple historical examination, it believes that Christian communities today (or some communities) live in a world that is similar to, if not identical with, the world in which Jesus himself lived. Hence the Christian community today can be related to its contemporary political context in exactly the same way that Jesus was related to his political context. According to this method, the Gospel story is reproduced in a contemporary context, with twentieth-century (modern) figures related to one another in the same way that the characters in the gospel story were related. Such a model, however, is undoubtedly naïve. It presupposes that history simply repeats itself. There is a lack of analogical *imagination* in this model.

The "correspondence of relationships" is the second model. This model (favored by C. Boff) will indeed attempt to see Jesus in dynamic relation to the context of his own times and will insist that the community's theological understanding of the text takes due account of that dynamic. It will also relate its theological reflection on the text to the sociological comprehension of its own context. Thus there is a distancing of ourselves from the text in order to see the dialectic within it, and also an identification with the dynamics of the text as we bring it to bear on our modern situation. The correspondence of relationship expresses and channels the element of analogy implicit in all hermeneutics and it relates the correlation to the dynamics within the text (Boff 1987, 147–149; McDonald 1993, 217).

From Response to Responsibility

Christian ethics has a responsorial character.[16] The starting point is God's words and deeds. Our moral life is a response to what God is doing in the world. This response leads to responsible acts on our part. In other words, God's love comes to us first and our actions correspond to the character of that love. In this sense we might speak of "Scripture as basis for responding love" (Spohn 1995, 94–126).[17] Christian ethics is an ethic of responsibility.[18] Christian moral reflection moves from patterns that are central to biblical narrative by analogy to discern appropriate ways of being and acting in the present situation.

This move from response to responsibility presupposes that one takes into consideration the discontinuity as well as the continuity between "then" and "now." I suggest a procedure that has three steps: listening, learning, and living. (1) the first task is *listening* carefully to the two texts: the "text" of the Bible and the "text" of life; (2) the second task is *learning*. From our listening to the biblical text and to our own context we should learn to discern what is God's will in the present situation. Ethical decision is a question of discernment (cf. Rom. 12:2), a learning process which is a communal rather than an individual task (Deidun 1998, 37–38); (3) the *living* in front of the text. The task is not simply that of copying the example of Jesus, not of repeating mechanically the words of Jesus. It is to live faithfully and responsibly in a new situation.

Because the Bible addresses communities rather than individuals, the appropriate moral response is discerned within the Christian community. In other words, the moral formation is closely related to moral community. The crucial question is: How are we to respond to our challenges in ways analogous to the responses that the first Christian communities made to their challenges? There is the double task of reading the biblical text and reading the world (Fowl and Jones 1991, 42–45). On the one hand, the Bible as Scripture forms the life of Christian communities. Christians will need to learn to read the Scriptures "over-against ourselves" rather than simply "for ourselves." We must be willing to be interrogated *by* Scripture in addition to interrogating it. On the other hand there are the readings of the world: The process of faithfully embodying an interpretation of Scripture presupposes that Christian communities have already analyzed and diagnosed the contexts in which they find themselves.

Conclusion: Readers and Disciples

To conclude this essay I relate my reflections on Bible and ethics to the issue of reader response criticism. Traditionally, classic exegesis presupposed "objective," dispassionate readers, but the very project of such neutrality has been called into serious question by new methods. The "interested" reader has replaced the "objective" reader.[19] As noted previously we are facing two opposed models for reading: a moderate form ("reader-reception") and a radical form ("reader-resistance"). In keeping with the first form I am giving priority to a "hermeneutics of hearing": We need to hear a voice other than our own or even our community (Snodgrass 2003, 9). Yet, this is not say that the text should be seen as a "meaning container." Rather, the text offers "potentialities of meaning" that can be actualized in a reading process that makes the text "meaningful" (Patte 1995, 94).

The preceding analysis of Bible and ethics shows that the biblical text claims our attention, teaches us, moves us, convinces us, empowers or degrades us.[20] Richard Hays rightly notes that the world we know is reconfigured when we "read" it in counterpoint with the New Testament. The hermeneutical task is to relocate our contemporary experience on the map of the New Testament story. By telling us a story that overturns our conventional ways of seeing the world, the New Testament provides images and categories in light of which the life of our community is interpreted (Hays 1997, 302).

At this point it might be useful to add a few notes on the authority of the Bible in relation to the committed readers, the Christian community (Nissen 2003b, 656–657). There is a dialectic between the "text" of life (experience) and the text of Scripture, and this dialectic is the kernel of the interpretive enterprise. The community of Christians formed and shaped the Bible, and the Bible in turn forms and shapes the community. However, if the Bible represents the self-understanding of the community that produced it, it is by no means an idealized statement of Christian propaganda. Rather, the Bible is a series of critique of the very community that produced it.

If the Bible is considered to have authority, the reader becomes the listener, seeking to enter into dialogue with the text, to enter personally in the story, to live it, to take part in it, to re-live it.[21] In this understanding, the embodiment of the text in the life of the readers is of great importance. They read and perform the text in the hope that their life will be transformed. When this occurs, they as readers are becoming disciples. A hermeneutic of hearing will include a hermeneutics of action, knowing that texts are the result of actions and are intended to produce action (Snodgrass 2003, 27). There is a move from the emphasis on the act of reading to a focus on the practices of the people of God fostered by that reading.

Notes

1. The main focus of this essay will be on the literary aspect of the biblical texts. This is not to say that the literary methods should be employed in any exclusive way when approaching the Bible, for they have to be supplemented with historical analysis. There is a need for a model that can integrate literary and historical methods.

2. For a more detailed analysis see Kevin J. Vanhoozer, "The Reader in New Testament Interpretation," in *Hearing the New Testament: Strategies for Interpretation*, ed. Joel B. Green (Grand Rapids, MI: Eerdmans), especially 304–312.

3. Cf. Klyne Snodgrass, "Reading to Hear: A Hermeneutics of Hearing," *Horizons in Biblical Theology*, 34 (2003): 21. "What we are interested in, as Ricoeur was right to emphasize, is the 'world' projected by the text, a world which may be inhabited or rejected."

4. As Fish puts it: "The interpretation constrains the facts rather than the other way around and also constrains the kinds of meaning that one can assign to those facts" (Stanley Fish, *Is There a Text in This Class? The Authority of Interpretive Communities* [Cambridge: Harvard University, 1980], 293).

5. Cf. Johannes Nissen, *New Testament and Mission: Historical and Hermeneutical Perspectives* (Frankfurt: Verlag Peter Lang, 1999), 15. On the problem of self-asserting Bible reading see my remarks on Luke 4:16–30; Nissen, *New Testament and Mission*, 68–69.

6. A more detailed investigation of the different types is given in my Danish book on Bible and ethics (Johannes Nissen, *Bibel og etik. Konkrete og principielle problemstillinger* [Aarhus: Aarhus University Press, 2003a]). For other helpful classifications of the various approaches see the articles by Leroy Long, Gustafson, and Deidun.

7. Common to biblicism and casuistry is an approach that treats the Bible as a collection of commandments, rules, and advice that can speak to every possible contingency in the modern world.

8. See also Allen Verhey's criticism of the two approaches in Allen Verhey, *The Great Reversal: Ethics and the New Testament* (Grand Rapids, MI: Eerdmans, 1984), 160.

9. William C. Spohn, *What are they Saying about Scripture and Ethics*, revised and expanded ed. (New York/Mahwah, NJ: Paulist Press, 1995), 7. See also Lisa S. Cahill, *Sex, Gender and Christian Ethics* (Cambridge: Cambridge University Press), 121. "Christian ethics today should encourage forms of behavior which serve an analogous function, without necessarily replicating the precise practices the NT records."

10. In this parable there is a "decentering of perspective" as in many other stories from the Gospels, especially Luke's Gospel. A sinful woman (Luke 7:34–50), a tax collector (Luke 19:1–10), and an outsider (Luke 10:30–37) represent the signs of the Kingdom of God; Johannes Nissen, "Jesus, the People of God, and the Poor: The Social Embodiment of Biblical Faith," in *New Directions in Biblical Theology*, ed. S. Pedersen (Leiden: E.J. Brill, 1994), 240.

11. Stephen E. Fowl and Gregory Jones, *Reading in Communion: Scripture and Ethics in Christian Life* (London: SPCK, 1991), 60. According to these authors "there is no formulaic pattern to the types of readings Paul gives. He does not follow a method designed to yield meaning which he then applies to a particular situation. Rather, he interprets his canon in the light of the particular situation he is addressing. His interpretation would then be confirmed as the believers embody it in their particular social contexts."

12. "Jesus' language is powerful, not because of his aesthetic brilliance or paradoxical quality, but because of the experience of God it mediates and the kind of life Jesus himself lived. What he spoke of in the parable he lived" (John R. Donahue, *The Gospel in Parable: Metaphor, Narrative, and Theology in the Synoptic Gospels* [Philadelphia: Fortress Press, 1988], 11).

13. The Lord's Supper "provided more occasions on which the implications of that special identity for appropriate modes of behavior could be impressed on the participants" (Wayne A. Meeks,

The Origins of Christian Morality: The First Two Centuries [New Haven: Yale University Press, 1993], 96).

14. Thomas F. Best and Martin Robra, *Ecclesiology and Ethics: Ecumenical Ethical Engagement, Moral Formation and the Nature of the Church* (Geneva: Would Council of Churches, 1997), 61. An ability to discern *mal*formation needs to be part and parcel of any true, ecclesial, formational Christian ethic; cf. Lewis S. Mudge, *The Church as Moral Community: Ecclesiology and Ethics in Ecumenical Debate* (New York/Geneva: Continuum and World Council of Churches, 1998), 92.

15. Clodovis Boff, *Theology and Praxis: Epistemological Foundations* (New York: Orbis Books 1987), 145–147. For a more detailed discussion see also Christopher Rowland and Mark Corner, *Liberating Exegesis: The Challenge of Liberation Theology to Biblical Studies* (London: SPCK, 1990), 54–65.

16. Sometimes German ethicists play on the words: "*Wort*" (word), "*Antwort*" (response), and "*Verantwortung*" (responsibility).

17. Another way of expressing this responsorial character of ethics is to adopt a "relationality-responsibility model" that "views the moral life primarily in terms of the persons' multiple relationships with God, neighbor, world, and self and the subject's actions in this context" (Charles E. Curran, *Moral Theology: A Continuing Journey* [Notre Dame, IN: University of Notre Dame Press], 44).

18. Cf. C. Freeman Sleeper, *The Bible and the Moral Life* (Louisville: Westminster/John Knox Press, 1992), 164–166. Sleeper favors an ethic of responsibility even though "responsibility" is not a biblical term or concept.

19. In the new model of interpretation meaning emerges as the result of an encounter between socially and historically conditioned text and a socially and historically conditioned reader. Fernando F. Segovia, "Cultural Studies and Contemporary Biblical Criticism: Ideological Criticism as Mode of Discourse," in *Reading from this Place, Vol 2: Social Location and Biblical Interpretation in Global Perspective*, ed. F. Segovia and M.A. Tolbert (Minneapolis: Fortress Press 1995), 8.

20. We tend to forget this function of the text because we are fascinated by our own interpretive prowess. Daniel Patte, *Ethics of Biblical Interpretation: A Re-evaluation* (Louisville: Westminster/John Knox Press, 1995), 98.

21. Cf. W. Vogels, "The Role of the Reader in Biblical Authority," *Theology Digest*, 47 (2000): 223. The author also notes: "As with any other text, the Bible has no authority in itself. The reader decides if and to what extent he or she will give it authority. But if the reader decides to take up the Bible, the rules of the game must be respected. This means respect of the communitarian authority of the Bible as canon and respect of the literary authority as a literary product" (225). See also Johannes Nissen, "Scripture and Community in Dialogue: Hermeneutical Reflections on the Authority of the Bible" in *The Biblical Canons*, ed. J.M. Auwers and H.J. de Jonge (Leuven: Leuven University Press, 2003b), 657–658.

Works Cited

Barth, Karl. *Church Dogmatics II/2.* Trans. G.W. Bromily et al. Edinburgh: T & T Clark, 1957.

Barton, Stephen. "New Testament Interpretation as Performance." *Scottish Journal of Theology* 52 (1999): 179–208.

Best, Thomas F., and Martin Robra. Eds. *Ecclesiology and Ethics: Ecumenical Ethical Engagement, Moral Formation and the Nature of the Church.* Geneva: Would Council of Churches, 1997.

Birch, Bruce C., and Larry L. Rasmussen. *Bible and Ethics in the Christian Life.* Minneapolis: Augsburg Publishing House, 1976.

Boff, Clodovis. *Theology and Praxis: Epistemological Foundations.* New York: Orbis Books, 1987.

Cahill, Lisa S. *Sex, Gender and Christian Ethics.* Cambridge: Cambridge University Press, 1996.

Curran, Charles E. *Moral Theology: A Continuing Journey.* Notre Dame, IN: University of Notre Dame Press, 1982.

Deidun, Tom. "The Bible and Christian Ethics." In *Christian Ethics. An Introduction.* Ed. B. Hoose. London: Cassell, 1998. 3–46.

Donahue, John R. *The Gospel in Parable: Metaphor, Narrative, and Theology in the Synoptic Gospels.* Philadelphia: Fortress Press, 1988.

Fiorenza, Elisabeth Schüssler. *Bread Not Stone: The Challenge of Feminist Biblical Interpretation.* Chicago: University of Chicago, 1984.

Fish, Stanley. *Is There a Text in This Class? The Authority of Interpretive Communities.* Cambridge: Harvard University, 1980.

Forrester, Duncan. *The True Church and Morality: Reflections on Ecclesiology and Ethics.* Geneva: World Council of Churches, 1997.

Fowl, Stephen E., and L. Gregory Jones. *Reading in Communion: Scripture and Ethics in Christian Life.* London: SPCK, 1991.

Green, Joel B. "The Practice of Reading the New Testament." In *Hearing the New Testament: Strategies for Interpretation.* Ed. J.B. Green. Grand Rapids, MI: Eerdmans, 1995. 411–427.

Gustafson, James M. "The Place of Scripture in Christian Ethics: A Methodological Study." *Interpretation* 24 (1969): 430–455.

Hays, Richard B. *The Moral Vision of the New Testament: A Contemporary Introduction to New Testament Ethics.* Edinburgh: T & T Clark, 1997.

Lash, Nicholas. *Theology on the Way to Emmaus.* London: SCM, 1986.

Long, Edward Leroy, Jr. "The Use of the Bible in Christian Ethics: A Look at Basic Options." *Interpretation* 19 (1965): 149–162.

Long, Thomas G. *The Witness of Preaching.* Louisville: Westminster/John Knox Press, 1989.

McDonald, J.I.H. *Biblical Interpretation and Christian Ethics.* Cambridge: Cambridge University Press, 1993.

Meeks, Wayne A. *The Origins of Christian Morality: The First Two Centuries.* New Haven: Yale University Press, 1993.

Mudge, Lewis S. *The Church as Moral Community: Ecclesiology and Ethics in Ecumenical Debate.* New York and Geneva: Continuum and World Council of Churches, 1998.

Nelson, Paul. *Narrative and Morality: A Theological Inquiry.* University Park/London: Pennsylvania State University, 1987.

Nissen, Johannes. *Poverty and Mission: New Testament Perspectives on a Contemporary theme.* Leiden: Interuniversity Institute of Missiology and Ecumenism, 1984.

——. "Jesus, the People of God, and the Poor: The Social Embodiment of Biblical Faith." In *New Directions in Biblical Theology.* Ed. S. Pedersen. Leiden: E.J. Brill, 1994. 220–242.

——. *New Testament and Mission: Historical and Hermeneutical Perspectives.* Frankfurt: Verlag Peter Lang, 1999.

——. *Bibel og etik. Konkrete og principielle problemstillinger.* Aarhus: Aarhus University Press, 2003a.

——. "Scripture and Community in Dialogue: Hermeneutical Reflections on the Authority of the Bible." In *The Biblical Canons.* Ed. J.M. Auwers and H.J. de Jonge. Leuven: Leuven University Press, 2003b. 651–658.

Patte, Daniel. *Ethics of Biblical Interpretation: A Re-evaluation.* Louisville: Westminster/John Knox Press, 1995.

Ricoeur, Paul. *Hermeneutics and the Human Sciences.* Ed. John B. Thompson. Cambridge: Cambridge University Press, 1981.

Rowland, Christopher, and Mark Corner. *Liberating Exegesis: The Challenge of Liberation Theology to Biblical Studies.* London: SPCK, 1990.

Sanders, Jack T. *Ethics in the New Testament*. London: SCM, 1975.

Schillebeeckx, Eduard. "Erfahrung und Glaube." In *Christlicher Glaube in Moderner Gesellschaft*. Vol. 25. Ed. F. Böckle et al. Freiburg: Herder, 1980. 72–116.

Schneiders, Sandra. *The Revelatory Text: Interpreting the New Testament as Sacred Scripture*. San Francisco: HarperCollins, 1991.

Segovia, Fernando F. "Cultural Studies and Contemporary Biblical Criticism: Ideological Criticism as Mode of Discourse." In *Reading from this Place, Vol 2: Social Location and Biblical Interpretation in Global Perspective*. Ed. F. Segovia and M.A. Tolbert. Minneapolis: Fortress Press, 1995. 1–17.

Sleeper, C. Freeman. *The Bible and the Moral Life*. Louisville: Westminster/John Knox Press, 1992.

Snodgrass, Klyne. "Reading to Hear: A Hermeneutics of Hearing." *Horizons in Biblical Theology* 34 (2003): 1–32.

Spohn, William C. *What are they Saying about Scripture and Ethics* (Revised and expanded edition). New York/Mahwah, NJ: Paulist Press, 1995.

———. *Go and Do Likewise: Jesus and Ethics*. New York: Continuum, 1999.

Vanhoozer, Kevin J. "The Reader in New Testament Interpretation." In *Hearing the New Testament: Strategies for Interpretation*. Ed Joel B. Green. Grand Rapids, MI: Eerdmans, 1995. 301–328.

Verhey, Allen. *The Great Reversal: Ethics and the New Testament*. Grand Rapids, MI: Eerdmans, 1984.

Vogels, W. "The Role of the Reader in Biblical Authority." *Theology Digest* 47 (2000): 219–225.

Weber, Hans-Ruedi. *The Book that Reads Me*. Geneva: World Council of Churches, 1995.

West, Gerald. *Contextual Bible Study*. Pietermaritzburg: Cluster Publications, 1999.

PART 3

Reading and the Literary

CHAPTER SEVEN

The Playwright, the Novelist, and the Comedian: A Case Study in Audience Responsibility

DIRK VISSER

Introduction

The starting point for this essay is formed by a series of events that took place in the Netherlands at the end of the twentieth century.

When in the 1980s a Dutch theater group wanted to perform Rainer Werner Fassbinder's play *Garbage, the City and Death*, they met with vehement protests, not least from the Jewish community, who perceived the play as anti-Semitic. One of the protesters, Jules Croiset, a Dutch Jewish actor, went so far as to stage his own kidnapping in protest against the play, claiming that he had been kidnapped by neo-Nazis who had read Fassbinder's play as an incitement to anti-Jewish violence.

A decade later, the Dutch author Harry Mulisch published a novel based on Jules Croiset's staged kidnapping. The performance artist Freek de Jonge took exception to this novel, arguing that it was nothing but a rehabilitation of an impostor, and announcing that he would publicly burn the novel during his next performance. Thus the Fassbinder affair was rekindled and a nationwide discussion on art and ethics ensued. Public figures discussed representation of Jews in theater and literature, an artist's freedom of expression, and the right of one artist to burn another artist's work in public.

This essay analyzes the various events, claiming that reader responsibility is what connects them. Through a discussion of public responses to various works of art and artists' comments on what they expect from their audiences, I argue that a truthful understanding of a work of art can only be arrived at when both artist and audience take their respective responsibilities.

Key Words

Fassbinder, Rainer Werner, Jonge, Freek de, Mulisch, Harry, anti-Semitism, book-burning, audience responsibility, freedom of artistic expression.

★ ★ ★

In order to promote the book trade in the Netherlands, the Stichting Collectieve Propaganda van het Nederlandse Boek (Foundation for the Joint Promotion of the Dutch Book) organizes the annual "Book Week." Every year, a renowned author is invited to write a novel (the so-called Book Week Gift) which will be distributed as a free gift for every customer who buys another book, and a famous artist is invited to put on a show on the opening night of the Book Week. In the year 2000, the comedian Freek de Jonge wrote and performed a one-man show on this night. The comic high-point of the show was an alleged conversation that the artist had with the Dutch crown prince, in the royal "library" (which consists only of one Ikea bookcase containing a handful of nonliterary books and periodicals). However, contrary to what the audience might expect, the conversation between the artist and the prince does not stick to the trivial, but turns to the topic of good and evil. De Jonge argues with the prince about the weapons which good is allowed to use in its struggle against evil.

Natuurlijk heeft goed precies dezelfde wapens als kwaad tot zijn
    beschikking, anders kan 'ie het wel schudden. Maar mag goed die
    wapens dan ook gebruiken?
"Natuurlijk," zegt de prins, "mag 'ie die wapens gebruiken. Waar het
    doel heilig is neemt de liefde de plaats van de doofpot in en mag goed
    heel even kwaad zijn."
Er valt een ongelofelijk lange stilte.
En nu is de hamvraag: hoe lang kan goed kwaad zijn voor hij voorgoed
    kwaad is?
Met andere woorden:
Wanneer wordt een provocerende kunstenaar antisemiet?
Wanneer wordt een fantaserende schrijver een leugenaar?
Wanneer wordt iemand die de vrijheid van kunst aantast, een fascist?

[Of course good has exactly the same weapons at its disposal as evil, or it
is doomed. But is good allowed to use those weapons?
"Of course," the prince says, "it is allowed to use those weapons. Where
the end is justified, love is a cover-up and good is allowed to be evil
for a while."
There is an unbelievably long silence.
And the main question is now: How long can good be evil before it
becomes evil for good?
In other words:
When does a provocative artist become an anti-Semite?
When does a fantasizing author become a liar?
When does someone who attacks the freedom of art become a fascist?]
(Jonge 2000)

In this speech, which in the show is immediately followed by yet
another comic turn, Freek de Jonge touches upon one of the most
important ethical questions about art. How far does the freedom of the
artist reach? Can an artist create a provocative work in order to serve a
greater good or is there a limit to what he or she can do? Can a work of
art even be evil in character to serve a greater good?

Freek de Jonge was not posing a hypothetical question. In the weeks
preceding his performance, he had caused a furore about a book that was
published on the occasion of the same Book Week. In 2000, the Book
Week Gift was a novel written by the renowned author Harry Mulisch,
by the title of *Het Theater, De Brief en De Waarheid (The Theatre, the Letter
and the Truth)*. The plot of this novel is based on what is known in the
Netherlands as the "Fassbinder affair."

In 1987, a Dutch theater company planned to stage Rainer Werner
Fassbinder's play *Der Müll, Die Stadt und Der Tod (Garbage, the City
and Death)*. Some ten years earlier, rehearsals of this play in Germany
had to be halted because of charges of anti-Semitism. Protesters
against the play took offence at one of the characters, the anonymous
"rich Jew," which according to them confirmed all prejudices against
Jews. A similar protest occurred in the Netherlands, Freek de Jonge
joining the ranks of those who wanted to prevent the Fassbinder play
from being performed in Rotterdam. One of the protesters, the actor
Jules Croiset, himself a Jew, was so upset that this play was being
performed, that he staged his own kidnapping, supposedly by neo-
fascists. By his staged kidnapping he wanted to demonstrate that anti-
Semitism was still very much alive, and was fuelled by Fassbinder's
play. In an essay that he wrote many years later he accounts for his

actions as follows:

> Ik had . . . geen persoonlijk belang nagestreefd; er stond mij een veel algemener belang voor ogen. Ik wenste door mijn handelen de geloken ogen van de samenleving te openen voor het, in mijn ogen, verblindend onrecht van de menselijke onverdraagzaamheid in het algemeen en het antisemitisme, het naar mijn mening altijd en overal latent aanwezig zijnde antisemitisme, in het bijzonder. Ik wenste zicht te verschaffen, inzicht.

> [I had not pursued any personal interest; I had a much more general interest at heart. By my actions I wished to open the shut eyes of society to the blinding injustice of human intolerance in general and anti-Semitism, always and everywhere latently present, in particular. I wished to provide sight, insight.] (Croiset 13, 1989)

At the same time of the kidnapping, dozens of Jewish families, among whom was the family of Freek de Jonge, had received anti-Semitic threatening letters. Later, Jules Croiset confessed that he had not only staged his own kidnapping but that he was also responsible for sending the letters.

Harry Mulisch based his novel, *Het Theater, De Brief en De Waarheid* on the story of Croiset's staged kidnapping. Freek de Jonge was enraged by this novel, which he saw as a rehabilitation of Croiset, and publicly called for Mulisch's novel to be burned. He promptly changed the original title of his one-man show into *De Conferencier, Het Boekenweekgeschenk en De Leugen (The Comedian, the Book Week Gift and the Lie)*, and thus made the De Jonge—Mulisch controversy the main theme of the show. The big question before the performance was: Will he burn the book on stage or not?

Meanwhile, Harry Mulisch seemed unperturbed by De Jonge's rage. He claimed that his novel, although based on fact, was a work of fiction.

> Mijn tekst is geen beeld of interpretatie van zijn [Croiset's] even fantastische als reële onderneming, die destijds veel opzien baarde, maar uitsluitend de aanleiding tot mijn eigen literaire avontuur. Ik heb mijn verbeelding er op losgelaten, en zoals het er nu ligt heeft het nauwelijks nog iets te maken met zijn lotgevallen. Mijn verhaal is niet waar of onwaar, zoals een feitenverslag,—als literair verhaal is het zijn eigen feit.

> [My text is no image or interpretation of his (Croiset's) enterprise, which is as fantastic as it is real, and which at the time caused a great furore, but only the starting point of my own literary adventure. I have

let my imagination run away with it, and as it is now there is hardly any link with his fortunes. My story is not true or untrue, as a factual report is,—as a literary story it is its own fact.] (Mulisch 2000, 85)

Mulisch clearly makes a distinction between the real-life events that inspired his novel and the contents of the novel itself. His novel, according to him, is an autonomous work which should be valued on its own, artistic merits and not on its source of inspiration. He even deems it unsavory for someone to bring up the Croiset affair in connection with his novel.

Mijn boek is een roos. Dan begin je toch niet over de mest onder de grond?

[My book is a rose. Why bring up the manure under the soil?] (Mulisch in "Freek de Jonge verwart fictie Van Mulisch met weskellij Kheid," *Trow*, February 23, 2000)

Mulisch's choice of words is significant here. He describes his book as a beautiful rose, which was nurtured by the manure of the Croiset affair. Manure in itself is a foul substance, but when used properly, it can help a rose to grow. Mulisch here seems to claim that an artist can make use of sources of inspiration that are ugly, or even morally corrupt in themselves, but that it is the artist's task to create something beautiful (a rose) on the basis of that manure.

Freek de Jonge saw things differently. He evidently considered the title of Mulisch's novel, *Het Theater, De Brief en De Waarheid* as a novelist's claim to representing the truth about the Fassbinder affair. Hence through the title of De Jonge's show, *De Conferencier, Het Boekenweekgeschenk en de Leugen*, which suggests that by means of his show, De Jonge wished to expose the lie behind Mulisch's novel.

However, one might wonder whether De Jonge's view was indeed warranted. If one analyzes Mulisch's novel, it appears to be one big game with the concept of "truth." The complete title of the novel is: *Het Theater, de Brief en de Waarheid. Een Tegenspraak. (The Theatre, the Letter and the Truth: A Contradiction.)* The novel consists of two parts. Part I is mainly taken up by a dramatic monologue by Herbert, speaking on the occasion of his wife's cremation. The character of Herbert is clearly based on Jules Croiset. In his monologue he tells those attending the ceremony that his self-staged kidnapping was inspired by worry for his wife's health. After having received an anti-Semitic letter, at the time of the Fassbinder affair, his wife had been so upset that Herbert decided to make it seem that he had written the letter himself. He staged his own kidnapping and later confessed to the police that both the kidnapping and the hate-mail had risen from his own imagination, and were lies. In this way, he had hoped to put his wife's mind at rest.

Part II of *Het Theater, de Brief en de Waarheid* consists mainly of a dramatic monologue by Magda, Herbert's wife, speaking at her husband's funeral. She also refers to the Fassbinder affair and tells the audience that it was she who had written the anti-Semitic letter, in order to reassure her husband that his worries about the anti-Semitic effects of the staging of Fassbinder's play in Rotterdam were not unfounded. However, it was this letter that led to Herbert's self-staged kidnapping and his eventual suicide.

Both Herbert and Magda's monologues are frequently interrupted by the narrators (who pose as mourners attending the ceremony), who make clear that their account is fictitious but true.

> Dit zei Magda die middag in de aula niet, ik verzin het er nu bij, want het is de waarheid.

> [Magda did not say this on that afternoon in the auditorium; I am making it up now, because it is the truth.] (Mulisch 2000, 76)

Signs like these abound in the novel, making it clear to the readers that they need to take the novel's claim to truth with a pinch of salt. Of course, the plot of the novel is also far from realistic, if not plainly impossible. As Harry Mulisch himself remarks:

> Zonder het tweede deel is het eerste mogelijk, en het tweede zonder het eerste. Maar hun combinatie is onmogelijk. Het zijn twee complementaire werelden, die elkaar uitsluiten. . . . Is het dus een absurd hersenspinsel? Misschien. Maar misschien ook niet. Misschien toont het juist nu de volledige waarheid.

> [Without the second part the first part is possible, and the second without the first. But the combination of the two is impossible. They are two complementary worlds, which exclude each other. . . . Does that make it an absurd fabrication? Perhaps. But perhaps not. Perhaps it is only now that it shows the entire truth.] (Mulisch 2000, 84)

By giving his novel this extraordinary form, Harry Mulisch draws attention to the fact that "truth" in fiction is an entirely different concept from factual truth. In order to make a truthful comment on life, art sometimes needs to present facts in such a form that they appear untrue in real life. Thus, an artist uses what would be considered a lie in a court of law as a means to present a truth. This is the very contradiction that Mulisch refers to in the subtitle of his novel.

It can be discerned from their argument that Mulisch and De Jonge have a different view on art. For Mulisch, the truth of art does not lie in a minute and factual representation of the events, but in its beauty. Even from a squalid affair such as Croiset's self-staged kidnapping, a thing of beauty can grow (a rose). And in Mulisch's view, it is this thing of beauty, the work of art that counts and the manure that fertilized it should not be brought up again. Apparently, the work of art is autonomous, and has cut itself loose from the factual events on which it has been based. A work of art should be judged, therefore, on its own merits, and not on its supposed factual truth or untruth.

De Jonge takes a different view. According to him, a work of art *does* indeed say something about life, and even claims to tell some truths about life. Mulisch's novel, although a work of fiction, has a clear link with reality, and as such presents a view on reality which it holds to be true. When another artist (in this case De Jonge) perceives that truth as false, it is his moral duty to correct the view put forward in that work of art by creating another work of art that will expose the other artist's lies and present a different, "real" truth. Also, the mendacious work will have to be destroyed in public.

The Freek de Jonge—Harry Mulisch controversy exposes some fundamental questions on art and responsibility. In what way should a work of art be truthful? And is there a limit to the freedom of art if it is found not to be true?

For a possible answer to this question it is necessary to go back to the very origin of the affair: Fassbinder's play *Garbage, the City and Death*. When defending the play against his critics, Fassbinder claimed that it was because his play was a true representation of real life that it contained a character like the rich Jew. Presenting negative and hateful characters on stage can, by holding up a mirror toward the audience, be a moral lesson for that audience or, failing that, at least tell a truth about life, that is, that life is not always pleasant and beautiful. In an open letter to his readers (in absence of a theater audience for his play) Fassbinder phrases this as follows:

> Gegen mein Stück *Der Müll, die Stadt und der Tod* wird der Vorwurf erhoben, es sei "antisemitisch." Unter dem Vorwand dieses Vorwurfs werden von bestimmter Seite Thesen und Deutungen vorgetragen, die mit mir und meinem Stück nichts zu tun haben. Zum Stück: Er gibt in der Tat unter den Figuren in diesem Text einen Juden. Dieser Jude ist Häusermakler; er trägt dazu bei, die

Stadt zu ungunsten der Lebensbedingungen der Menschen zu verändern; er macht Geschäfte. Die Verhältnisse, unter denen diese Geschäfte gemacht werden können, hat er nicht geschaffen, hat nicht er zu verantworten; er benutzt diese Verhältnisse.

[My play, *Garbage, the City and Death*, is often criticized for being anti-Semitic. Under the pretence of this reproach statements and interpretations are put forward which have got nothing to do with my play. About the play: Indeed, among the characters in this text there is a Jew. This Jew is an estate agent; he contributes to changing the city to the disadvantage of the living conditions of the people: he is doing business. He did not create the circumstances in which business like this can be made; he is not responsible for them: he uses these circumstances.] (Fassbinder 1984, 108)

In short, Fassbinder defends his portrayal of the rich Jew by stating that, although this Jew is indeed rich because of the shady business that he is in, the Jew is only making use of the way society is structured: a Jew's only way to survive is doing business, simply because he is not allowed to enter any other realm of society. It is this aspect of life that puts the alleged anti-Semitism of the play into an entirely different light, according to Fassbinder.

Zu betrachten wären die Beweggründe derjenigen, die sich dagegen wehren, dass über diesen Sachverhalt gesprochen wird. Sie sind die wahren Antisemiten. Zu prüfen wäre, warum man, statt die realen Sachverhalte zu untersuchen, gegen den Autor eines Stückes mit Sätzen argumentiert, die er—um bestimmten Zustände kritisierbar zu machen—für seine Figuren erfunden hat.

[It is the motives of those who resist discussion about this state of affairs that should be considered. They are the true anti-Semites. It should be examined why, instead of studying the real state of affairs, people argue against the author of a play with sentences that he has—in order to criticize certain situations—invented for his characters.] (Fassbinder 1984, 108)

In other words, the truth of Fassbinder's play lies in the fact that he holds up a mirror to the audience. It is by shocking them by the portrayal of a rich Jew that he wants to question the status quo of society, which he considers to contain anti-Semitic elements. In his view, it is not he who is the anti-Semite; it is the people who succeeded in banning his play who are the real anti-Semites.

From the confusion surrounding the perceived truths and untruths of Fassbinder's play and Harry Mulisch's novel, it becomes clear that a search for truth in art is getting us nowhere. What one person sees as truth, the other considers a lie. However, in defending his play, Fassbinder brings up an aspect of art which is a much more useful tool if we want to make an ethical judgment on art, and that is the integrity of the author and the work. In short, it is the responsibility of the author to create a work—however provocative and shocking it may be—of integrity, of sound intentions.

In the 1970s the majority of Fassbinder's audience decided that he had taken his artistic freedom too far in his portrayal of the rich Jew. However, Fassbinder defended himself by saying that his intentions were pure and that if the audience put this play into the perspective of his earlier works they would have understood that.

Es gibt in diesen Stück auch Antisemieten; es gibt sie aber nicht nur in diesem Stück, sondern, beispielsweise, auch in Frankfurt. Selbstverständlich geben diese Figuren—ich feinde es eigentlich überflüssig, das zu betonen—nicht die Meinungen des Autors wieder, dessen Haltung zur Minderheiten aus seinen anderen Arbeiten hinreichend bekannt sein sollte.

[There are also anti-Semites in this play: however, they do not only exist in this play but also, for example, in Frankfurt. Of course, these characters—actually I find it superfluous having to stress this—do not represent the opinions of the author, whose attitude toward minorities should be clear enough from his other works.] (Fassbinder 1984, 109)

According to Fassbinder, the anti-Semites in his play are those who enforce the Jew to make his living in the housing trade. The anti-Semites in the outside world (here: in the city of Frankfurt) are those who in real life treat minorities in a similar manner. In his open letter, Fassbinder assumes the posture of someone who is genuinely amazed that his audience could find his play anti-Semitic in the first place: if they knew his previous works they should know that his attitude toward minorities is far from anti-Semitic. The problem, of course, is that apparently Fassbinder's audience found his play so confusing that they started to worry about the motives that might have brought an author, whose attitudes they had always thought to be quite in order, to write an apparently anti-Semitic play such as *Der Müll, die Stadt und der*

Tod. The meaning they distilled from the play was clearly different from the intended meaning of the author.

   It is here that we touch upon another main problem when discussing art and ethics: communication between the artist and his audience. Many artists and theorists have drawn attention to the fact that a work of art does not have a fixed meaning. A play does not *mean*, meaning has to be constructed by the audience, using representational systems: the signs of the play and the codes of language and culture. In the words of Harold Pinter,

> Meaning begins in the words, in action, continues in your head and ends nowhere. There is no end to meaning. Meaning which is resolved, parcelled labelled and ready for export is dead, impertinent—and meaningless. (Scott 1986, 80)

Pinter, and many artists with him, wants to create works of art whose meaning is not obvious at a first glance. Instead, he wants the audience to make a conscious effort to grasp the meaning of a performance.

   A similar comment is made by the Argentine-German composer Mauricio Kagel, whose music is characterized by its creation of ambiguities, and seeming lack of meaning. Many a concert of his has left the audience in a state of bewilderment or even anger. However, Kagel claims that he creates this confusion with a specific purpose in mind.

> Wissen Sie, man macht mir oft den Vorwurf, meine Musik sei so geladen, so intensiv und kompakt, daß der normale Hörer davon abgestoßen werde. Darin siehe ich durchaus keine Mangel; darauf bin ich im Gegenteil sehr stolz. So darf ich nämlich verlangen, daß mit der gleichen Ernsthaftigkeit, mit der ich meine Musik schreibe, der Hörer sie aufnimmt, und daß er beim Hören ebenso produktiv ist wie ich es beim Komponieren bin. Ich will keine Hörer, die im Konzert bloß zerstreuung suchen. Unter keinen Umständen. Ich verlange, daß der Hörer arbeitet. Aber das ist nicht autoritär gemeint, sondern mit größter Güte. Denn er arbeitet nicht für mich, sondern für sich. Wenn er, der Hörer, sich anstrengt, wenn er denkt, mitdenkt, dann gewinnt er etwas.

> [You know, I am often reproached for making my music so multi-layered, so intense and compact, that the ordinary listener is repelled by it. I don't consider that a defect at all, instead I pride myself on this. In this way I can demand that the listener perceive my music with the same seriousness as with which I write it, and that he is just as productive in the process of listening as I am during the process of composing. I don't want listeners who only

seek entertainment at a concert. Not at all. I want the listener to work. But I don't mean that in an authoritarian manner, but with the best of intentions. Because he is not working for me, but for himself. When he, the listener, exerts himself, when he is thinking, thinking along, then he gains something.] (Pauli 1971, 93–94)

Kagel is making an ethical statement rather than a statement on aesthetics here. He says that the purpose with which he creates confusing moments in his music is deliberately to estrange the listeners. However, he does not want his audience to turn its back on his music in revulsion. Instead, he demands his listeners to be as productive in the listening process as he was during the composition of the piece. Only then will the audience gain something from the performance. In other words, Kagel inflicts pain on his audience for its own good.

In his inflicting pain on his audience, Kagel takes a similar attitude toward his audience as Fassbinder and Mulisch. And strikingly, in his case perceived anti-Semitism proves to be a stumbling block for many a listener. When his choral work *Ein feste Burg ist unser Gott (A Mighty Fortress is Our God)* was performed during a church service in the Netherlands, one member of the congregation issued a vehement protest.

> De muzikale versie van Luthers *Ein feste Burg* van de componist Mauricio Kagel had nooit geschreven mogen worden. De fascistoïde wijze waarop de tekstgetrouwe woorden "Das Reich" zijn getoonzet is een regelrechte verheerlijking van "Das Dritte Reich."

> [The musical version of Luther's *Ein feste Burg* by the composer Mauricio Kagel ought never to have been allowed to be written. The fascist manner in which the scriptural words "Das Reich" have been put to music is a downright glorification of the Third Reich.] (Tjallingii 1987)

Clearly, this churchgoer felt hurt to the core when a hymn which he perceived as having fascist overtones was sung during a church service. What he failed to notice in his hurt and anger, however, was the fact that Kagel himself is a Jew. Once one realizes this, one should think again why Kagel would choose to set a well-known Lutheran hymn in this particular way (having the choir militantly shout the words of the hymn through megaphones). He must have had a different purpose in mind when he wrote this composition, which was clearly intended to shock. Instead of glorifying the Nazi era he holds up a mirror in front of his audience, showing them what the triumphalist voice in which the church has often sung "A mighty fortress" can lead to and has led to, as

Hans Ruiter, the clergyman who presided at this particular service, explained in a radio interview.

> Na de dienst sprak ik iemand die zich dodelijk had geërgerd aan het op deze wijze zingen van "Ein feste Burg". Hij noemde het fascistoïde, en dat klopte. Alleen, hij vond het spotten . . . terwijl Kagel eigenlijk iets anders doet. Hij houdt gewoon een spiegel voor, van "Hoor eens mensen, zo zingen jullie wel eens, met zoveel christelijk triomfalisme wat aan het fascistoïde denken grenst," om het vrij voorzichtig te zeggen.

> [After the service I spoke to someone who had taken great offence at the manner in which "Ein feste Burg" had been sung. He called it fascist, and he was right. Only, he considered this a blasphemy . . . whereas Kagel in fact does something else. He holds up a mirror, saying "Listen people, this is how you sing sometimes, in such a Christian triumphalist voice that borders on the fascist," to put it mildly.] (Ruiter 1987)

The responses to Kagel's setting of *Ein feste Burg* differ to a great extent. Tjallingii is clearly hurt to the core by hearing it performed during a church service, whereas Ruiter senses that it can serve a useful purpose in this way. However, the essence of their reactions lies not in their rejection or acceptance of Kagel's choral work, but in reader responsibility.

Tjallingii's reaction is a gut reaction. Shocked by Kagel's piece and taking it at face value, he lashes out in anger against it by sending a letter to the editor of a regional newspaper, in which he goes so far as to say that such a work should never have been allowed. He might, however, have taken Kagel's advice to heart and have taken the trouble to reflect on the meaning of this work and to find out why the people behind the church service allowed it to be sung on that occasion. Such an effort could, for instance, have involved a study of Kagel's personal background and of some of the main ideas behind his music.

Ruiter is clearly someone who did make a study of Kagel's music. His response to *Ein feste Burg* is not a knee-jerk reaction but a realization on that a listener can indeed, as Kagel says, gain something from listening to his music and working hard in order to grasp its meaning. As Ruiter points out, a listener who would not take the hymn at face value, but who would give it some thought, might realize that he, as a churchgoer, was being confronted with severe criticism of the Christian Church. Reflection on the hymn might even lead the churchgoer to a mea culpa, a prayer of penitence. In short, Kagel's setting of *Ein feste Burg* is not an anti-Semitic work, but a work which harshly criticizes anti-Semitic tendencies within the Christian church. However, it is only a listener (reader) who takes his responsibility who will grasp this deeper meaning. The Kagel incident resembles the Fassbinder affair to a great extent. Public reaction to Fassbinder's *Der Müll, die Stadt und der Tod* was, like Tjallingii's response to Kagel's *Ein feste Burg*, an accusation of anti-Semitism, an accusation which Fassbinder denied when he said that his audience should have known better. If they had taken the trouble to go beyond their gut reaction and closely examine the motives of the author and his previous work, they would have realized that *Der Müll, die Stadt und der Tod*, instead of encouraging anti-Semitism, criticizes anti-Semitic attitudes that he saw in contemporary German society. Fassbinder clearly felt that readers who did not take the effort to closely study his work and his personal motives were dodging their responsibility. Thus, he would undoubtedly have accused those who protested against the intended performance of his play in Rotterdam, amongst whom were Freek de Jonge and Jules Croiset, of relying too much on their gut reactions and not acting as responsible readers.

In the Freek de Jonge—Harry Mulisch controversy history seemed to repeat itself. When Mulisch published his novel *Het Theater, de Brief en de Waarheid*, which De Jonge perceived as an unjust rehabilitation of Jules Croiset, De Jonge reacted too swiftly and irresponsibly by changing the title of his show and calling for a public burning of Mulisch's book. In his call for a public burning of *Het Theater, de Brief en de Waarheid* he seemed to have lost his sense of distinction between fact and fiction. Thus he came to see Mulisch's novel as an unambiguous rehabilitation of Jules Croiset, without pausing too long to think whether the impossibilities and contradictions in the novel might call for a possibly more profound meaning. Like the churchgoer who took offence at Kagel's *Ein feste Burg* and the protesters against Fassbinder's *Der Müll, die Stadt und der Tod*, De Jonge did not stop and think what deeper meaning might lie hidden in Mulisch's novel, but angrily lashed out against it. After having attempted to curb the freedom of artistic expression in his protest against the Fassbinder play, he now took his crusade one step further in his call for a public burning of Mulisch's book.

As it turned out, however, Freek de Jonge showed himself very much aware indeed of the non-fixed meaning of art and a master at wrong-footing his audience. In the weeks leading up to his show, he called for a public burning of Harry Mulisch's book, causing an international outcry. De Jonge was accused of wanting to fight alleged anti-Semitism with Nazi methods. Debates in the various media ensued, dividing the audience into those who thought De Jonge's proposed action was justified and those who advocated the complete freedom of art. As the debate raged, the big question in the weeks leading up to the performance was "will he burn the book on stage or won't he?"

On the evening of the performance, Freek de Jonge began his show by coming on stage carrying a jerrycan in one hand and a bunch of wood in the other and asking Mulisch, who was the guest of honor, for some matches. His show then developed into a complex narrative in which comic elements were intertwined with his memories of the self-staged kidnapping of Jules Croiset, and his feelings of having been betrayed and abused by Croiset, of having been tricked into curbing the freedom of artistic expression (that is Fassbinder's play) by a fraud. As his show approached its climax, he discussed the media hype around his intended book-burning.

> Zoals antisemitisme taboe is, is boekverbranden ook taboe. Je denkt toch niet dat ik de illusie heb dat ik de geest van de kunst wil doden? Nee, eindelijk krijg ik de gelegenheid door een boekje te verbranden goed te maken wat ik ooit in Rotterdam verpest heb. Ik zal net als Fassbinder het taboe doorbreken om de burgerij te sarren en te provoceren. Om precies de juiste mensen de verkeerde dingen te laten zeggen.
>
> Want in de kunst staan tussen droom en daad geen wetten in de weg en geen praktische bezwaren. En daarom zal dit boek branden, in de geest van Rainer Werner Fassbinder, die de kunst niet zag als een spel met de waarheid, waar je een pijpje naar believen bij aansteekt, maar die de kunst zag als een gevecht met de waarheid met je eigen leven als inzet.
>
> En daarom zal dit boek branden. Hier sta ik, ik kan niet anders.

> [As much as anti-Semitism is a taboo, book-burning is taboo. Don't think I have the illusion that I want to kill the spirit of art. No, at long last, by burning a book, I am getting the opportunity to rectify what I ruined in Rotterdam. Just like Fassbinder, I'll break down a taboo in order to antagonize and provoke the *bourgeoisie*. To make the right people say the wrong things. For in art there are no laws or practical objections between dream and deed. And that is why this book will burn, in the spirit of Rainer Werner Fassbinder, who did not consider art a game with truth, during which one can light a pipe at one's leisure; but who saw art as a struggle with truth, with one's own life at stake. And that is why this book will burn. Here stand I, I can do no other.]
> (Jonge 2000)

With these words, Mulisch's book caught fire by means of an impressive coup-de-theatre, but from its ashes arose a phoenix. By solving the De Jonge—Mulisch controversy in this way, De Jonge again demonstrated his skill at kicking back at his audience. Whereas in previous shows he loved telling a bad-taste joke and then telling his audience off for laughing at such an unacceptable joke, in *De Conferencier, het Boekenweekgeschenk en de Leugen* he took things a step further. In his speech preceding the book-burning he put his conflict with Harry Mulisch in an entirely different perspective. The De Jonge—Mulisch controversy disappeared into the background, and the question of the freedom of art and and the responsibility of the audience came to the fore. The burning of Harry Mulisch's novel no longer served to expose the lie of the book, but to open the eyes of the audience to their knee-jerk reaction to De Jonge's announcement that he would set fire to the book. At the same time, it was an apology for De Jonge's own rash reaction to the performance of Fassbinder's play in Rotterdam. The closing lines of De Jonge's speech are a tribute to Fassbinder, the artist for whom telling the truth sometimes meant a provocation of his audience, and whom De Jonge once tried to stifle.

Contrary to what his audience had been led to believe by the media hype preceding his performance, Freek de Jonge's show was not an attempt to silence another artist. During his show he at one point explicitly ridiculed his audience for taking at face value the media hype that followed his announcement that the Mulisch book ought to (and would be) burned. Apparently, De Jonge had cleverly turned the frenzy into a part of his performance, and thus turned the tables on both the press and his audience. Whereas many people thought that De Jonge's call to arms had put him into an impossible position (an artist could not possibly destroy the work of another artist in public and get away with it) it was De Jonge who put his audience on the spot. He taught his audience not to use art to jump to quick conclusions, but to put a conscious effort into grasping its meaning, the truth that it is trying to get across.

It might appear that De Jonge was playing a game with his audience all along. However, from his speech preceding the book-burning it can be discerned that it is a game which he takes very seriously. Art is not a game with truth, but a struggle with truth, in which one's own life may ultimately be at stake. The book-burning thus served a double purpose. It was a mea culpa for Freek de Jonge's own protest against Fassbinder (one of the songs in the show, cleverly disguised as a ridicule of the Dutch crown prince's fiancée, Princess Máxima, had as its refrain "*mea culpa maxima*") and, for his audience, was a lesson in responsibility.

Rainer Werner Fassbinder, Harry Mulisch, and Freek de Jonge: three artists with different views on life and different modes of artistic expression. However, in their outlook on art they share an important similarity. They all advocate the necessity of artistic freedom. An artist should be free to express his truth in his own peculiar, artistic manner, without having to explain himself to his audience. Fassbinder, Mulisch, and De Jonge would undoubtedly all subscribe to the epigram of Harry Mulisch's novel, a quote from Diderot's "Paradox about the Actor": "He who wishes to be understood should give no explanation."

The Fassbinder affair and the ensuing De Jonge–Mulisch controversy illustrate the importance of reader responsibility. In the words of Mauricio Kagel, it is only when a reader exerts himself in his struggle to grasp the meaning of a work of art that he can gain something. In other words, Jules Croiset and Freek de Jonge as readers of Fassbinder ought to have taken their responsibility and sought for Fassbinder's motives in writing *Der Müll, die Stadt und der Tod*, Freek de Jonge as a reader of Mulisch should have grasped the meaning of *Het Theater, de Brief en de Waarheid*, and the audience at large should have looked beyond the media hype surrounding *De Conferencier, het Boekenweekgeschenk en de Leugen* in order to learn from the game that De Jonge was playing.

As much as it is the responsibility of the artist to handle sensitive topics with care, it is the responsibility of the audience not to jump to quick and easy conclusions. It is then that a phoenix can rise from the ashes of a scandal, and that from the manure of a squalid affair a beautiful rose can grow.

Works Cited

Croiset, Jules. *Met Stomheid Geslagen*. Amsterdam: Toth, 1989.

Fassbinder, Rainer Werner. *Der Müll, die Stadt und der Tod*. Frankfurt am Main: Verlag der Autoren, 1984.

"Freek de Jonge verwart fictie van Mulisch met werkelijkheid." *Trouw*. February 23, 2000.

Jonge, Freek de. *De Conferencier, het Boekenweekgeschenk en de Leugen* (Oneman show) Amsterdam. March 14, 2000.

Mulisch, Harry. *Het Theater, de Brief en de Waarheid*. Amsterdam: De Bezige Bij, 2000.

Pauli, Hansjörg. *Für wen komponieren Sie eigentlich?* Frankfurt am Main: S. Fischer Verlag, 1971.

Pinter, Harold. "A Letter to Peter Wood." In *Harold Pinter. The Birthday Party, The Caretaker, The Homecoming. A Casebook*. Ed. Michael Scott. London: Macmillan, 1986.

Ruiter, Hans. Radio Interview During the Programme *Liturgie en Kerkmuziek*. IKON Radio. May 17, 1987.

Scott, Michael. *Harold Pinter: The Birthday Party, the Caretaker & the Homecoming. A Casebook*. London: Macmillan, 1986.

Tjallingii, Ulbe. "Nieuwe Muziek." *Friesch Dagblad*, Letter to the Editor, April 29, 1987.

CHAPTER EIGHT

Dialogue in Gandhi's Hind Swaraj *or Indian Home Rule or the Reader as Truth-Seeker*

CLARA A.B. JOSEPH

Introduction

This essay[1] examines Gandhi's *Hind Swaraj*, particularly its dialogic form, in order to highlight several theoretical implications for a study of the literary reader. The Gandhian reader is, above everything else, committed and honest: one who might sleep but one who never pretends to sleep. Such a reader is ever-ready for dialogue (for monologue is intrinsically violent), yet not necessarily to agree but to understand even at the point of difference. This unusual understanding can to some extent be explained with the help of Habermas' theory of communication that is summed up in his four "universal validity claims": uttering something intelligibly, giving (the hearer) something to understand, making herself thereby understandable, and coming to an understanding with another person (Habermas 1998, 22). In Gandhi, however, a theory of the reader while it covers Habermas' grounding in the rational goes further to encompass the relevance of the transcendental, what Gandhi calls Truth. The reader, then, is defined as a Truth-seeker. In following up on this theme, this essay establishes the reliance of *Hind Swaraj* on a discretionary Gandhian reading of the Bhagavad Gita and argues for the centrality of the reader as a Truth-oriented human person rather than primarily a reading process.

Key Words

Dialogue, Satyagrahi, Habermas, Bhagavad Gita, empathetic difference, swaraj.

★   ★   ★

But what is political and what is religious? Can life be divided into such watertight compartments? The whole machine is run by one person from one place. If that person and that place are clean and pure, then all the activities will also be clean and pure; if they are both tainted, then all the activities will also be tainted. I am amused at such distinction of our various activities, because my experience has been different.—M.K. Gandhi (CWMG 31: 443)

A study of Mahatma Gandhi's *Hind Swaraj or Indian Home Rule* has to begin with at least a brief narrative of how, when, and why it was written, before the work can be analyzed for its form and content, or an argument can be developed for a Gandhian theory of representation that is also a literary theory of cognition, expression, and praxis—a literary theory of the integrated human person as author and reader. Hence, to the narrative.

The year is 1909. Gandhi is on a ship, the *Kildonan Castle*, on his way back to South Africa from England. He had, as on his previous visit, in 1906, spoken to numerous British and Indian activists in England. The members of India House, a youth group led by Vinayak Damodar Savarkar with whom Gandhi had talks in 1906, came once again to his attention. Gandhi had been impressed by their zeal and commitment, but he found their espousal of violence as a means to achieve the independence of India both illogical and counterproductive. Members of the Indian National Congress who had aligned themselves neatly into two categories—the Extremists (or Nationalists as they referred to themselves) and the Moderates—too did not meet with Gandhi's approval (nor did he with theirs). Numerous talks that Gandhi had had with these various groups in England and South Africa came back to him during his ten-day sea trip. Seized by the violent storm of convictions that had been seething in him for quite some time now, Gandhi wrote almost without ceasing—he wrote with his left hand when his right tired—and produced on that ship, between November 13 and 22, this "little book" *Hind Swarajya* in the Gujarati language. This is a book that Gandhi in a letter to *Young India* in January 1921 claimed could be placed in the hands of a little child. Yet, the Bombay government which governed the regions speaking Sindhi, Gujarati, Marathi, and Kannada banned the book. Gandhi's response was to publish from Natal, South Africa, an English translation of the book as *Indian Home Rule* and to make it available to those he called his "English friends" (CWMG 10: 457). Gandhi kept the dialogue format of the original, a dialogue between two characters: the Reader and the Editor.

Indian Home Rule was criticized, even by friendly readers, not only for its content but even more immediately for its form. The dialogue came across as a thoroughly inappropriate literary form to deal with the serious topic of politics. If Gandhi adopted the form precisely for its potential for simplicity and clarity, that is, its communicative possibility, intellectuals who read the work in English felt let down by that unsophisticated style. Gandhi felt pressured to give an explanation for employing the form of the dialogue and so, in his "Preface to the English Translation," he writes:

> Some of the friends who have read the translation have objected that the subject matter has been dealt with in the form of a dialogue. I have no answer to offer to this objection except that the Gujarati language readily lends itself to such treatment and that it is considered the best method of treating difficult subjects. Had I written for English readers in the first instance, the subject would have been handled in a different manner. Moreover, the dialogue, as it has been given, actually took place between several friends, mostly readers of *Indian Opinion*, and myself. (Parel 1997, 6)

The claim to the intrinsic suitability of Gujarati to dialogue reflects Gandhi's own comfort with the language as mother tongue in which mainly daily conversations flowed. It was following the publication of *Hind Swarajya* that Gandhi began to use Gujarati as a literary language, chiefly in translations of the many edifying English works he came across. Thus John Ruskin's *Unto This Last* and Leo Tolstoy's *The Kingdom of God Is Within You*, works that influenced and affirmed Gandhi's political philosophy at the turn of the century, were translated into Gujarati (Gandhi 1993, 299). The liberty that Gandhi took in translations, in forsaking transliteration for the sake of communication, suggests that his principle of translation was always to capture the spirit of the original. He believed that language was not simply made up of sounds and words but of whole cultures and values so that translations could linguistically deviate from the original in order to convey the message. Accordingly, he was adamant about speaking to his children in Gujarati much against the counsel of his close friends. He argues, "It has always been my conviction that Indian parents who train their children to think and talk in English from their infancy betray their children and their country. They deprive them of the spiritual and social heritage of the nation, and render them to that extent unfit for the service of the country" (312). In the *Hind Swaraj*, the Editor asks English speakers of India to "teach morality to their progeny through their mother-tongue" (Parel 1997, 104). Gandhi's belief in a certain intrinsic nature of language that convinced him to use the dialogue form when writing *Hind Swarajya* in Gujarati also leads him to consider the inappropriateness of that form in the English language: "Had I written for English readers in the first instance, the subject would have been handled in a different manner." That Gandhi did not feel at home with English, in spite of extensive, even editorial, function in that language, becomes apparent when in *Young India* he writes, "I frankly confess that to me editing a newspaper in English is no pleasure" (CWMG 19: 37).

If the form of the dialogue does not suit English the way it does Gujarati, there is, according to Gandhi, a nonlinguistic and yet formal nature that is capable of permeating different languages. The dialogue as a form has qualities that go beyond a particular language. Thus, as a literary form of communication, the dialogue is "the best method of treating difficult subjects," in *any* language. Not surprisingly, in *Indian Opinion*, dated 15–2–1908, under the title, "A Dialogue on the Compromise" Gandhi responds to the numerous letters (of objection) to the editor in the form of a dialogue (in English) between the Reader and the Editor.[2] In the preface to this "dialogue," he identifies his readers: the sleepy reader he can wake and to whom the piece is addressed, and the reader who feigns sleep whom he knows he will never wake, never have as a participant in a dialogue. Although for Gandhi, as a Satyagrahi (loosely translated as an upholder of Truth) and responsible seeker through relative truths of the Absolute Truth, the dialogue as both an external and internal or meditative means of communication and discovery must never stop, the formalistic judgment in favor of the dialogue rises from Gandhi's ethical principles of simplicity and honesty where the yeas are yeas and the nays are nays—simple and straightforward where dialogue, as a form of communication, has to adhere to this simplicity and honesty in order to meet its own criteria for communication—so that the other can understand, a point that Gandhi stresses in the preface to both *Indian Home Rule* and the aforementioned dialogue on the compromise. Gandhi himself drew inspiration from dialogues that he had read, not only of Plato but also of "the tortoise and his mate" (CWMG 24:330); about a year before his death, he regretted not being able to write a "dialogue" on "the delicate subject of the evil habits of children" for a certain "Mrs. Stanley Jones" (94: 335–6). Jürgen Habermas' theory of communication that critics such as Edward Said, Michael Hardt, and Antonio Negri have critiqued for its lack of grounding in either "a moral center" (Viswanathan 2001, 205) or the historicity of imperialism (Hardt and Negri 2000, 33–34), can, as Homi K. Bhabha says, be bent to our purposes (Bhabha 1994, 171) to help understand the sociopolitical function of communication and to, in turn, theorize the dialogical aspects of literary representation. In *On The Pragmatics Of Communication*, Habermas lists four "universal validity claims" that determine the condition to communication: "uttering something intelligibly," "giving (the hearer) something to understand," "making herself thereby understandable," and "coming to an understanding with another person" (Habermas 1998, 22). The first of these has to do with the manner of expression or form. The speaker has to carefully choose a form that facilitates mutual comprehension. Second, for the hearer to comprehend, the speaker must deal with truth. Third, the speaker must communicate truthfully. Finally, the speaker must speak from within a "right" context, that is, "a recognized normative background" (23) to be understood. These conditions of communication bind the form of the dialogue. Gandhi's decision to keep this form in *Indian Home Rule* arises from the theoretical possibility of the form determining both the language and the message.

As a writer and statesman Gandhi was acutely aware of the substantiality of form and genre; for him, the manner in which a message was dressed was of utmost importance. Writing about the duty of editors and journalists, Gandhi advises, "The editors and their assistants have to be extra careful about the news they give and the manner in which they dress it" (Hingorani and Hingorani 1985, 232). In Gandhi's case, his choice of the clichéd metaphor, of the form as dress or outer covering, significantly points to his fundamental principle of Truth so that if later on in life Gandhi felt impelled to adopt the dress code of the half-naked fakir, it was out of a "WYSIWYG" ("what you see is what you get") conviction that the essence was often proportionate to that which was perceived, the external form.

Finally, Gandhi's reply to those who criticized his use of the form of the dialogue is that the dialogue is "real," namely that he has recorded conversations with readers of his South African journal *Indian Opinion*. In the *Aryan Path—Special Hind Swaraj Number* published in September, 1938, Gandhi writes, "Let the reader bear in mind that it [*Hind Swaraj*] is a faithful record of conversations I had with workers, one of whom was an avowed anarchist. He [the reader] should also know that it stopped the rot that was about to set in among some Indians in South Africa" (CWMG 73: 290). Thus, the dialogue involved real life meetings with anarchists in England and in South Africa and therefore, although imaginatively rendered, was not fictitious. In *Moral Consciousness and Communicative Action*, Habermas explains that universal validity claims that are normative possess cognitive meaning and can be comprehended "*like* claims to truth." Habermas' italicized "like" recognizes the elusiveness of ideological structures that determine the normative while refusing to dismiss the relevance of truth claims within realities. Further, according to him, the discourse cannot assume either a monological or fictional debate: "the justification of norms and commands requires that a real discourse be carried out and thus cannot occur in a strictly monological form, i.e., in the form of a hypothetical process of argumentation occurring in the individual mind" (Habermas 1990, 68). Whereas Habermas' are primarily critical theories with minimal practical agenda, Gandhi's understanding and use of literary communication are integral to his social and political action and to his identity and role as a Satyagrahi. As Thomas Pantham notes, "Habermas' practico-political discourse is a thought experiment in practical truth. It has rationalistic overtones. Gandhi's *satyagraha* is not a mere thought experiment but a mode of truth-centered direct action, which consists of both rational and extra-rational elements" (Pantham 1987, 308).[3] The preface to *Hind Swaraj or Indian Home Rule* by invoking claims to truth makes clear the legitimate conditions of the discourse involving Satyagrahis, but through an understanding of ahimsa (nonviolence).

Gandhi's choice of the form of the dialogue acknowledges the play of interpretations that as an author Gandhi strives to make finite through ethico-aesthetic principles of communication. If in the *Hind Swaraj* Gandhi stresses the inseparability of what he calls "means" and "ends," his use of the form of the dialogue foregrounds the significance of this inalienability at the level of ethics and aesthetics. Responding to the Reader's argument that a good goal ought to be arrived at by any means (including violence), the Editor says: "The means may be likened to a seed, the end to a tree; and there is just the same inviolable connection between the means and the end as there is between the seed and the tree" (81). Alluding to both the Bhagavad Gita and the New Testament,

Gandhi brings to focus the inherence of truth in method affirming the Habermasian principle that goals and their means "share the same life form" (Holub 1991, 64). Such inherence matters to the Satyagrahi for whom Absolute Truth or God is the end and nonviolence the only means:

> Satya and ahimsa are like the two sides of a coin, or rather of a smooth unstamped metallic disc. Who can say which is the obverse, and which is the reverse? Nevertheless, ahimsa is the means; truth is the end. Means to be means must always be within our reach, and so ahimsa is our supreme duty. If we take care of the means, we are bound to reach the end sooner or later. When once we have grasped this point, final victory is beyond question. (CWMG 49: 409)

Where the end of Satya (as Absolute Truth) is not immediately accessible, the only reliable and reachable means is nonviolence as not only the refusal to cause harm to another but also to, if necessary, suffer in one's own person, and to actively love the other. It introduces the interactive element of literary representation, denoting interaction not only between the author and the reader but also extending such action in the service of the world, in the service of "the poorest and the weakest" (96: 311).[4] Taking care of this means (of ahimsa) will, according to Gandhi, certainly lead to the supreme end of Satya. The discussion between the Editor and the Reader immediately foregrounds the artistic function of the dialogue in not only handling the topic of means and ends, but in itself enacting (performing) in its very form and in its communicative capacity—that compels not only the reason but also "the heart" and therefore the action of the other—the inseparability of those means and ends.

Gandhi's philosophy of unity of means and ends as well as his experience as a journalist determine his choice of the characters, the Reader and the Editor, of *Hind Swaraj* and the dialogue between the two. Gandhi had already spent about four years running the South African weekly, *Indian Opinion*. While the journal proved a useful medium for his work and philosophy, including the first publication of *Hind Swarajya* in its Gujarati sections, his experience editing and financing it was far from a profitable business venture. He was more concerned that the journal should hold a mirror to the soul of the Editor, reflecting the changes in one's life. In his autobiography he writes, "*Indian Opinion* in those days, like *Young India* and *Navajivan* today, was a mirror of part of my life. Week after week I poured out my soul in its columns, and expounded the principles and practice of Satyagraha as I understood it." In fact, continues Gandhi, "Satyagraha would probably have been impossible without *Indian Opinion*." The unity of life and writing makes *Indian Opinion* a study of human nature. Gandhi makes possible this study, he says, by "establishing an intimate and clean bond between the editor and the readers" (Gandhi 1993, 286). An "intimate and clean bond," a thoroughly idealistic and arguably relativistic status, introduces the ethical portion to his practice of journalism while journalism assumes the form of a dialogue between the readers and the editor.

The intricate relationship between the dialogue form implicit in journalism, Gandhi's reliance on this form to not only express his truth-ideas but also to live and experience such truth in his life, and his growing awareness of the need for harmony between his own thoughts, words, and deeds (even as Gandhi often failed in their daily demands in his exercise as a truth-seeker or Satyagrahi) is best understood in the following excerpt from an editorial in *Navajivan*:

> With much striving I have formulated some principles for my life and put them into practice. The happiness I have found that way, I think, I have not seen in others. Many a friend has testified to this. It is my sincere aspiration to place these principles before India and share my happiness with her. A newspaper is one means to that end.
>
> For me, satyagraha is not a mere copy-book maxim: it is my very life. To me nothing but truth has any interest. I am convinced that the country can never benefit by untruth. In any case, I am firmly of the view that, even if untruth should seem profitable for the time being, we must not abandon truth.
>
> I have been a seeker of this truth ever since I began to understand things. I have been trying to practice it for 40 years. Even so, I know that I have not attained perfect harmony in thought, word and deed.
>
> What does it matter, though? The more we strive to realize an ideal, the farther it recedes. To pursue it the more vigorously is the only object worthy of endeavor. We may stumble and fall, but shall rise again; it should be enough if we did not run away from the battle. (CWMG 18: 345)

Hind Swaraj becomes an instance of the literary representation of the intimate tie between the dialogical aspects of journalism and the writerly and readerly roles of a Satyagrahi as a human person whose function is not only textual but also social and spiritual. For Gandhi there is no representation other than the expression of truth; its cognition and praxis rely heavily on a dialogue between the editor and the reader.

However, what Gandhi saw around him were readers entranced by what was a monologue of the dominant sections of society through the newspapers. He felt that readers gave the newspapers the unquestioning belief that only the scriptures had had until then. In *My Picture of Free India*, Gandhi writes, "The newspapers have taken the place of the *Gita*, the *Bible* and the *Quran* with the people. For them, the printed sheet is gospel truth" (Hingorani 1985, 232). That the trust of the readers was so whole was a call to the editors and newspaper writers to the highest sense of responsibility. Gandhi argued that when the people were turning more and more to the newspaper for facts and truth, the power of the newspaper was immense and that, therefore, journalists and editors needed to learn restraint, of all virtues. *Indian Opinion* was for Gandhi "a training in self-restraint" (Gandhi 1993, 286). "The newspaper press is a great power," wrote Gandhi in his autobiography, "but just as an unchained torrent of water submerges whole countrysides and devastates crops, even so an uncontrolled pen serves but to destroy" (287). The newspapers had become the instrument of (mis)communication during colonialism. The two English newspapers that began in India in 1780, the *Bengal Gazette* and the *Indian Gazette*, were strategically located in Calcutta, the then headquarters of the British East India Company. Numerous other newspapers, in English and the vernacular, soon took their place. In less than a century, the British Reuters agency became the chief provider of news for the Indian newspapers until other national agencies were formed such as the Indian News Agency (INA) in 1900 and the Associated Press of India (API) of 1905. The leading writers of these agencies kept in close contact with the colonial administrators; many famous colonial administrators were at some time or the other themselves journalists and, thus, both the INA and the API worked closely with the Viceroy of India, Lord Curzon who as George Nathaniel Curzon had in turn worked as a journalist. The British Reuters' services in South Africa began in 1861 and the most publicized correspondent of the Boer Wars was none other than Winston Churchill.[5] Freedom fighters such as Lokmanya Balagangadhar Tilak and Swadeshabhimani Ramakrishna Pillai were also themselves journalists and editors who fought fiercely for the freedom of the press. Gandhi too was like Tilak and Swadeshabhimani in his conviction that a free press was the lifeblood of a society; he believed that government censure of the press would prove "more poisonous than want of control."

Sedition was the most frequently invoked charge against many freedom fighters, Tilak and Gandhi included, and the censure of *Hind Swaraj* itself was more than a symbolic curbing of the dialogic privilege of the Reader and the Editor. However, Gandhi also believed that restraint "exercised from within" (287) alone could save the press and ultimately, society, for he knew that many newspapers succumbed to political and economic pressures and readily engaged in distortion of facts which unsuspecting and gullible readers considered gospel truth. The alibi was to adopt the model of the dialogue where all participants spoke and were heard.

Again, Gandhi's philosophy and practice of journalism throws light on what "representation" meant for him. If the symbols in his life such as the *charka* and the flag signified principles of concern for the poorest of the poor, home industries, and unity, literary representation for him acknowledged the symbolic power of the word (invariably made flesh) to lead to Truth. In his autobiography Gandhi writes, "To describe truth, as it has appeared to me, and in the exact manner in which I have arrived at it, has been my ceaseless effort. The exercise has given me ineffable mental peace, because, it has been my fond hope that it might bring faith in Truth and Ahimsa to waverers." Gandhi's ethical and spiritual stance, that "There is no other God than Truth" (503), and his choice of representation of his relative truths by the written or spoken word as much as by one's own life, place a heavy onus on readers and writers, and on the Reader and the Editor in *Hind Swaraj*.

The dialogue that Gandhi dramatically represents in *Hind Swaraj* captures the tension between representation and application. It is the Reader who begins the dialogue, by providing the context of the title topic, Home Rule, and posing an open question: "Will you explain your views in this matter?" The Editor's answer is preceded by acts of listening, acknowledging, and considering. These three processes of the dialogue also become the points of the Editor's response in an analysis of the objectives of a newspaper, thereby legitimizing the presence of the specific characters. The listening and acknowledging—receiving "the popular feeling" in order to represent it—is a function of the newspaper. As a modern medium of interaction and dialogue, the newspaper further has the onus of praxis, "to arouse among the people certain desirable sentiments" and "to expose popular defects." The Editor sees a functional link between what the newspaper does and the process of answering the Reader's question: "The exercise of all these three functions is involved in answering your question" (Parel 1997, 13).

In this way, the form of the dialogue, the literary mode that permits questions and answers, is intricately bound up with what is being discussed, the content.

In *Moral Consciousness and Communicative Action* Habermas lists three modes of language use: cognitive, interactive, and expressive, that correspond to issues of truth, justice, and taste (Habermas 1990, 137). Literary theories focus mainly on the last of these, namely the expressive, in the concept of literary representation. Examining the form and the content of *Hind Swaraj* in terms of the ethico-aesthetic requires a study of ethical questions of truth and justice as only the other side of the expressive. It is in following up on some of the textual allusions in *Hind Swaraj*, chief of which is the Bhagavad Gita,[6] that such a study is made possible.

Gandhi's reading of the Bhagavad Gita is allegorical. This reading of the Gita determines to a great extent the form and content of *Hind Swaraj*. The Gita forms part of Book VI of the epic *Mahabharata* and is written in the form of a dialogue between Prince Arjuna and his charioteer Lord Krishna. Whereas the immediate context of the Bhagavad Gita is the imminent war between kin, the Pandavas and the Kauravas, and the dilemma is whether or not to kill one's own, the dialogue sweeps widely and covers issues of duty, knowledge, and devotion. Arjuna, who as a good Kshatriya has always entered the battlefield without hesitation, now hesitates when confronted with the prospect of kin for enemies. Krishna's advise is a reminder of Arjuna's dharma (duty)— his vocation as a Kshatriya. In a sustained dialogue between Krishna and Arjuna, the topic expands into theology and how human beings can know God. Many Indian Freedom Fighters against colonialism relied heavily on a historical interpretation of the Gita that ultimately saw themselves as bound, like Arjuna, to commit themselves for the greater good. Those such as Lokmanya Bal Gangadhar Tilak, the early Aurobindo Ghose, and Vinayak Damodar Savarkar privileged a historical interpretation that permitted them to use violence, if necessary, for the greater good. Gandhi's espousal of nonviolence (ahimsa), on the other hand, required him to seek greater literary freedom with the scripture.

A historicized and non-allegorical reading of the Bhagavad Gita would be a reading that privileges a righteous and divine bloodshed in the battle of Kuruskshetra. Such a reading was especially prescribed by the Hindu nationalists of whom Tilak is perhaps the best known. In his commentary on the Bhagavad Gita, Tilak stressed karma (action) as the supreme dharma and relegated spirituality to the back burner. According to him, the colonial times called not for piety but military action.

His *Srimad Bhagavadgita-Rahasya* written in a British jail is a simple reminder to imitate Krishna to achieve *lokasamgraha* or, as he puts it in Benthamite terms, "the greatest good of the greatest number—the unification of humanity in universal sympathy" (Tilak 1971, 688). While the circumstances of colonial and penal invigilation obviously curbed any apparent militant and "extremist" rendering of the Gita, the book remained, at the turn of the century, an invocation to an anticolonial struggle, thus confirming Tilak's thesis that nationalism and religion were inseparable. In *20th Century Indian Interpretations of BHAGAVADGITA: Tilak, Gandhi and Aurobindo*, P.M. Thomas argues that there was "a remarkable sense of history in Tilak's interpretation of the *Gita*" and that this world vision (of even though a relative reality) made him an "activist" or "extremist" (Thomas 1987, 71). Aurobindo Ghose's reminder: "To shrink from bloodshed and violence under such circumstances is a weakness deserving as severe a rebuke as Sri Krishna addressed to Arjuna when he shrank from the colossal civil slaughter on the field of Kurukshetra" (Ghose 1952, 29), like Tilak's, is also premised on a historical reading of the Gita. The militant action that these commentators demand of colonized people had no use for what they saw as the spiritualizing tendencies of those such as Sankara, Gandhi, or Sarvepalli Radhakrishnan.

As an Indian national leader of the "extremist" wing, Tilak, like Aurobindo, Lala Lajpat Rai, and Bankim Chandra Chatterjee encouraged Indians to return to India's ancient greatness and further marked this movement into the past with the revival and popularization of religious festivals such as the Ganapathy Puja which contributed to Indian nationalism becoming Hindu nationalism (Thomas 1987, 56). Tilak's translation and commentary of the Gita trace the political philosophy of his religious study and practice, the essence of which is to be found in the concept of *Karmayoga*. His translation of the Bhagavad Gita (II.50) defines *Karmayoga* as follows: "[he] who is steeped in the (equable) Reason remains untouched both by sin or merit in this (world); therefore take shelter in Yoga. The cleverness (skillfulness or trick) of performing Action (without acquiring the merit or sin) is known as (*Karma*) *Yoga*." In an article published in *The Journal of Asian Studies* about a decade after Indian independence, D. MacKenzie Brown argues that through an interpretation of the Gita that stressed *Karmayoga*, Tilak rallied the Indian intelligentsia and the masses against the colonial government: "The one scripture that he found eminently suited to this role was the *Bhagavad-Gita* . . . it stressed the doctrine of *Karma-yoga* (action)—insisting upon the warrior's duty to fight" (Brown 1958, 197). This duty, for Tilak, is determined by a superior "desireless, equable and unattached Reason of the doer" that is justified by attitude, not consequence. "The *Gita* in discriminating the doable and the not-doable, attaches a higher importance to the desireless, equable and unattached Reason of the doer, than to the external result of the action . . . and the welfare of all created beings resulting from such a mode of life is the external or concomittant result of that equability of Reason" (Tilak 1971, 531). Within this interpretation it is equally possible for a *karmayogi* to engage in acts of violence and possess a clear conscience. Tilak's commentary *Gita-Rahasya* published in 1915 became one of the first anticolonial applications of the scripture. That the similarities between Tilak's and Gandhi's Gita are few accounts for some of the stylistic and topical characteristics of the *Hind Swaraj*.

Gandhi's much later translation and commentary of the Gita is similar to Tilak's in its emphasis on *Karmayoga* founded on the principle of desirelessness or work without desire for fruit—*nishkamakarma*. But Gandhi, unlike Tilak, is reluctant to give absolute theological or historical credence to the Gita. For Gandhi, all scriptures are mediated, thereby requiring of the devotee reason and discretion in their reading, interpretation, and application. In the *Harijan* of December 5, 1936, Gandhi writes, "I exercise my judgement about every scripture, including the *Gita*. I cannot let a scriptural text supersede my reason. . . . Nothing in them [the scriptures] comes from God directly" (quoted in Thomas 1987, 84). Second, Gandhi chooses to do a literary rather than a literal interpretation of the Gita by arguing for the less than historical nature of the text. In *The Teaching of the Gita*, Gandhi argues as follows: "By ascribing to the chief actors superhuman or subhuman origins, the great Vyasa made short work of the history of Kings and their peoples. The persons therein described may be historical, but the author of the *Mahabharata* has used them merely to drive home his religious theme" (Gandhi 1971, 19). Privileging the reader over the text, Gandhi makes way for some unorthodox readings of the Gita that challenge the approval of violence.

Gandhi's refusal to interpret the Gita literally has multiple implications for the understanding of *Hind Swaraj* as text and for a theory of literary representation. According to Gandhi, "Krishna is the Dweller within, ever whispering to a pure heart . . . Under the guise of physical warfare."[7] Arjuna, then, represented higher impulses and struggles against evil (Fischer 1951, 48). This allegorical reading of the Bhagavad Gita invokes in turn a reading of *Hind Swaraj* that recognizes dignity and divinity in *both* the Reader and the Editor. An instance of this recognition is the discussion on Home Rule itself.

"How can India be free?" This is the high level and political question that prompts Gandhi to define "Hind Swaraj" at the turn of the century. The question becomes the title of chapter XIV. Earlier on, chapter IV bears a more direct title: "What is Swaraj?" But, in the dialogue that ensues, this chapter turns out to be an exposition of what *swaraj* is *not* according to Gandhi. The Reader, who in speech comes closest to a Gandhian style, as in the courteous request to the English to "Please leave our country" (Parel 1997, 26), and in the use of provocative similes to suggest the unquestionable danger of the English presence in India, "It is similar to the question whether there is any harm in associating with a tiger" (27), is furthest away, from the Gandhian interpretation of swaraj. In responding, the Editor underscores the void between what swaraj is to him and what it is to the Reader: "You want the tiger's nature, but not the tiger; that is to say, you would make India English, and, when it becomes English, it will be called not Hindustan but Englistan. That is not the Swaraj that I want" (28). This dialogue by negation depicts at best the struggle-stage or "Arjuna stage" of both the Reader and the Editor. What immediately precedes or follows this chapter also examines the "condition" of both the English and the Indians. Options are measured, found wanting, rejected. No enlightenment as such emerges, as yet.

In chapter XIV, though, once again, as in the case of the Bhagavad Gita, by rejecting history, an attempt is made to define swaraj: "if we become free, India is free. And in this thought you have a definition of Swaraj. It is Swaraj when we learn to rule ourselves" (73). The immediate effect of this definition that stands at odds with definitions based on right rather than duty is of course to raise further questions. In his essay, "What is Swaraj? Lessons from Gandhi" Fred Dallmayr produces a list of seven questions beginning with "If *swaraj* is identified with moral self-rule or self-restraint, why should such self-restraint be hampered or obstructed by British colonialism (or any other political regime)?" And ending with, "Yet, if moral restraint is deemphasized in favor of popular politics, does self-rule not shade over into a simple strategy of national independence, and swaraj into a synonym for the pursuit of nationalist goals (perhaps to the detriment of neighbors and the global community)?" (Parel 2000, 108). Dallmayr finds his own answers through Parel's commentary that emphasizes the individual dimension of swaraj. The metaphor of the "oceanic circle" (Parel 1997, 189)—of the potential of the good to radiate from within to without and of self-government to expand through the *panchayat* (or village government) to the wider levels of government—that Gandhi used in an interview in 1946, annotates Gandhi's definition of *swaraj*. However, the definition may not stand the test of historical evidence or backing. As the Reader says, "But it has not occurred in history." The Editor's reply is, "The condition of India is unique" (74). Again the Reader asks, "Is there any historical evidence as to the success of what you have called soul-force or truth-force?"[8] And the Editor replies by resorting to a poet, Tulisidas, whose *Ramacharatamanas* was second only to the Bhagavad Gita for Gandhi (88). On another instance Gandhi poses the question and answers as follows: "What is the meaning of *Hind Swaraj*? It means rule of *dharma* or *Ramarajya*" (CWMG, 32: 489). Again, swaraj is ahistorical. If it has to be brought into social reality it will have to be done through morality and spirituality, and through the literary dialogue of the *Hind Swaraj* in which both the Editor and the Reader never "feign sleep."

In a critique of Gandhi's *Hind Swaraj* in *Nationalist Thought and the Colonial World: A Derivative Discourse*, Partha Chatterjee compares Gandhi to several nationalists of the time and concludes that Gandhi "does not feel it necessary to even attempt a historical demonstration of the possibilities he is trying to point out." "Indeed," notes Chatterjee, "he objects that the historical mode of reasoning is quite unsuitable, indeed irrelevant, for his purpose" (93). Chatterjee goes on to interpret Gandhi's critique of history as a record of quarrels as pointing to the ahistoricity of Truth: "History therefore, does not record the Truth. Truth lies outside history; it is universal, unchanging. Truth has no history of its own" (Chatterjee 1986, 94). This is not to suggest that Gandhi had no sense of history. The Editor's definition of "history," in *Hind Swaraj*, using the Gujarati meaning, "it so happened" (Parel 1997, 89) permits a wider and more wholesome understanding of the past and of life perceived in Truth. Gandhi's philosophy of Truth gains significance when juxtaposed with his interpretation of the Gita. In his "Introduction: The Message of the *Gita*," Gandhi explains:

> Even in 1888–89, when I first became acquainted with the *Gita*, I felt that it was not a historical work, but that, under the guise of physical warfare, it described the duel that perpetually went on in the hearts of mankind, and that physical warfare was brought in merely to make the description of the internal duel more alluring. This preliminary intuition became more confirmed on a closer study of religion and the *Gita*. (Bakker 1993, 29)

That the concept of swaraj, the fundamental thesis of the book, stands outside history, "as a record of the wars of the world" (Parel 1997, 89), is due in part to its conception in Gandhi's allegorical and ahistoricized reading of the Bhagavad Gita.

The allegorical interpretation of the Gita lends itself to a social and spiritual movement founded on nonviolence. *(A)himsa* seals the difference between one such as Tilak for whom ultimate goal takes priority over means and Gandhi for whom the means has to be in keeping with principles of truth and nonviolence. For Tilak the Gita serves to bring about the break between means and ends: "If thieves enter our house and we have not sufficient strength in our wrists to drive them out, we should without hesitation, shut them up and burn them alive." He continues, "Do not circumscribe your visions like frogs in a well. Get out of the Penal Code, enter into the extremely high atmosphere of the *Bhagavad Gita* and then consider the actions of great men" (quoted in Brown 1958, 205). The Reader of the *Hind Swaraj* alludes to this solution to thievery: "Shall I think of the means when I have to deal with a thief in the house? My duty is to drive him out anyhow" (Parel 1997, 80). In the chapter titled "Brute Force," the Editor responds at length by examining the pros and cons of using "soul force" against "brute force" in the case of the Reader's hypothetical thief. The Former attempts to unsettle the latter's complacency by introducing a shocking possibility: "If it is my father who has come to steal," says the Editor, "I shall use one kind of means" (82). The possibilities are numerous between an armed father and an armed stranger, proving to the Reader that the ultimate goal is "*not* to drive away the thief by any means you like" (83).

Gandhi's youth experience of theft and the role of a father in introducing the lesson of ahimsa in the middle of that crime perhaps accounts for his narrative of the paternal thief. As Gandhi narrates in his autobiography, he was fifteen years old, a married youth, when he stole some gold ostensibly for a good purpose—to pay his brother's debt. Gandhi writes,

> I was trembling as I handed the confession to my father. . . . He read it through, and pearl-drops trickled down his cheeks, wetting the paper. . . . Those pearl-drops of love cleansed my heart, and washed my sin away. . . . This was, for me, an object-lesson in *Ahimsa*. Then I could read in it nothing more than a father's love, but today I know that it was pure *Ahimsa*. When such *Ahimsa* becomes all-embracing, it transforms everything it touches. There is no limit to its power. (Gandhi 1993, 28)

As if to answer a lifetime's question—"What would I have done, were my father in my position?"—Gandhi considers the effect that his father as thief would have had on him. The writer of the letter is also the writer of *Hind Swaraj*, both (variously) aspirants to Truth—Satyagrahis. The reader, though, is different: in the one case it is the writer's father and in the other, an anarchist who is also a friend. The reader of the letter is moved to tears in an experience of empathetic difference: unable to condone the crime, yet fully understanding the spirit of the confession. Such reading, as it were miraculously, transforms the writer who witnesses the means of "pure Ahimsa" so that decades later, "The strength of my father [as thief] would make me weep" (Parel 1997, 82), says the Editor in *Hind Swaraj*. Empathizing with the Reader, the Editor continues, "the strength of the armed man would rouse in me anger, and we should become enemies" (82–83). It is at this moment, however, that the Editor invokes ahimsa's soul force: "I myself seem clearly to see what should be done in all these cases, but the remedy may frighten you" (83). The application of soul force and ahimsa on the perpetrator and the criminal is, to say the least, frightening. But, according to Gandhi, all else is misreading and interpolation, even so in the ethics of the Bhagavad Gita.

The nonliteral reading of the Gita and the reliance of this method in the writing of *Hind Swaraj*, also contributes to a Gandhian theory of reading that affirms the dialogical nature of reader-response but only in so far as the participants are Satyagrahis. As Gandhi's famous biographer, Louis Fischer, notes, "Gandhi decides that loyalty to the *Gita* entitles him to amend it" (Fischer 1951, 49). While this violent[9] reading of the Bhagavad Gita. is at the basis of the disputes between the Reader and the Editor in *Hind Swaraj*, it also makes possible the very process of dialogue between the two. The battle on the colonial *Kurukshetra* can assume a historical himsa for the Reader or an allegorical ahimsa for the Editor. The purpose of the dialogue, however, is to make possible an understanding about the opposite plan of action.

Dialogue neither presupposes nor produces an elimination of differences. On the contrary, the personal pronoun—the Me[10] talking to the You—functions grammatically so that the speaker and the listener become each other's "alter ego." So, in the Gita, when Krishna says, "My dear Arjuna, only by undivided devotional service can I be understood as I am, standing before you; and I can thus be seen directly. Only in this way can you enter into the mysteries of My understanding" (Bhaktivedanta 1968, 236),[11] Arjuna has to "enter" Krishna's understanding without ceasing to be Arjuna. For Habermas, dialogue not only poses no threat to differences in speaker perspectives but also recognizes those differences as almost a condition for dialogue: "The intersubjectivity of linguistically achieved understanding is by nature porous, and linguistically attained consensus does not eradicate from the accord the differences in speaker perspectives but rather presupposes them as ineliminable." The alter ego as a recognition of the self in the other has a prerequisite—a "consciousness" of "absolute difference and irreplaceability" (Habermas 1998, 48). An understanding that moves toward solidarity and yet is not, never, free of conflict, privileges the practice of dialogue.

According to Gandhi, scripture must be submitted to an art of understanding or hermeneutics[12] rather than to tradition: "The written word undoubtedly helps, but even that has to be interpreted, and when there are conflicting interpretations, the seeker is the final arbiter" (CWMG 62: 290). Reading is thus not a monologue subject to tradition and authority, but a dialogic process that moves toward understanding though not necessarily agreement. Ultimately, the onus is on the reader. The "Reader" of *Hind Swaraj* is, thus, empowered as a Satyagrahi or "seeker"—a key term in Gandhi's vocabulary. (See "Seeker After Truth" in 31: 228–229). The "Editor" too, then, can move to the place of "final arbiter" only as a Satyagrahi/seeker willing to brace up to conflicting interpretations of the Gita and consequently of the *Hind Swaraj*. For Gandhi, "A poet's meaning is limitless. Like man, the meaning of great writings suffer [sic!] evolution. On examining the history of languages, we notice that the meaning of important words has changed or expanded. This is true of the *Gita*. The author has himself extended the meanings of some of the current words" (46: 174). Thus, reading must take into consideration the "limitless" extent of the meaning of the poet/author, the evolving sense of discourse, and the change of language. These three determinants of reading are, in fact, not mutually exclusive. As Gandhi sees it, a perceptive author "extends" the use of words. The word "sacrifice" in the Gita then signifies not animal sacrifice, but the sacrifice of body labor, the word having been extended by the poet (Desai 1970, 133). If for Gandhi the process of reading is itself creative through a dialogue, for Tilak the author places a check on the reader's free play of interpretations. In a speech on his *Gita Rahasya* Tilak considers the monologic process of reading, "Various commentators have put as many interpretations on the book, and surely the writer or composer could not have written or composed the book for so many interpretations being put on it. He must have but one meaning and one purpose running through the book, and that I have tried to find out"

(Tilak 1922, 233). What Tilak finds out is the message of the subservience of all *yogas* to *Karmayoga* or the yoga of action rather than the yoga of sole knowledge (*jnanayoga*) or of devotion (*bhakthiyoga*). Interestingly, the Gita leads Gandhi too along the path of *karmayoga* rather than any form of renunciation. In his conclusion to "Discourses on the 'Gita'," Gandhi notes that the Gita does not give "the central importance to karma, nor to *jnana* nor to *bhakti*." However, as he continues his argument he acknowledges that "the Gita has stressed karma" although "*bhakti* and *jnana*, too, are essential" (CWMG, 32: 351). Gandhi's insistence on a dialogical reading process, however, distances itself from the violence (*himsa*) of a monologue. The former functions within structures of creative understanding even as it dips deeply into what the participants already share while the latter by foreclosing itself to that dialogue insists on the unrelenting "one meaning" and "one purpose."

The dialogue is thus subject to the presence of a "normative background," that is, the speaker and the hearer should be accessible to each other. Habermas' definition of normative background as a space of empathy can rationalize some of the choices of topics in the dialogue between the Reader and the Editor in *Hind Swaraj*. Habermas defines normative background as follows: "A speaker can in a performative attitude address himself to a hearer only under the condition that he learns to see and understand himself—against the background of others who are potentially present—from the perspective of his opposite number, just as the addressee for his part adopts the speaker's perspective for himself" (Habermas 1998, 24). Suggestive, once again, of Krishna's invocation to understand, the participants in a dialogue can function only through empathetic difference. Habermas proceeds to examine meditations on the "self" by philosophers such as Søren Aabye Kierkegaard and Dieter Henrich. For the purposes of this essay, it is sufficient to become aware of the presence of access points in the dialogue between the Reader and the Editor that facilitate understanding. What permits the dialogue of *Hind Swaraj* is the presence of verbal meeting points located on a scriptural (con)text. Three such obvious points are of nonviolence (ahimsa), patriarchy, and home rule (*swaraj*), and yet another shared but nontraditional structure is modernity that in a manner invades the traditional structures thereby highlighting the gap between the speakers. It is necessary for both the Reader and the Editor to base their discussion not only on but also *within* each of these concepts to be understood in a dialogue.

If the Reader in *Hind Swaraj* envisions a home rule that would take off on "arms and ammunitions," for which there is historical precedence as

in the case of Japan and England (Parel 1997, 27), the Editor's speech too
is not without the vocabulary of violence. Were it without the vocabulary
of violence, it would not be understood, that is, be part of a dialogue.
The "passive resistance" that the Editor proceeds to define startles even
the Reader: "You would then disregard laws—this is rank disloyalty.
We have always been considered a law-abiding nation. You seem to be
going even beyond the extremists" (91). The Editor's response is to rub
it in: "a man devoid of courage and manhood can never be a passive
resister" (93). The Editor appropriates the presumed qualifications of
himsa—courage and manhood (*insaniat* and *mardai*)[13]—and announces
satyagraha or truth force as actually qualified by those characteristics,
thereby exposing that which is not satyagraha as both cowardice and
effeminate. Again, if the Reader's attitude is of hate, the Editor's too is
of hate. Only the target varies: the Reader hates the English, the
Editor—the English civilization.

Another point of entry is the patriarchal diction shared by both the
Reader and the Editor: words such as "manhood" and "effeminate"
reach a climax in the feminization of the British parliament by the
Reader as "the Mother of Parliaments" (29) and by the Editor as "sterile woman and prostitute" (32). The scriptural categorizing of women as
either godly or ungodly enhances the exercises of speaking and listening
for the Reader as for the Editor. Both characters are eager to protect
women. When the Reader worries over the ills of child marriage, the
condition of widows, the polyandry of women, and the exploitative
system of *niyog*, the Editor too would protect those women (70–71) and
can yet argue through that diction for an un-widowed condition of
postcolonial India that, however, clearly verbalizes the harm that can
come from the English protecting a female India (113). Patriarchal
ideology draws a bond of communication between the Reader and the
Editor even at the point of differences. While the Reader would readily
mimic the English and their institutions to bring about a parallel
autonomous state in India, he finds the Editor's use of gendered
metaphor pleasing if not persuasive. When the Editor is done drawing a
picture of the English parliament as a prostitute who is "under the
control of ministers who change from time to time" (30), and as a "sterile
woman" who is selfish and lazy, one who is seen to "stretch . . . and to
doze" (31)[14] (where, incidentally, infertility is a case of lack of initiative
and will power even when the exercise of both are historically denied to
women at large), the Reader's response is encouraging: "You have set
me thinking; you do not expect me to accept at once all you say. You
give me entirely novel views. I shall have to digest them. Will you now

explain the epithet 'prostitute'?" (32). The dialogue moves toward an understanding of the novel in terms of the old. What the Reader asks to hear is not about the English parliament, but of the English parliament as "prostitute." The already known about a prostitute may open the way for the unknown about the English parliament.

That Gandhi regretted the use of these sexist terms in deference to "a lady," presumably Annie Besant (30), who challenged him and yet did not undertake to delete them even from his 1938 edition, perhaps points to the rhetorical viability of a "moral patriarchy,"[15] one grounded in the scriptures, as a point of entry in this dialogue.[16] The corruption of women is not simply a matter of shame and control. In the context of the Gita, it has grave scriptural bearings and social consequences. Chapter I and verse 40 of the Bhagawad Gita runs as follows, "When irreligion is prominent in the family, O Krsna, the ladies of the family become corrupt, and from the degradation of womanhood, O descendant of Vrsni, comes unwanted progeny" (Prabhupada 1968, 14).[17] The condition of the absence of *dharma*—*adharma*—here is the disintegration of one of the four ideals of *purushartha*, namely *dharma*, the other three being wealth (*artha*), desire (*kaama*), and release (*moksha*). Arjuna here displays his piece of wisdom and Krishna does not contradict him, but moves on to the need to kill the elders of the family of the Kauravas in this case. The elders who normally are in charge of "protecting" women and children and ought to be respected have to be done away with for the sake of a higher *dharma*. For Gandhi and for those such as Tilak[18] who placed a high stance on the *dharma* of *varna* and *ashrama* (*varnashramadharam*) or the "natural" division of society into *Brahmin, Kshatriya, Vaisya,* and *Sudra* and built their mission prioritizing one or more of the four stages of life, *Brahmacarya, Grahastha, Vanaprastha,* and *Sanyasa,* the chastity and loyalty of women was fundamental to a stable society. Out of loyal and chaste women alone could come an untainted population, namely one in which the four varnas kept their place. Thus, to compare England's supreme legislative body to a whore is to prophesy the ultimate moral and hence social destruction of that nation. Both the "Editor" and the "Reader" can now be said to be at compatible wavelengths.

A third point of access is the concept of *swaraj*. The term *swaraj* provides a common language for the dialogue even if concepts of "home" and "rule" are variously conceived. Parel notes that in the Gujarati Gandhi consistently uses the term "swaraj," but that in the English he replaces it with terms such as "home rule," "self-rule," "independence," "freedom of the individual," "liberty," "rights," "fundamental rights," and "economic freedom," and sometimes with "swaraj" as an English word (Parel 2000, 3). Each term acquires a definite sense within the context of its use. In his note on the history of *Hind Swaraj*, Parel writes that on the title page of the 1910 English translation of this book, Gandhi changed "Hind Swarajjya" to "Hind Swaraj" (Parel 1997, lxiii). The change in title further emphasizes the difference between the concept of home rule as nationalist jingoism and home rule as that nationalism which is a by-product of love and truth in the concept of "self-rule," the rule *of* the self, rather than only *by* the self. The difference between "rajya" and "raj" was the difference between geographical space or place and practice and Gandhi's work sought to define the latter even as it acknowledged the former, emphasizing duty over rights. The transition from place to practice is also a consequence of the ahistoricized and allegorical reading of the Bhagavad Gita. The *punya bhumi* (holy land) of the Gita—the Mahabharath or India—is the contested territory of "*swaraj.*" Both the Reader and the Editor are then on common ground. However, a historicist interpretation leads the Reader to argue as follows: "At first, we will assassinate a few Englishmen and strike terror. . . . We may have to lose a quarter of a million men, more or less, but we will regain our land. We will undertake guerrilla warfare, and defeat the English." The Editor's reply subverts this interpretation: "That is to say, you want to make the holy land of India unholy" (77). Within such a hermeneutics, if the land being conquered by Arjuna is to be holy, it will have to be the nonviolent inner space of the self, where the conquest would have to be made by soul force and not sword force. *Swaraj* then is "home rule" based on "self-rule." The dialogue proceeds through an understanding of these disagreements but from within shared ideological structures of aggression, patriarchy, and nationalism.

Linking the various structures is also the ideology of modernity that the Editor in *Hind Swaraj* denounces as "Western" and "Non-Christian." "According to the teaching of Mahomed" says the Editor, modern civilization, "would be considered a Satanic civilization. Hinduism calls it the Black Age [*Kali Yug*]" (37). The *kali yug* is the period of *adharma*. In its greed and corruption modern civilization is, in spite of its claims to reason, monologic and authoritarian as well as manipulative and mercenary. Modern civilization penetrates the aforementioned propensity for violence, tradition of patriarchy, and patriotic zeal, equally threatening the ancient civilization of India as well as Christian ideals. "Women, who should be the queens of households, wander in the streets, or they slave away in factories," says the Editor, lifting the veil on the famous suffragette movement that accompanied modernity (37). Suggestive of the numerous anti-globalization cries of today, the *Hind Swaraj* in one breath denounces modern civilization and yet stakes hope in it being "not an incurable disease" (38). Through the form of the dialogue, *Hind Swaraj* checks the demonizing of concepts and representatives of the Moderate and Extremist groups and becomes in turn an early instance of an actual dialogue with terrrorism in the wake of modernity. The Reader wittily sums up the complicitous and ambiguous relationship of the Editor to modernity in the question, "Is it a good point or a bad one that all you are saying will be printed through machinery?" (110). Once again, modernity as normative background makes literally possible the dialogue between the Reader and the Editor.

Facilitated by the normative background, the participants of the dialogue are ultimately invited into an understanding of Truth as Absolute Truth, but more immediately through relative truths that draw a correspondence between what is or what is not and one's honest acknowledgment of that fact even when the "fact" changed (psychologically, ideologically, etc.). The ultimate goal, however, is to reach the capitalized Truth. In his youth Gandhi reasoned and believed in that which decades later he would theorize as follows:

> In "God is Truth" "is" certainly does not mean "equal to" nor does it merely mean "is truthful." Truth is not a mere attribute of God but He is That. He is nothing if He is not That. Truth in Sanskrit means Sat. Sat means "Is." Therefore Truth is implied in "Is." God is, nothing else is. Therefore the more truthful we are, the nearer we are to God. We are only to the extent that we are truthful. (CWMG 56: 128)

While both the Reader and the Editor are required to wade through relativism "truthfully," that truthfulness does not contain the ultimate Truth. Gandhi does not seek the "rationally grounded consensus" which for Habermas is "the ultimate criterion of the truth of (empirical) statements or the rightness of social norms or standards" (Pantham 1987, 295), rather, for him, both consensus and dissent must be grounded in one's own truthfulness. In 1924, Gandhi made clear what was for him the priority of Truth in art: "I see and find Beauty in Truth and through Truth" (CWMG 25: 249). Such insistence on the relevance and place of the reader or author as a Truth-oriented human being (a Satyagrahi), has implications today for poststructuralist theories and their master narratives of relativism, constructivism, and textualism. Whereas deconstructive critics engage in critique to let loose diverse and opposed meanings, and poststructuralists recognize the relevance of the historical, but then deconstruct it because language is unstable and unreliable, a Gandhian process utilizes the relativist aspect of writing, reading, and interpreting not as an end in itself but as the path of the Satyagrahi whose goal is "Is." This presence is very much unlike the Derridian center that is absent. If through Claude Levi-Strauss and Michel Foucault, Roland Barthes progressed from "the pleasure of the text" to "the death of the author," for Gandhi "pleasure without conscience" is only one of the seven social sins (33: 135) and the author functions as the editor of a "dialogue" that always contains a "plot" (39: 403 and 41: 52). Dealing in Truth/truth, the author as a Satyagrahi is an "editor," a seeker of truth who is also skilled in the art of putting forth (truth) to the world, as suggested in the etymology of "edit" (also see 11: 15–17); Gandhi's plot-based "dialogue" (samvaad) can ill-afford the looseness of a "conversation" as the former facilitates dissent empathetically and becomes in turn a metaphor for sustained communication; in literary representation it is the locale of the ideal relationship between an author and a reader as Satyagrahis, dozing perhaps, but never pretending to be.

The normative background is also the Truth/truth element that sustains, in some ways, a Habermasian dialogue in Hind Swaraj, just as ahimsa marks the element of Justice, and the integration of form and content the aesthetic, Beauty. The threefold unity—of Truth, Justice, and Beauty—in the dialogue of Hind Swaraj calls for a theory of literary representation that stresses not only the expressive mode of language use, but also the cognitive and the interactive. Understanding becomes the touchstone of such literature where reader-response is qualified by empathetic difference and the identity of both the reader and the author as Satyagrahis challenges theories that would convert such identity into a "function." Interestingly, several references by Gayatri Spivak to Gandhi's function in "the discursive field of the Hindu religious Imaginary" or in "the sign-system of bourgeois politics" (Landry and McLean 1996, 207) or as "a political signifier within the social text" (206) appear as poststructuralist attempts to circumvent the personhood of an author.

In conclusion, Gandhi's quasi-fictional and journalistic work relies heavily on the reality of dialogue as a mode of communication at the point of difference. Where form and message, truth and simplicity, means and ends evolve as a humanistic and integrated whole that recognizes a moral and spiritual core in the concept of the Satyagrahi, it then becomes crucial for readings and interpretations to move toward the literary because the allegorical has ratified both means and their ends. Here, swaraj makes meaning through ahimsa, even in an encounter with injustice, and the dialogue places the onus on readers to respond through that which can already be perceived, the normative background, as well as from worlds of differences.

Notes

1. I am grateful to Anthony Parel for commenting on an earlier draft of this essay.
2. Where a "compromise" was initiated by Gandhi in offering voluntary registration by the Transvaal Indians instead of submitting to a law that forced all Indians to provide ten finger printings. See (CWMG), *The Collected Works of Mahatma Gandhi* (New Delhi: Publication Division, Ministry of Information and Broadcasting, 1958–1994), 8: 136–147.
3. Truth is the first condition of Satyagraha. Many more conditions follow. See CWMG, 9: 339–342 for a detailed introduction to the concept. For the purpose of this essay, the Truth condition should suffice.
4. I am indebted to Varghese Thekkevallyara for making explicit this connection between the role of the reader/author and Gandhi's concern for the least privileged in society. The following is known as Gandhi's "talisman": I will give you a talisman. Whenever you are in doubt, or when the self becomes too much with you, apply the following test. Recall the face of the poorest and the weakest man whom you may have seen, and ask yourself if the step you contemplate is going to be of any use to him. Will he gain anything by it? Will it restore him to a control over his own life and destiny? In other words, will it lead to swaraj for the hungry and spiritually starving millions? Then you will find your doubts and yourself melting away (CWMG, 96: 311).
5. See Robert W. Desmond's *Windows on the World: The Information Process In a Changing Society 1900–1920* (Iowa City: University of Iowa Press, 1980), 147–169.
6. In "Gandhi and the Bhagavadgita," J.T.F. Jordens writes: "In his autobiography, Gandhi recalled his first meaningful encounter with the work when in 1889, at the end of his second year in England, two Theosophists invited him to read with them the *Gita* in Sir Edwin Arnold's translation. Although he was greatly impressed by the work at first reading, he did not start studying it more closely until 1903" (J.T.F. Jordens, "Gandhi and the Bhagavadgita," in *Modern Indian Interpreters of the Bhagavad Gita*, ed. Robert Minor [Albany: SUNY Press, 1986], 88]. Jordens also concludes that "textual references to it [the Gita] are very rare in his writings of the South African period, and at no stage do they suggest any attempt at interpreting the meaning of the work or reflecting on the basis of its authority" (89). My reading of the *Hind Swaraj* suggests otherwise.
7. Balagangadhar Tilak's historical reading of the Gita too recognizes that Arjuna's dilemma was the dilemma of the righteous (Balagangadhar Tilak, *Srimad Bhagavadgita-Rahasya*, 3rd ed. [Poona: Tilak Brothers, 1971], 41–54).
8. The Editor does not use this term here, but Gandhi many a time defines "Satyagraha" as "soul force": "Satyagraha is pure soul-force. Truth is the very substance of the soul. That is why this force is called satyagraha. The soul is informed with knowledge. In it burns the flame of love. If someone gives us pain through ignorance, we shall win him through love. 'Nonviolence is the supreme dharma' [Ahimsa *Paramo* Dharmah] is the proof of this power of love" (CWMG, 16: 10).
9. The reading of a Satyagrahi is necessarily not passive. See my discussion of the normative background of the vocabulary of violence. Also, the moral and spiritual strength that is the source of any activity of a satyagrahi (including writing and reading) is violently active: It is absurd to suggest that satyagraha is being resorted to only by those who are deficient in physical strength or who, finding physical strength unavailing, can think of no alternative but satyagraha. Those who

hold such a view, it may be said, do not know what this fight means. Satyagraha is more potent than physical strength, which is as worthless as straw when compared with the former. Essentially, physical strength means that a man of such strength fights on the battlefield with little regard for his body, that is to say, he knows no fear. A satyagrahi, on his part, gives no thought whatever to his body. Fear cannot touch him at all. That is why he does not arm himself with any material weapons, but continues resistance till the end without fear of death. This means that the satyagrahi should have more courage than the man who relies on physical strength (CWMG, 9: 340).

10. Habermas borrows the concept from George Herbert Mead's essay, "The Social Self" in *Selected Writings* (Chicago: University of Chicago Press, 1964). Note that the subject here is neither in the first nor third person, but in the second person. Habermas defines this second person as the status of "recognizing-oneself-in-the-other" (Mead, "Social Self", 175). This, Habermas explains, is not the objectified third person (the target of a "gaze"). The "me" as "original self-consciousness" is generated in communication or through dialogue (177).

11. Gandhi's version runs: "But by single-minded devotion, O Arjuna, I may in this Form be known and seen, and truly entered into, O Parantapa!" (Mahadev Desai, *The Gospel of Selfless Action or The Gita According to Gandhi* [Ahmedabad: Navajivan Publishing House {1946} [1970], 306).

12. General hermeneutics as defined by Friedrich Schleiermacher is an "art of understanding" (Friedrich D.E. Schleiermacher, "The Hermeneutics: Outline of the 1819 Lectures," in *The Hermeneutic Tradition: From Ast to Ricoeur*, ed. Gayle L. Ormiston and Alan D. Schrift [Albany: State University of New York Press, 1990], 85).

13. I am obliged to Anthony Parel for pointing out the relevant Gujarati equivalent used by Gandhi.

14. For a psychoanalysis of this scene see Eric H. Erikson, *Gandhi's Truth: On the Origins of Militant Nonviolence* (New York: W.W. Norton & Company, Inc., 1969), 219–220.

15. Contemporary feminist critics such as Kumari Jayawardena, Lata Mani, Suruchi Thapar, and Ketu H. Katrak take issue with Gandhi's concept of Satyagraha that, according to them, places women at a disadvantage when the female is seen as the ideal sufferer.

16. It is probable that Gandhi may not be the editor of the edition.

17. Gandhi's translation differs somewhat: With the destruction of the family perish the eternal family virtues, and with the perishing of these virtues unrighteousness seizes the whole family (1.40). When unrighteousness prevails, O Krishna, the women of the family become corrupt, and their corruption, O Varshneya, causes a confusion of *varnas* (1.41), Desai, *Gospel of Selfless Action*, 146.

18. "*Lokasamgraha* according to the *Gita* means, giving to other people a living example of how one can perform desirelessly all the various activities, which are allotted to one, according to the arrangement of castes" (Tilak, *Srimad Bhagavadgita-Rahasya*, 462).

Works Cited

Bakker, Hans J.I. *Gandhi and the Gita.* Toronto: Canadian Scholar's Press, 1993.

Bhabha, Homi K. *The Location of Culture.* London/New York: Routledge, 1994.

Bhaktivedanta, A.C. (Swami). *The Bhagavad Gita As It Is.* New York: Collier Books, 1968.

Brown, D. MacKenzie. "The Philosophy of Bal Gangadhar Tilak: *Karma* vs. *Jnana* in the *Gita Rahasya.*" *The Journal of Asian Studies* 1.2 (February 1958): 197–206.

Chatterjee, Partha. *Nationalist Thought and the Colonial World: A Derivative Discourse.* Minneapolis: University of Minnesota Press, 1986.

(CWMG). *The Collected Works of Mahatma Gandhi.* New Delhi: Publication Division, Ministry of Information and Broadcasting, 1958–1994.

Desai, Mahadev. *The Gospel of Selfless Action or The Gita According to Gandhi.* Ahmedabad: Navajivan Publishing House [1947], 1970.

Desmond, Robert W. *Windows on the World: The Information Process in a Changing Society 1900–1920.* Iowa City: University of Iowa Press, 1980.

Erikson, Eric H. *Gandhi's Truth: On the Origins of Militant Nonviolence.* New York: W.W. Norton & Company, Inc., 1969.

Fischer, Louis. *The Life of Mahatma Gandhi.* New York: Granada, 1951.

Gandhi, M.K. *The Teaching of the Gita.* Ed. Anand T. Hingorani. Bombay: Bharatiya Vidya Bhavan, 1971.

———. *An Autobiography: The Story of My Experiments with Truth.* Boston: Beacon Press, 1993.

Ghose, Aurobindo. *Speeches.* Pondicherry: Sir Aurobindo Ashram, 1952.

Habermas, Jürgen. *Moral Consciousness and Communicative Action.* Cambridge, MA: MIT Press, 1990.

———. *On The Pragmatics of Communication.* Cambridge, MA: MIT Press, 1998.

Hardt, Michael, and Antonio Negri. *Empire.* Cambridge, MA: Harvard University Press, 2000.

Hingorani, Anand T., and Ganga A. Hingorani. *The Encyclopaedia of Gandhian Thought.* New Delhi: All India Congress Committee (I), 1985.

Holub, Robert C. *Jürgen Habermas: Critic in the Public Sphere.* London: Routledge, 1991.

Jayawardena, Kumari. *Feminism and Nationalism in the Third World.* London: Zed Books, 1986.

Jordens, J.T.F. "Gandhi and the Bhagavadgita." In *Modern Indian Interpreters of the Bhagavad Gita.* Ed. Robert Minor. Albany: SUNY Press, 1986. 88–109.

Katrak, Ketu H. "Decolonizing Culture: Toward a Theory for Post-colonial Women's Texts." *Modern Fiction Studies* 35 (Spring 1989): 157–179.

Landry, Donna, and Gerald Mclean. Eds. *The Spivak Reader.* New York: Routledge, 1996.

Mani, Lata. "Contentious Traditions: The Debate on Sati in Colonial India." In *Recasting Women: Essays in Colonial History.* Ed. Kumkum Sangari and Sudesh Vaid. New Jersey: Rutgers, 1990.

Mead, George Herbert. "The Social Self." In *Selected Writings.* Ed. Andrew J. Reck. Chicago: University of Chicago Press, 1964.

Pantham, Thomas. "Habermas' Practical Discourse and Gandhi's Satyagraha." In *Political Discourse: Explorations in Indian and Western Political Thought.* Ed. Bikhu C. Parekh. Sage: New Delhi, 1987. 292–310.

Parel, Anthony J. *Gandhi: Hind Swaraj and Other Writings.* Cambridge: Cambridge University Press, 1997.

———. *Gandhi, Freedom, and Self-Rule.* Oxford: Lexington Books, 2000.

Prabhupada, A.C. Bhaktivedanta (Swami). *Bhagavad-Gita As It Is.* New York: Bhaktivedanta Book Trust, 1968.

Ruskin, John. *Unto this Last: Four essays on the First Principles of Political Economy.* London: Smith, Elder, 1862.

Schleiermacher, Friedrich D.E. "The Hermeneutics: Outline of the 1819 Lectures." In *The Hermeneutic Tradition: From Ast to Ricoeur.* Ed. Gayle L. Ormiston and Alan D. Schrift. Albany: State University of New York Press, 1990. 85–100.

Thapar, Suruchi. "Women as Activists; Women as Symbols: A Study of the Indian Nationalist Movement." *Feminist Review* 44 (Summer 1993): 81–96.

Thomas, P.M. *20th Century Indian Interpretations of BHAGAVADGITA: Tilak, Gandhi and Aurobindo.* Delhi: ISPCK, 1987.

Tilak, Bal Gangadhar. *Bal Gangadhar Tilak, his Writings and Speeches.* (Appreciation by Babu Aurobindo Ghose), 3rd ed. Madras: Ganesh & Co., 1922.

——. *Srimad Bhagavadgita-Rahasya.* 3rd ed. Poona: Tilak Brothers, 1971.

Tolstoy, Leo. *The Kingdom of God is Within You; What is Art?; What is Religion?* New York: Crowell, 1899.

Viswanathan, Gauri. Ed. *Power, Politics, and Culture: Interviews with Edward W. Said.* New York: Pantheon Books, 2001.

CHAPTER NINE

Responsibly Performing Vulnerability: Salman Rushdie's Fury and Edgar Laurence Doctorow's City of God

ERIK BORGMAN

Introduction

Salman Rushdie's novel *Fury* (2002) presents modernity as intrinsically religious. *Fury* creatively twists and reverses the Koranic story of Abraham (Ibrahim) sacrificing his son by presenting its main character Malik Solanka as attempting to avoid the rage that urges him to murder his son. The postmodern chaos of New York, however, is itself a theater of frustration, aggression, and violence. The novel pictures this as the breaking loose of the furies, the unbounding of the religious energies once contained within religions. In the end Malik Solanka surrenders to his vulnerability, accepting to depend on the love of his son. A parallel is drawn between Rushdie's *Fury* and the Critical Theory of Theodor W. Adorno: both criticize religion in order to hold on to a central religious notion. In Rushdie's case the notion is vulnerability, in Adorno's case it is the always remaining absence of truth and meaning. This essay argues that simply stressing the need to surrender to one's vulnerability is not enough for the question to what or to whom one surrenders is inescapable. Edgar L. Doctorow's novel *City of God* (2000) addresses this issue. It shows how, after Auschwitz, sticking to one religious story, simply because it happens to be one's own, is inadequate. Religion should function as the memorial of suffering and resistance to it. *Memoria passionis* (Remembrance of the Passion) is the task of the Christian tradition according to the interpretation of Metz's New Political Theology.

From this viewpoint, art in general and literature especially can be considered as "concretion" (Adorno) of the *memoria* of God's absence and the hope of God's coming presence.

Key Words

Salman Rushdie, Edgar L. Doctorow, New Political Theology (Johann Baptist Metz), Abraham/Ibrahim, Auschwitz, religion, and vulnerability.

★ ★ ★

Responsibility in relation to literature is first of all responsibility in reading.[1] But, as Jacques Derrida made clear in his work on literature and reading, this implies a certain "profession," a dedication to the never simply present meaning of the text, a taking up of the responsibility to bring the text to its meaning.[2] Thus, reading is a way of enacting life performatively and recreating it in an event of meaning, making sense of the world by behaving as if sense is at the origin of the world and giving it the possibility to reveal itself.[3] It is an act of resistance to what "just happens" senselessly, meaninglessly, and seemingly without any reference to justice.[4] As ritual studies have recently made clear, religious rituals reshape life by performing it in a certain form, thus enabling interpretation and critique.[5] In this sense reading is a religious activity, the performance of a religious ritual that gives one a position in the world from where to interpret it. It is akin to what in the Jewish tradition is called "to mend the world": restoring and discovering the meaning of human lives and the reality they are part of, even if they seem to have no meaning at all, by performing them in a certain way through reading about it.

All this is to say that reading is religious in a sense.[6] In what sense exactly is to be discovered and I hope to shed some light on this issue by presenting in this essay a reading of Salman Rushdie's *Fury*[7] and one of Edgar Laurence Doctorow's *City of God*.[8] As I show, this reading is in a particular sense a religious practice and theologically relevant.

Salman Rushdie's Fury

Before I start the presentation of my reading of Rushdie's novel *Fury*, it seems worthwhile to remember a remarkable aspect in the history of Rushdie's novel. Before it was published in English, in September 2001, *Fury* was published in Dutch in March as the so-called boekenweekgeschenk.[9] In the ten days that are called "boekenweek," the collective publicity effort of the book business, from writers to bookshop owners, everyone who spends the minimum of something like €11.11 on books gets a specially published gift book. This is the *boekenweekgeschenk*. Usually this is a rather small booklet by a Dutch writer, but in the sixty-sixth boekenweek the translation of Rushdie's novel, about three times as voluminous as the usual boekenweekgeschenk was given away in 725,000 copies. The response of Dutch literary critics was extremely critical. It was considered bad promotion of Dutch literature to make the boekenweekgeschenk a translation of a book that would shortly be published in its original English also. But, more importantly, Salman Rushdie's *Fury* was considered not to be a good book to seduce the general public into reading, which is what the Foundation for the Collective Promotion of the Dutch Book that organizes the boekenweek is supposed to do. It was seen as too difficult, too literary.

Rushdie's *Fury* was also judged by Dutch literary reviewers as not being a very good book. In this they were joined by the international critical community after the publication of the English edition. Reading the critical appraisals of the book gives one the impression that its significance was not noted. This is very strange, given the fact that the book was published on September 7, 2001. It could have been read as an exploration of the fury behind the tragedies occurring in the United States four days later, and behind the furious reactions to these tragedies. That this did not happen seems to me due to the fact that reviewers fail to consider the religious aspect in reading a novel like *Fury*.

Let us turn to the novel, then.[10]

Abraham in Reverse

Salman Rusdhie's *Fury* is very much about exactly that: fury, anger, rage, the feeling of spite because of humiliations, lost opportunities, expectations not met, and desires not fulfilled. It is about the anger that seems to be everywhere, present in everything and everybody in our global culture. It is in particular about the rage that inhabits, and time and again overcomes, the protagonist of the novel. Rushdie describes him in the very first sentence of his book as: "Professor Malik Solanka, retired historian of ideas, irascible dollmaker and since his recent fifty-fifth birthday celibate and solitary by his own (much criticized) choice." In "the digested read" of *The Guardian*, the plot of the novel is ultimately summarized as "self-regarding fifty something man dumps his wife, moves to New York, meets the most beautiful woman in the world and writes about it." Many reviewers have limited their interpretation to the surface level and suggested the novel presents Rushdie's wet dream. It is read as the rather improbable story of a middle-aged Indian man who moved to the United States—as Rushdie himself did—not just falling in love with but loved in return by a young woman of Indian origin who is so overwhelmingly beautiful that wherever she appears, men are throwing themselves in all kind of catastrophes: they walk into lampposts, they throw themselves under cars, they fall off ladders. But to reduce the novel to this would be like summarizing the biblical and koranic story of Abraham as "very old man becomes father unexpectedly, tries to get rid of his son by stabbing him, but changes his mind," which, if we changed the name of Abraham into Malik Solanka, could also be a summary of Rushdie's *Fury*.

Malik Solanka in *Fury* is Abraham in reverse. Solanka is not only a retired professional historian of ideas, but he embodies the ideas of our historic episode by being a travesty of Abraham—Ibrahim—in the Koran. Solanka leaves his wife and son in Hampshire, England, for the United States of America after he has found himself with a knife in his hand, ready to kill his sleeping son, whom he loves. "Then We gave him the glad tidings of a prudent boy," writes the Koran about Abraham, but after a while Abraham said: "My son, I have seen in a dream that I should sacrifice you" (Koran 37:100–101). Malik Solanka flees in order to avoid killing his son, but his son is stubbornly willing to surrender himself to his father, as is said about Abraham's son in the Koran: "O father, do what you are ordained to do." After Malik Solanka has left his wife and son, afraid of what he might do, his son—who is called Asmaan, that is Urdu for heaven—begs him over and over again to please come home, daddy. Because of Abraham's readiness to kill his son, the Koran says that he is remembered by generations to come and is called by God "one of Our believing servants"—that is, a Muslim. Malik Solanka however is not ready to kill his own son and tries to flee from the fury that had almost made him do exactly that. In New York, he hopes to lose himself amidst the amalgam of life stories and attempts to be successful that are populating this metropolis. But he himself becomes a pathologically successful doll maker instead.

Here the real travesty begins. According to the Koran Abraham is not a maker, but a destroyer of dolls. Sûrah 21 tells how he turns against the worshipping of idols by "his father and his people," saying:

> "What are these statues to which you pay devotion?" They said: "We found our fathers worshipping them." He said: "You and your fathers are in manifest aberration. . . . But our Lord is the Lord of heaven and earth who originated them; and to that I am among the witnesses. And by God, I will surely contrive against

your idols after you have gone away turning your back." Then he reduced them to fragments, all but the great one of them. . . . They said: "Have you done this to our gods, O Abraham?" He said: Nay, it was this great one of them that has done it. So question them, if they can really speak.". . . Then they returned to him hotheaded, saying: "You know that these do not speak." He said: "Do you then worship, apart form God, that which neither avails you anything nor hurt you? Fie on you and on what you worship, apart from God. Do you not comprehend?" (Koran 21:51–53; 55–57; 61–63; 65–66)

By staging a little puppet show in which the statues of the idols are smashed, according to the Koran Abraham makes clear that they are powerless and that even their worshippers in fact do know that. They do not believe in the ability of the idols to really do something and to influence their lives. In Rushdie's novel, on the other hand, Malik Solanka becomes a doll maker, translating the history of ideas and the contemporary conflicts in puppet shows on television and the Internet. Thus he makes clear how in today's world the idols do have enormous powers and are fervently believed in. According to the Koran, the people were outraged at Abraham after he had exposed their foolishness:

They said: "Burn him and stand up for your gods . . ." [But] We [= God] said: "O fire, be you a coolness and a safety for Abraham." And they desired to contrive against him, but We made them the worst losers. (Koran 21:67–69)

According to Rushdie, however, the people are very grateful to Malik Solanka for providing the idols they can believe in, making it possible for them to make sense of an otherwise senseless world. But this by no means rescues Solanka. On the contrary, it puts him amidst a rather hot and threatening fire of fury that rules the contemporary world and confronts him with the fury in himself he intended to escape. In other words, and in the imagery of Rushdie's novel, it puts him under the spell of the Furies, the Greek goddesses of wrath that in the narrator's view are responsible for the turbulence we today live in and by.

The view of the contemporary world presented in *Fury* is ultimately religious. Not only does it use religious motives to fathom the current situation, but it also presents that situation as ultimately a religious situation. The forces working in it are in its presentation of a religious nature. The novel suggests there is no gap between modernity and postmodernity on the one hand and religious myths on the other. Far form it, the only way to understand our postmodern situation is to use the myths of the religious traditions, be it in a subversive manner, thus unveiling the religious significance of the present.

The Furies

In and through the way it uses religious motives, the ultimate issue Salman Rushdie's *Fury* addresses is how to live responsibly in an apparently religious present. He does this by confronting monotheism and polytheism. On the one hand—and very much in line with *The Satanic Verses*[11]— Rushdie presents monotheism first and foremost as violence. In the parody of Abraham's sacrifice in Malik Solanka's impulse to kill his son, he portrays monotheism as a violent act of exclusion, of repressing the plurality of meaning and the uncertainties of life. What *The Satanic Verses* symbolize in Mohammed's attempt to write the one book of true meaning, *Fury* attributes to Abraham as the common father of the three monotheistic world religions. Abraham's attempt to destroy all gods to the benefit of one, univocal center of meaning is presented as not only living on in Judaism, Christianity, and Islam, but also in modern ideologies that in the name of the one true liberation enforce on their followers the obligation to absolute faith. In an explicit reference to the case of Galileo, Rushdie makes the leader of the prototypical revolutionary movement in the prototypical Caribbean country Lilliput Blefusco say that a period of discipline is needed in which, if the leader tells his people that the earth is flat, it is flat, and if he decrees tomorrow that the sun goes around the earth, it will be the sun that goes around.[12] Our current cultural polytheism makes clear in Rushdie's view that the repression of plurality, ambivalence, and uncertainty cannot hold. The once smashed idols are remade into the images and icons of our popular culture; the once tamed furies are on the loose again.

This to Rushdie is an unavoidable development, but by no means simply positive. He reminds his readers of the ways in which the Greeks made the furies, representing the unfocussed, uncontrollable, and therefore scaring forces in the universe and in history, part of their pantheon of gods and goddesses. This way they reassure themselves by encapsulating that which is by definition incoherent in a coherent story. But in our days, Rushdie concludes:

> the goddesses, less regarded, were hungrier, wilder, casting their nets more widely. As the bonds of family weakened, so the Furies began to intervene in all of human life. From New York to Lilliput Blefusco there was no escape from the beating of their wings.[13]

This is *Furies* way to account for, among other things, the chaotic speed and unpredictability of cultural and social developments, and the individual and collective frustration resulting in violence always seemingly just about to come to an outburst. Rushdie brilliantly expresses the general mood in the monologues of the Islamic taxi driver Ali Majnu, who rides the streets of New York screaming things like "Unclean offspring of a shit-eating pig, try that again and the victorious jihad will crush your balls in its unforgiving fist,"[14] without even being aware of it. Here Rushdie is not accusing Islam of being an undue aggressive religion, but presents the rage of Muslims as an expression of the inexplicable fury that inhabits the course of the events and the people who are part of it, in ways they do not themselves understand or even really know. It is a caricature of course, but it is a caricature of a world that is undeniably ours, a world that is often its own caricature.

Ours is a polytheistic world, *Fury* points out by making Malik Solanka a puppeteer and his puppet shows on television and Internet hugely successful. In its view we are reinstalling that what was thrown down at the beginning of Western civilization. Ours is a more dangerous world because of its polytheism, the novel adds by narrating how Solanka's puppet shows, how television and computer games make explicit the violence implicit in our culture, and how reality imitates fiction in the seemingly random outbursts of violence that characterize our historical situation. Monotheism is unable to stop this violence, in the novel's view, because it is itself a violent attempt to kill plurality, to suppress the multiplication of centers of thinking and acting, to prevent autonomy of the other because autonomy makes him or her uncontrollable. In other words, Abraham's willingness to sacrifice his son and Malik Solanka's urge to stab his son, reveal the essence of monotheism as the author of *Fury* sees it: hatred of and fear for what will ultimately be beyond control. This hatred and this fear are in itself understandable enough. Rushdie slowly uncovers the deepest source of Malik Solanka's inability to surrender to what he did not invent and does not control, even if it is to the son he loves more dearly than anything in the world. As a child Malik was a victim of a particular humiliating form of sexual abuse. Leaving all possible other levels of meaning of this theme aside, this at the very least makes clear that the world being what it is, to abstain from violence and to let the other be other, means the risk of becoming victim of violence oneself. *Fury* shows how we ultimately depend on the benevolence of others who are beyond our control, which is always and by definition uncertain and unwarranted, and even dangerous.

Galileo Galilei

If there is a hero in Rushdie's *Fury*, it is Galileo Galilei. That is to say, not the actual Galilei of history who retracted his claim that the earth was going around the sun, but Galilei as he could and should have been: standing up for his deepest conviction. Galilei is in *Fury* not just the lonely and heroic autonomous scientist, shaking off the religious prejudices and only believing what he can himself verify. He is not an Abraham for modernity, breaking the idols of his contemporaries and being threatened because of it. The significant paradox is that Galilei autonomously discovered that we are *not* autonomous. Galilei discovered that the earth, humankind, the individual human being is *not* the center of the universe, the source, and goal of everything of importance and the origin and focus of all meaning. That this is what we have to understand and accept seems to be the message of the author of *Fury*: that we depend on something and someone else we cannot control. To know this and to surrender to it is presented as our only possible redemption.

After he had found himself ready to kill his son, Malik Solanka flees to America and the chaos and restlessness of today's world it embodies. He prays it (America) "to eat him and give him peace." He wants to be "free of attachments" as a postmodern sanyasi, and thus become free of fear, pain, anger, and the urge to hurt others. But what he almost did to his son Asmaan, he in the end has to let Asmaan do to him. Asmaan—the love of Asmaan, the pain of not being with him and not being seen by him—"twisted in him like a knife" we are told.[15] This was exactly what Malik Solanka subconsciously had tried to avoid when he almost stabbed his son. He could not handle the idea of not being the center of his own universe anymore and to depend on someone else. But what America, what the exposure to the modern and postmodern fury of ever-changing meanings and new idols, of unexpected success and influence but also equally unexpected deadly violence could not do, the knife of love ultimately succeeds in doing: it kills Solanka's self. At the end of *Fury* Malik Solanka surrenders to the discovery he shares with his onetime hero Galileo Galilei: that he is not the center of his own universe. Just as a son demands to be seen by his father, just as we are told Asmaan makes Malik Solanka notice how well he can bounce the bed, Malik Solanka in the very last paragraph of *Fury* begs his son to see him. Unannounced Malik Solanka travels back from America to England to his wife, her new lover, and his son. He finds them in the park near their home. There are funfairs in the park, among them a bouncy castle. "It was bright blue, bright as an iris," Rushdie informs his readers, the iris being the symbol of the Furies in Greek mythology. Although the castle is for kids only, Malik Solanka forces entry to it and starts bouncing and yelling his son's name:

> grand and high was his bouncing; and he was damned if he was going to stop leaping or desist from yelling until that little boy looked around, until he made Asmaan Solanka hear him . . . , until Asmaan turned and saw his father up there . . . flying against the sky, *asmaan*, the sky, conjuring up all his lost love and hurling it high up into the sky. . . . His . . . father taking flight like a bird, to live in the great blue vault of the only heaven in which he had ever been able to believe. "Look at me!" shrieked Professor Malik Solanka, his leather coat-tails flapping like wings. "Look at me Asmaan! I'm bouncing very well! I'm bouncing higher and higher."[16]

The last words are exactly what his son said to him while he bounced the bed during the time Malik Solanka was still living with him and his wife.

This last paragraph of *Fury* is almost a mystical text.[17] By changing the perspective from self-centered to other-centered—and in fact *asmaan*-centered, heaven-centered at that—Malik Solanka is liberated from the grip the Furies on the drift have on his live. His devastating and violent anger is changed in harmless bouncing, expressing the yearning for his son's love. The Furies who, as the novel tells us, according to Hesiod were born of Earth and Air, but among whose siblings were "Terror, Strife, Lies, Vengeance, Intemperance, Altercation, Fear and Battle,"[18] are reduced to their rather harmless origin: the human longing to be loved and thus to connect heaven and earth. Bouncing the bouncy castle, Malik Solanka is *Fury's* alternative to Abraham. To surrender to the longing to be loved, is the novel's alternative to monotheism and its violent tendency to kill the other, as well as to polytheism and its tendency to subject to and enhance the violence ruling the world already. It is a religious alternative, because it comes down to surrendering to the unknown, the uncontrollable, to the other and its benevolence. It means to be dependent; to know to be dependent, and to decide to accept to be dependent.

A New Expression of Religiosity

Modernist and postmodernist literature can be seen as a performance of human life revealing how living implies being part of a larger whole. The self-proclaimed autonomous modern subject is made visible not as the center of the universe, but a planet in a complex solar system.

This made religion and its traditions that express, reflect upon, and suggest ways to deal with human dependency, relevant in a new way to Nineteenth- and Twentieth-Century literature.[19] In line with this development, Rushdie's *Fury* can be called religious in character. This is not just because it creatively uses religious mythology, but because of the fact that it pictures human beings as dependent on what transcends them. Rushdie's novel shows how we can only understand ourselves by imagining the universe we are part of, as religious myths do. That is the reason why literature in general could be called "religious": it does in a sense what in ancient societies was done by myths.[20] But, more importantly, the point is ultimately that Rushdie portrays human beings as dependent on what transcends them. It is the task of human beings to deal with this dependency in a responsible manner. *Fury* makes clear how for human beings to deny their dependency is irresponsible behavior and that how we have to find our way to perform this dependency responsibly.

This is not to deny Rushdie's own presentation of his position as nonreligious. Rushdie clearly presents himself as a critic of religion. Although it is unethical reading to relate the anecdotes of Malik Solanka's life too closely to certain autobiographical details of Rushdie's, as many reviewers did, Solanka's skeptic, agnostic, and nonbelieving attitude is clearly Rushdie's own.

Theodor W. Adorno

As an Indian-Brit, Rushdie of course comes from an entirely different background, but I would like to suggest his approach to religion is akin to that of the Frankfurt School.

Leading philosopher Theodor W. Adorno was a skeptic and a nonbeliever vis-à-vis confessional religion, but he took from his ancestral Judaism the idea of God's absolute greatness and infinite sublimity, signifying that God can never be fully identified. For Adorno, God symbolizes the ultimate truth that is never present and always yet to be revealed, the ultimate meaning of the world still hidden and, after Auschwitz, definitely darkened by the excess of human suffering in history. God signifies the redemption that can only be present as absent and missed. For Adorno, confessional religion is almost by definition sacrilege and idol worship. Every image of God witnesses to the transgression of the second of the Ten Commandments in the Book of Exodus: "You shall not make for yourself a graven image, or any likeness of anything that is in the earth beneath, or that is in the water under the earth; you shall not bow down to them or serve them" (Ex. 20:4–5). The ban on imagining the Divine is the aspect of the Jewish religion Adorno wants to be faithful to.[21] For him it is the core for which he abandons the rest of the Jewish tradition as it is usually understood, because in his view it violates and compromises that very core. In an analogical way, for Rushdie the awareness that one is not the center of the universe but depends on the loving gaze of the other to be able to make sense of one's own life, is the core of religion he wants to hold on to. It is the hidden core confessional religions violate by projecting their own view of the world on the cosmos and reshaping reality in their image, excluding what does not fit. Thus they reproduce and re-enforce the dominant violence.

So Adorno's as well as Rushdie's is a religious iconoclasm, turning against religion for religious reasons. But there is also a major difference. This difference comes to light in the fact that Adorno sees his thinking in line with Abraham's smashing of the idols, while *Fury* breaks away from Abraham, suggesting that to a certain extent we have to go with the current tendency to polytheism. No doubt to a large degree this is caused by the differences in historical contexts. Adorno was resistant to the totalitarian worldview paradigmatically embodied by national socialism presenting itself not only in theory but also in practice as the ultimate and definitive truth. It not just excluded everything and everyone who were "other" symbolically, but Auschwitz witnesses to how it very literally destroyed and tried to annihilate him and her: the Jew, the gipsy, the mentally disturbed, in short everything marginal.[22] It made Adorno change Hegel's famous dictum "das Ganze ist das Wahre," the totality is the truth, to its opposite: "das Ganze ist das Unwahre," the totality is the untruth. In Adorno's view, truth is only present hidden in what is marginalized, excluded, and destroyed to make the totality total.[23] Starting from there, the idolatry of the dominant way of thinking has to be intellectually attacked. Rushdie, on the other hand, writes in a situation characterized not by marginalizing, exclusion, or silencing of stories threatening the dominant worldview, but by a superabundance of stories and claims to meaningful significance. He pictures a situation in which, as Michel de Certeau writes, the media constantly "transform the great silence of things into its opposite. Formerly constituting a secret, the real now talks constantly" in "news reports, information, statistics, and surveys,"[24] but also in the images, icons, and plots of popular culture. Although everybody is aware of the fact that what is written and imagined is manipulated and in turn manipulates reality, words and images nevertheless work as if they are the ultimate reality. In this situation it does not seem to make much sense to try to break the idols in order for the truth to reveal itself, in the tradition of Abraham and Adorno. Everything is already revealed and an extra story would just enhance the cacophony. The issue is how to deal with the cacophony in which the distinction between truth and falsehood has become virtually obsolete in the ever-changing, but in its flux always identical flow of images and stories.

Rushdie's *Fury* suggests that the appropriate and appropriately critical act in the current situation is to stop resisting the fact that we are created and shaped by stories out of our control. It means admitting that we as human beings have in a sense become marginal ourselves. We should stop trying to claim the center, being aware that it is not what we achieve that makes our lives worthwhile—everything we do is in the end as productive and impressive as a child bouncing the bed—but the fact that a loving eye sees us, transferring our passions and efforts from the area of meaninglessness to the realm of what is meaningful. This comes down to the paradox that to deal responsibly with our dependency means to stop resisting it and to accept it. But this in fact looks a little too much like avoiding the issue of responsibility altogether and drowning it in the overwhelming amount of stories which interpret our lives already long before we ourselves start giving meaning to it. As the apostle Paul points out, even if being a slave is unavoidable, it is still important to discriminate between being a slave of sin and being a slave of God and Christ in faith (cf. Rom. 6:20–23).

This takes us back to the issue maybe not of smashing, but at least of recognizing idols, of recognizing and criticizing idolatry. Paul suggests that we need to find the place where, amidst all falsehood, the truth lives and reveals itself. This takes us back to what Adorno calls his "Negative Dialectics": the stubborn attempts not just to speak about what is only present in its absence from Totality, but to speak about all of reality in a nontotalitarian manner, starting from this absent presence. The point is not just to accept our dependency on the stories that are told about us before we can even speak, the stories that speak to us and make us speak. We should also accept the protest incarnated in our rage against being merely subjected to the circumstances, the course of history, the current interpretation. The latter is not only expressing a desire to be loved for our own sake, as *Fury* suggests, but also an insight that the world we are part of is not the world as it should be, and that in the end we depend on whether or not this world will become what in biblical metaphor is called "a new heaven and a new earth" (Rev. 21:1). Therefore, it is our responsibility to contribute to that and to mend the world.

New Political Theology

Unsurprisingly theologians have seen a parallel to Adorno's idea of a Negative Dialectics in the Christian presentation of the history of Jesus' suffering and crucifixion as the parable of God's presence. The so-called New Political Theology of Johann Baptist Metz and his disciples stresses that in a violent and destructive world, to remember the victims and to protest against their suffering is the only possible resistance against its culture of victimization and the only faithful expression of hope for authentic, gracious life.[25] In the words of the apostle Paul:

> God chose what is foolish in the world to shame the wise, God chose what is weak in the world to shame the strong, God chose what is low and despised in the world, even things that are not, to bring to nothing things that are. (1 Cor. 1:27–28)

From death as the realm of ultimate exclusion a new and inclusive life is born, already present but veiled and hidden in the first creation in which we continue to live. This means that, for Political Theology, the Divine revelation and the human redemption still have to be completed and in the world as it is—a world in which Auschwitz could and did occur—can only be longed and hoped for. Confessing to Christianity can only be a "venture of non-identity" in the world as it is.[26]

Metz and his disciples are very critical of the postmodern stress on multiplicity and plurality.[27] To them, it means drawing away the attention from the crisis of meaning implicit in suffering and dying. The new, postmodern openness to religion for them witnesses to a misguided willingness to reconcile with what should be repudiated, and to find meaning in what should be considered meaningless and the crisis of all meaning. Peter Sloterdijk, the *enfant terrible* of German philosophy, has recently made the Frankfurt School, and Theodor Adorno together with Jürgen Habermas in particular, responsible for that philosophy's suffocating moralizing, making it almost impossible to really think through the difficult but unavoidable problems of our times. To take an ethical stand has become more important than to understand.[28] Although this was Sloterdijk's rather idiosyncratic response to the violent attacks on an essay of his on genetic engineering,[29] the tendency he points at is real. If stressing too heavily the dangers inherent in our cultural situation and to the philosophical and theological attempts to understand it, philosophers and theologians are in danger of condemning themselves to moralizing in the margins. New Political Theology started out in the late 1960s as an attempt to think critically about the actual situation from within the actual situation, in theological terms. It wanted to be an alternative to forms of theology that just repeated old answers in new words and considered that as criticism of the present.[30] But how might it escape the same predicament?

New Political Theology can best be understood as being an attempt to understand the current situation in theological terms. Thus it revealed and reveals the ever-surprising relevance of theology precisely in a time of secularization. Does that mean that it tragically looses its relevance in what is sometimes called a time of de-secularization, as Metz and some of his disciples sometimes seem to fear?[31] What we currently see, however, is not so much a denial of secularization, which in the views of New Political Theology is theologically legitimate and necessary, following the tendency in the Judeo-Christian tradition to consider human autonomy a gift of God. Instead, we are rediscovering the essentially religious aspects of life in a secularized society in which, in Friedrich Nietzsche's expression, God is dead.[32] This is what Rushdie also is exploring.

Metz's disciple Tiemo Rainer Peters has recently taken up the idea that we need a Christianity that is in the process of "re-foundation." The conviction that Christianity was in the need of a "re-foundation" was first expressed by Franz Overbeck (1837–1905), theologian, Church historian, and friend of Friedrich Nietzsche.[33] In Overbeck's view, such a "re-foundation," a reshaping of Christianity in order to allow it to have the same revolutionary impact in the second half of the nineteenth century in which he lived as it had in the first centuries, was tragically impossible. Peters thinks that such a "re-foundation" is possible and even suggests that Christianity in the process of "re-foundation" actually exists.[34] This implies an exhortation to go and search for it.

Edgar L. Doctorow's City of God

A Christianity in the process of its "re-foundation" is portrayed in Edgar Laurence Doctorow's novel *City of God*. Doctorow's oeuvre is mostly in the tradition of attempts to write the ultimate American novel, extending from John Dos Passos to Don DeLillo.[35] In his works Doctorow tries to capture the atmosphere of an era. In 1971, the ability displayed in his *The Book of Daniel* to capture the atmosphere of the late 1960s in narrative and voice, made him a writer of great esteem. In 1975 the attempt to do the same in a totally different manner for the first decennia of the twentieth century made his *Ragtime* a best seller. After his attempt at an autobiographical portrait of America in the wake of World War II in *World Fair* from 1985, after his cartography of the Depression by way of a parody of the pulp novel in *Billy Bathgate* from 1989, and after the detective story suggesting to unveil the riddles of the last quarter of the nineteenth century in *The Waterworks* from 1995, Doctorow in 2000 published in a novel called *City of God* his literary reflections upon the situation at the start of the new millennium, including his reflections upon writing in this situation.[36] The novel's central question seems akin to that of Augustine's famous treatise with the same title: where and how lives the people that, amidst the often rather despairing course of history, is or tries to be in the presence of God? If we are to believe Doctorow, they are hidden in very small and undistinguished synagogues, trying to reestablish the essence of their religious tradition, and in worn-down inner city churches with all but dissolved congregations and priests struggling fiercely with formal orthodoxy and the question of the intellectual and moral integrity of the Christian tradition.

Church and Synagogue

Doctorow's *City of God* has remarkable ambition. Not only is it meant to be, as the inside of its dust jacket informs its readers, "a defining document of our times, a narrative of the twentieth century written for the twenty-first," and it is not just "a quest for an authentic spirituality at the end of a tortured century." In trying to become these things, it deals freely with rather complicated and far-reaching theological and philosophical discussions. To create the space necessary to the literary imagination, Doctorow constructs a distance between the text and the subjects it treats by presenting the novel as a writer's notebook. It records sketches and ideas, accounts love affairs, reflects on cosmological processes, but especially contains notes on the story he thinks may grow into his next novel. According to that story a large brass cross mysteriously disappears from its place behind the altar of a run-down Episcopal church and reappears on the roof of the Synagogue for Evolutionary Judaism. What starts out as an attempt to find the people responsible for this desecration by the clergy of both religious institutions, develops into a reflection on the relationship between Judaism and Christianity and on their role and task in the contemporary and future world. As a result of the events Thomas Pemberton, the divorced priest of St. Timothy's Episcopalian Church, from where the crucifix disappeared and who is in long-term conflict with his bishop on doctrinal matters, becomes a Jew and marries Sarah Blumenthal, the widowed female rabbi of the Synagogue of Evolutionary Judaism. The fictional notebook ends with an idea for a movie in which, after a rather apocalyptic image of the growing deterioration of the city caused by people trying to reshape it by force of an idea or a semireligious vision, "we are introduced to the hero and heroine . . ., a vitally religious couple that runs a small progressive synagogue on the Upper West Side."[37] These two people represent religion not as a system of meaning forced on reality that is supposed to be meaningless, but as a defense of the clash of ideas and stories that characterizes the city.[38] In Doctorow's performative representation the city, as a collection of human attempts to find meaning and to lead a responsible and good life, is apparently a place of holiness. It is the chaotic plurality of lives that makes the city a city of God.

Of course the image of a crucifix stolen from a church and planted on the roof of a synagogue is rather shocking. For a brief instant the fictional author of the notebook the novel is, wants to write a detective story. His goal is in a literary manner to solve the mystery of who committed the crime and what the statement was they were making. But the text shifts rather quickly from focusing on the origin of the incident to focusing on its meaning. The question becomes: what happens because of it, and why? On the philosophical and theological level this is a very significant shift, one Doctorow's novel seems to propagate. The aim of the Synagogue of Evolutionary Judaism is to reduce the Jewish tradition to its bare core, to limit the theories and practices to what can be justified without relying on arguments from history and tradition. Thomas Pemberton remembers one of his teachers who rigidly searched for the true historical Jesus as the only source and origin of Christianity, but was lost in confusion. And on a more abstract level, the problem is present from the very first sentence of the book. The fictional author of the notebook is fascinated by matters of cosmology and Doctorow uses the theory of the Big Bang in much the same way as Rushdie uses the vision of Galilei: to express fundamental religious themes. What does it mean (the rather cryptic question in the opening paragraphs of the novel) that the "singular space/time point, a moment/thing, some original particulate event or quantum substantive happenstance" did not blast into being through space but that space, itself property of the universe, is what blasted out along with everything in it? . . . The universe expanding even now its galaxies of burning suns, dying stars, metallic monuments of stone, clouds of cosmic dust, must be filling . . . something. [. . .] Or is there no edge, no border, but an infinite series of universes expanding into one another, all at the same time?[39]

To stay within the metaphor, Doctorow's *City of God* is ultimately not about origin, but about this "something" in which the universes of meaning expand, blasting out from their centers. Thus the novel in fact states that there may be no meaning in the void, but that there always is significance, and it is worthwhile to look for it. There is an appeal to recognition and a desire for meaningfulness which are worthy of our attention.

Loosing any Fixed Identity

A crucifix getting stolen from a church is a powerful image of the Christian identity getting lost, and the empty spot the cross leaves behind symbolizes how what once was a powerful presence is transformed into nostalgia for what has been. Thomas Pemberton is portrayed as someone who even before the theft of the crucifix has come to see the Christian tradition as a story. He does not know any longer how to "distinguish our truth from another's falsity" except "by the story we cherish," but he cannot believe that God is incarnated in "our story of Him" that just happens to put Jesus at the center.[40] The disappearance of the cross from his church, that speeds up the process of its closing down, symbolizes the deterioration of Pemberton's faith in Christianity, that is at the same time his growing conviction that God is not enclosed in any tradition. God can only be found in dedication to life, trying to live it as responsibly as possible: this is what Pemberton finds in the Synagogue of Evolutionary Judaism, what unites him with Sarah Blumenthal and converts him to Judaism.

At the dance celebrating his marriage with Sarah, Pemberton delivers a speech in the form of a long monologue to God. In the speech he notes that "even among those of us clinging to a love of You and an irrepressible longing for Your love . . . there is a risen suspicion, that You are part of the problem" humanity has with letting people live good or even half-decent lives.[41] His conclusion is:

> I think we must remake You. If we are to remake ourselves, we must remake You, Lord. We need a place to stand. We are weak, and puny, and totter here in our civilisation. . . . We have only our love for each other for footing, our marriages, the children we hold in our arms, it is only this wavery sensation, flowing and ebbing, that justifies our consciousness and keeps us from plunging out of the universe. Not enough. It's not enough. We need a place to stand.
>
> I ask for reason to hope that this travail of our souls will find its resolution in You, Lord, You of Blessed Name. For the sake of all of us on this little planet of Yours I ask this. Amen.[42]

God is seen here as present in our necessary weak attempts to do the impossible: to lead a responsible life and have a responsibility to life, in a world marked by an excess of suffering and death. One could, I think, argue convincingly that this is very much in line with the Christian confession of God's incarnation in Jesus Christ, but Doctorow's *City of God* presents it as something that can only be fully expressed by breaking away from the Christian tradition.

Doctorow has a Jewish background. He knowingly brings up a very difficult and painful subject in *City of God* by imagining a crucifix planted on the roof of a synagogue. "Hello, Rabbi? Your roof is burning," says an anonymous caller announcing the fact that the cross was on the small and modest Synagogue of Evolutionary Judaism to Josua Gruen, then still alive husband of the later widowed Sarah Blumenthal. Bringing a cross to a synagogue is not just desecrating a place of worship of one tradition by bringing into it a sacred symbol of another, it is an act of symbolic violence. Jews were persecuted and killed for ages because of their supposed responsibility for the crucifixion of Jesus. In the course of the novel, it becomes clear however that after Auschwitz the proper place for what the cross is supposed to stand for, as a symbol of suffering and of persevering faithfulness to God in the severest of crises, is not the church but the synagogue. There is a long fragment in the novel in which Sarah Blumenthal's father tells the story of his life in a Jewish ghetto in an unnamed city in Central Europe, witnessing the individual and collective struggle to live an evil life responsibly and a humiliated life dignified. One of his tasks was to bring the chronicles on life in the ghetto, secretly written by one of the members of the Jewish council of the ghetto, to a church where they were hidden by the priest. The church presented as the secret repository of the Jewish mystery, in a certain analogy to the way in which Jerusalem, the holy city of Judaism, is holy according to the Christian tradition because it is the place of remembrance of the suffering and death of Jesus. What Christianity is unsuccessfully trying to express, is present in Judaism, Doctorow's *City of God* seems to suggest: God after his death living in solidarity with his people.

It seems to be in line with the what in his oeuvre the Jewish-American philosopher Emil Fackenheim tries to express.[43] In his *magnum opus*, entitled *To Mend the World*, Fackenheim writes:

> The Nazi logic of destruction was irresistible: *it was, nevertheless, being resisted.* This logic is a *novum* in human history, the source of an unprecedented, abiding horror: but resistance to it on the part of the most radically exposed, too, is a *novum* in history, and it is the source of an unprecedented, abiding wonder.[44]

Living as a Jew after Auschwitz means, according to Fackenheim, to obey its commanding voice not to grant Hitler a posthumous victory, not to let one's humanity be killed, and not to give in to the temptation to consider God dead if it means to consider God obsolete and irrelevant.

It means coming to life again and calling to God to come to life again. To Fackenheim "to hear and obey the commanding Voice of Auschwitz is [a] possibility, here and now, because the hearing and obeying was already [a] reality, then and there."[45] Therefore we can place our lives into the light of this second *novum*.

Doctorow's *City of God* presents Auschwitz as the event revealing the essence of human history and considers the resistance to its logic the moral and religious responsibility of all of us. Wherever this responsibility, taken up by Sarah Blumenthal and Thomas Pemberton, is met, there lives the city of God. According to Doctorow's novel, it proves to be impossible to retrieve the chronicles of the ghetto witnessing to what Fackenheim calls the second *novum:* the resistance to the Nazi logic of death and destruction. Ultimately that is not necessary. The whole of human history is permeated by echoes of this second *novum* that makes people try and live, responsibly performing their human vulnerability amidst the overwhelming presence of all kind of echoes of the first *novum*.

Radicalized "Religion of the Novel"

Tiemo Rainer Peters has called Metz's New Political Theology a "Theologie des vermissten Gottes,"[46] a theology of God missed, of God as present in people missing him, searching for him, crying for him. The history of which we are a part clearly indicates that God still has not fulfilled our human yearning, is not indisputably present even in Jesus as Christ. According to New Political Theology, in this situation to remember Jesus' suffering, death, and resurrection keeps open the unbridgeable gap between the liberating holiness of God's Name and our actual history. To speak of Jesus Christ as an incarnation of God's presence means to confess to that gap as not God's annihilation, but God's paradoxical presence, and to the idea that to try to perform one's life as a revelation of that gap means to perform one's life as a life dedicated to God. In this line of thought, responsibly performing vulnerability is not just, as it is in Rushdie's *Fury*, to acknowledge and to accept dependency on benevolence of the other to be able to live a good life. It is living life as searching for benevolence and goodness that are not yet there. They can only be missed, and thus be expected, and performed, and in a sense realized: as absent. In Doctorow's *City of God* Thomas Pemberton and Sarah Blumenthal embody the human search for a good life, and because of that they are in a sense already living the good life. They live life as it reveals itself in a world in which Auschwitz could occur and as New Political Theology see it revealed in Jesus' suffering on the cross: vulnerable, threatened, violated, desecrated, but commanding reference of those who are able to see holiness in weakness. This, I suggest, is a radicalized version of what literary historian Margaret Ann Doody has called "the religion of the novel."

In a famous essay published in 1945, Theodor W. Adorno strongly defends art's autonomy.[47] Against all romantic or downright reactionary attempts to reestablish its supposedly once close relationship with religion in order to save it from subjectivism, fragmentation, and arbitrariness, Adorno defends art's own logic that in his view differs fundamentally from the logic of religion. Religion here is understood by him as being a legitimizing expression of organic solidarity among a social or cultural group, projecting the structure of its society or culture on nature and thus providing the illusion that these structures are natural and God-given. Adorno's critical view on religion is strongly influenced by his aversion to the use made of quasi-religious motifs in Nazi Germany. In fact, however, in all his polemics against any attempt to subject art to religion, Adorno develops a connection to religion in the very core of modern art. In Adorno's view, art in general and literature in particular are religious in the dedication to the concrete. In opposition to the false universality of the religion he criticizes, in Adorno's view art (literature) finds its meaning through and in extreme "concretion." Literature comes to universal meaning, not by abstracting from concrete and always individual reality but by absolute dedication to narrating in convincing detail individual stories.

Half a century later, literary historian Margaret Anne Doody speaks of "the religion of the novel," a religion which has as at its core the conviction akin to the Christian idea of incarnation: ultimacy lives in what is concrete, finite, and contingent. The ultimate meaning of life therefore is not to be found by detachment from, but by attention to what happens in people's lives and histories. The religion of the novel— which is also in the heart of other genres of modern literature—is its dedication to the concrete and limited life stories of human beings, its profession to the finite in order to discover the infinite, the meaning of life and cosmos.[48] Rushdie and Doctorow are radicalizing Doody's approach by dedicating their writing to the weak, vulnerable, and contested lives of human beings in our era of mass atrocities, indifference, and lack of recognition. Doctorow radicalizes this dedication even more to lives explicitly performing their vulnerability and weakness, thus expressing their need of vindication. As Pemberton expresses it: "I ask for reason to hope that this travail of our souls will find its resolution in

You." This prayer is what the reader of novels like Doctorow's *City of God* and Rushdie's *Fury* implicitly perform while reading. The act of reading means being confronted with the travail of souls hoping for a resolution, or in theological parlance: redemption, grace. It means embodying their hope, taking up their yearning, feeling their abandonment as a religious act of surrendering to the presence of the absent God.

This is exactly why theology needs literature, why it needs to consider it and study it, why literature is theologically significant. According to the Jewish and Christian traditions, God's presence is not limited to the canonical writings of the Bible, the authoritative traditions, and the words, images, and ideas they contain and present. Ultimately, God is the God of creation and history, of human beings in their concrete lives, in their projects, in their passions and their fates. Even the most sacred of texts and the most sublime of visions show their legitimacy by enlightening the meaning of life as it is actually lived.[49] The religion of the novel, literature in the modern sense of the world, helps to remember exactly this point, which history shows to be easily forgotten. Literature is theologically significant in its stubborn dedication to the meaning present but hidden in the darkness of practices and performances, of the ongoing reinvention of everyday life. Exploring even the most meaningless of situations for its meaning and significance, literature can be theologically understood as trying to find traces of God after God's death in the Nietzschean sense, attempts to find God's presence, if it can be traced at all, hidden in what first of all seems to be and is God's absence. Reading literature shows concretely what a "Theologie des vermissten Gottes," a theology of a God missed and of missing God, entails: thinking, writing, living in vulnerability, performing a vulnerability that is open to and dependent on the meaning that makes life possible, as a dedication to waiting for God and a profession to the God who still has to come.[50] This, if really taken seriously, will prove to be changing theology almost beyond recognition.

Here, theology will not lose itself. It will discover itself anew.[51]

Notes

1. Geoffrey G. Harpham, "Ethics and Literary Study," in *Shadows of Ethics: Criticism and the Just Society* (Durham/London: Duke University Press, 1999), 18–37.
2. See especially Jacques Derrida, *Acts of Literature*, ed. David Attridge (New York/London: Routledge, 1992); cf. also Jonathan Culler, "Philosophy and Literature: The Fortunes of the Performative," *Poetics Today*, 21 (2000): 503–520.
3. Cf. Jacques Derrida, *L'université sans condition* (Paris: Galilée, 2001); translation in Jacques Derrida, "The University Without Condition," in *Without Alibi*, ed. and trans. Peggy Kamuf (Stanford: Stanford University Press 2002), 202–237.

4. Peggy Kamuf, "Introduction: Event of Resistance," in Jacques Derrida, *Without Alibi*, ed. and trans. Peggy Kamuf (Stanford: Stanford University Press 2002), 1–27.
5. See Roy A. Rappaport, *Ritual and Religion in the Making of Humanity* (Cambridge: Cambridge University Press 1999), 115–126; see for Ritual Studies Ronald J. Grimes, *Beginnings in Ritual Studies* (Washington: University Press of America, 1982); Ronald J. Grimes, *Research in Ritual Studies: A Programmatic Essay and Biography* (Chicago/Metuchen: American Theological Library Association/Scarecrow Press, 1985), revised ed. (Columbia: University of South Carolina Press 1994); Ronald J. Grimes, *Reading, Writing and Ritualizing: Ritual in Fictive, Liturgical and Public Spaces* (Washington: Pastoral Press 1993); Ronald J. Grimes, ed., *Reading in Ritual Studies* (Upper Saddle River: Prentice Hall, 1996).
6. For the typical characteristics of religious reading and its relation to a postmodern understanding of reading, cf. Paul J. Griffiths, *Religious Reading: The Place of Reading in the Practice of Religion* (New York/Oxford: Oxford University Press, 1999).
7. Salman Rushdie, *Fury* (London: Vintage, 2001).
8. Edgar L. Doctorow, *City of God: A Novel* (London: Little, Brown 2000).
9. Salman Rushdie, *Woede* (Amsterdam: Contact, 2001).
10. For interpretations of other works in Rushdie's oeuvre, cf. Roger Y. Clark, *Stranger Gods: Salman Rushdie's Other Worlds* (Montreal/Kingston: McGill-Queens University Press, 2001); S. Hassumani, *Salman Rushdie: A Postmodern Reading of his Major Works* (Madison/London: Fairleigh Dickinson University Press/Associated University Presses, 2002); Madelena Gonzalez, *Fiction after the Fatwa: Salman Rushdie and the Charm of Catastrophe* (Amsterdam/New York: Rodopi, 2005), has a section on Rushdie's *Fury*, 177–196. As the title of this chapter— "Fury: Devoured by Pop"—already suggests, the emphasis is on the way the novel adapts to pop culture and is devouring all distinctions between true and false, reality and phantasy: *Fury* "tempts us to enjoy fiction as a consumer item rather than a lasting challenge to perseption" (195). The religious motives that are central in my interpretation do not get any attention.
11. Salman Rushdie, *The Satanic Verses* (Harmondsworth: Viking 1989).
12. Rushdie, *Fury*, 244.
13. Ibid., 251.
14. Ibid., 66.
15. Ibid., 126.
16. Ibid., 259.
17. Cf., in contrast, Gonzalez, *Fiction after the Fatwa*, 195: ". . . the 'bouncing' leitmotif taken up again in the past paragraph . . . fails to elevate the hero's fate above the banal. On the contrary, it seems an example of indiscriminate intertextuality. . . . Literary reaching for the sky (Asmaan is 'sky' in Urdu), the ending falls (intentionally?) flat . . ."
18. Ibid., 251.
19. Cf. my "Missing Links between the Arts, Religion, and Reality: An Introductory and Exploratory Essay," in *Missing Links: Art, Religion and Reality*, ed. J. Bekkenkamp, S. Van Mass, and M. Valente (Münster: Lit, 2000), 1–14.
20. This issue is explored by Jean-Luc Nancy in his reflections on literature. The Heyendaal Institute Nijmegen had planned a research project on Nancy's idea of a "deconstruction of Christianity."
21. Cf. for background, Michel Traubel, Die Religion in der kritische Theorie bei Max Horkheimer und Theodor W. Adorno, unpublished dissertation, Freiburg in Breisgau 1978; Werner Brändle, *Rettung des Hoffnungslosen: Die theologischen Implikationen der Philosophie Theodor W. Adornos* (Göttingen: Vandenhoeck & Ruprecht, 1984); René Buchholz, *Zwischen Mythos und Bilderverbot: Die Philosophie Adornos als Anstoss zu einer kritischen Fundamentaltheologie im Kontext der späten Moderne* (Frankfurt: Lang, 1991); Ralf Frisch, *Theologie im Augenblick ihres Sturzes: Theodor W. Adorno und Karl Barth; zwei Gestalten einer kritischen Theorie der Moderne* (Wien: Passagen-Verlag, 1999); Mattias Martinson, *Perseverance Without Doctrine: Adorno, Self-critique, and the Ends of Academic Theology* (Frankfurt: Peter Lang, 2000).

22. Cf. Z. Bauman, *Modernity and the Holocaust* (Cambridge: Polity, 1989); Z. Bauman, *Wasted Lives: Modernity and its Outcasts* (Cambridge: Polity, 2004).

23. See especially Theodor W. Adorno, *Negative Dialektik* (Frankfurt am Main: Suhrkamp, 1966).

24. Michel de Certeau, *The Practice of Everyday Life* (Berkely/Los Angeles/London: University of California Press, 1988), 185.

25. Johann-Baptist Metz, *Glaube in Geschichte und Gesellschaft: Studien zu einer praktische Fundamentaltheologie* (Mainz: Matthias-Grünenwald-Verlag, 1977), especially 87–103 ("Zukunft aus dem Gedächtnis des Leidens: Zur Dialektik des Fortschritts") and 104–119 ("Erlösing und Emanzipation"); Joahnn Baptist Metz, "Im Eingedenken fremden Leids: Zu einer Basiskategorie christlicher Gottesrede," in *Gottesrede*, ed. J.B. Metz, J. Reikerstorfer, and J. Werblick (Münster: Lit, 1996), 3–20. For a good overview of Metz's theological project in English, see J. Garcia Martinez, "Johann Baptist Metz: Political Theology," in *Confronting the Mystery of God: Political, Liberation and Public Theologies* (New York: Continuum, 2001), 21–88.

26. Cf. the title of the Festschrift for Metz's seventieth birthday: Johann Reikerstorfer, ed., *Vom Wagnis der Nichtidentität* (Münster: Lit, 1998). For a surprisingly analogical position, cf. J.D. Caputo, "Undecidability and the Empty Tomb: Towards a Hermeneutics of Belief," in *More Radical Hermeneutics: On Not Knowing Who We Are* (Bloomington/Indianapolis: Indiana University Press, 2000), 220–248.

27. Johann Baptist Metz, "Theologie versus Polymythie oder: Kleine Apologie des biblischen Monotheismus," in *Einheit und Vielheit*, ed. Odo Marquard (Hamburg: Meiner Verlag, 1990), 170–186; Johann Baptist Metz, "Die letzten Universalisten," in *Zum Begirf der neuen Politischen Theologie 1967–1997* (Mainz: Matthias-Grünenwald-Verlag, 1997), 156–159. Cf. also Jürgen Manemann, *Monotheismus* (Jahrbuch Politische Theologie, 4), Münster: Lit, 2002.

28. Peter Sloterdijk, "Die kritische Theorie ist Tod," *Die Zeit*, September 9, 1999.

29. See his "Regeln für den Menschenpark" (1999), reprinted in Peter Sloterdijk, *Nicht gerettet: Versuche nach Heidegger* (Frankfurt am Main: Suhrkamp, 2001), 302–337. For commentaries, see Peter Sloterdijk, *Regeln für den Menschenpark* (Frankfurt am Main: Suhrkamp, 1999).

30. Cf. Johann Baptist Metz, *Zur Theologie der Welt* (Mainz: Matthias-Grünenwald-Verlag, 1968); cf. also the programmatic articles form the early period of New Political Theology, reprinted in Metz, *Zum Begriff der neuen politische Theologie 1967–1997*, 9–84.

31. For the—in my view rather misleading—term, cf. Peter L. Berger, *The Desecularisation of the World: Resurgent Religion and World Politics* (Grand Rapids: Eerdmans, 1999).

32. The idea that what appears as the return of religion is in fact expressing the death of God in the Nietzschean sense, is developed in Gianni Vattimo, *Belief* (Oxford: Polity, 1999 [1996]); Gianni Vattimo, *After Christianity* (New York: Colombia University Press, 2002).

33. Tiemo Rainer Peters, "Evangelische Räte—therapeutische Räte," in *Gottespassion: Zur Ordensexistenz heute*, ed. Johann Baptist Metz and Tiemo Rainer Peters (Freiburg/Basel/Wien: Herder, 1991), 68–103, especially 73–78: "Christentum im Prozess der Neugründung"; cf. also Tiemo Rainer Peters, " 'Eine Religion beweist sich stets selbst'—Zur Aktualität Overbecks und seine theologiekritischen Anfragen," in *Mystik und Politik: Theologie im Ringen um Geschichte und Gesellschaft*, ed. E. Schillebeeckx (Mainz: Matthias Grünenwald-Verlag, 1988), 218–234.

34. For Peters this Christianity in the process of "re-foundation" exists in the various forms of the religious life. He does not make it very clear how he sees this.

35. Cf. John Dos Passos, *U.S.A.* (New York: Random House, 1937); Don DeLillo, *Underworld* (New York: Scribner, 1997).

36. For Doctorow's oeuvre, cf. Douglas Fowler, *Understanding E.L. Doctorow* (Columbia: University of South Carolina Press, 1992); John G. Parks, *E.L. Docotorow* (New York: Continuum, 1991).

37. Doctorow, *City of God*, 272.

38. Something similar has been done, from a more orthodox Jewish theological standpoint, in Jonathan Sacks, *The Dignity of Difference: How to Avoid the Clash of Civilizations* (New York: Continuum, 2003).

39. Doctorow, *City of God*, 3–4.
40. Ibid., 14.
41. Ibid., 266.
42. Ibid., 268.
43. Cf. Emil L. Fackenheim, *God's Presence in History: Jewish Affirmations and Philosophical Reflections* (New York: Harper and Row, 1970).
44. Emil L. Fackenheim, *To Mend the World: Foundations of Post-Holocaust Jewish Thought* (Bloomington/Indianapolis: Indiana University Press, 1994 [1982]), 25.
45. Ibid.
46. Cf. the subtitle of Tiemo Rainer Peters, *Johann Baptist Metz: Theologie des vermissten Gottes* (Mainz: Matthias-Grünenwald-Verlag, 1998).
47. Theodor W. Adorno, "Theses upon Art and Religion Today," in *Noten zur Literatur* (Frankfurt am Main: Suhrkamp, 1974), 647–653.
48. Margaret Anne Doody, *The True Story of the Novel* (London: HarperCollins, 1997). Doody studied what she sees as the origin of the novel in late antiquity. In that era, the novel was revolutionary because its subject were "ordinary" stories that were not considered to be worthy of literature. The same point can be made if one locates the birth of the novel at the beginning of modernity. Today's poetry and today's drama are "prosaic" in the way once only the novel was "prosaic."
49. This is at least the claim in the tradition of Catholic theology to which I subscribe; cf. my *Edward Schillebeeckx: a Theologian in his History, Part I, A Catholic Theology of Culture (1914–1965)* (London: Continuum, 2002).
50. For the structure of "profession" seen as depending on a truth that still has to come and in a sense even has to be produced, cf. Derrida, *L'université sans condition*.
51. This is written from the context of the Heyendaal Institute Nijmegen. It is the mission of our institute to do research on the interface of theology and other academic disciplines. In my experience this does not just mean engaging in interdisciplinary dialogue, but in this process also reinventing theology.

Works Cited

Adorno, Theodor W. "Theses upon Art and Religion Today." In *Noten zur Literatur*. Frankfurt am Main: Sührkamp, 1974. 647–653.

———. *Negative Dialektik*. Frankfurt am Main: Suhrkamp, 1966.

Attridge, David. Ed. *Jacques Derrida: Acts of Literature*. New York/London: Routledge, 1992.

Bauman, Zygmund. *Modernity and the Holocaust*. Cambridge: Polity, 1989.

———. *Wasted Lives: Modernity and its Outcasts*. Cambridge: Polity, 2004.

Berger, Peter L. *The Desecularisation of the World: Resurgent Religion and World Politics*. Grand Rapids: Eerdmans, 1999.

Borgman, Erik. "Missing Links between the Arts, Religion, and Reality: An Introductory and Exploratory Essay." In *Missing Links: Art, Religion and Reality*. Ed. J. Bekkenkamp, S. Van Maas, and M. Valente. Münster: Lit, 2000. 1–14.

———. *Edward Schillebeeckx: A Theologian in his History*. Part I. *A Catholic Theology of Culture (1914–1965)*. London: Continuum, 2002.

Brändle, Werner. *Rettung des Hoffnungslosen: Die theologischen Implikationen der Philosophie Theodor W. Adornos*. Göttingen: Vandenhoeck & Ruprecht, 1984.

Buchholz, René. *Zwischen Mythos und Bilderverbot: Die Philosophie Adornos als Anstoss zu einer kritischen Fundamentaltheologie im Kontext der späten Moderne*. Frankfurt: Lang, 1991.

Caputo, John D. "Undecidability and the Empty Tomb: Towards a Hermeneutics of Belief." In *More Radical Hermeneutics: On Not Knowing Who We Are*. Bloomington/Indianapolis: Indiana University Press, 2000. 220–248.

Clark, Roger Y. *Stranger Gods: Salman Rushdie's Other Worlds*, Montreal/Kingston: McGill-Queens University Press, 2001.

Culler, Jonathan. "Philosophy and Literature: The Fortunes of the Performative." *Poetics Today* 21 (Fall 2000): 503–520.

De Certeau, Michel. *The Practice of Everyday Life*. Berkely/Los Angeles/London: University of California Press, 1988.

Derrida, Jacques. *L'université sans condition*. Paris: Galilée, 2001; translation in Derrida, Jacques, *Without Alibi*. Ed. and trans. Peggy Kamuf .Stanford: Stanford University Press, 2002. 202–237.

Doctorow, Edgar L. *The Book of Daniel*. New York: Random House, 1971.

———. *City of Love*. New York: Random House, 1971.

———. *World's Fair*. New York: Random House, 1985.

———. *Billy Bathgate*. New York: Random House, 1989.

———. *Ragtime*. New York: Vintage, 1991.

———. *The Waterworks*. New York: Random House, 1994.

———. *City of God: A Novel*. London: Little, Brown, 2000.

Doody, Margareth Ann. *The True Story of the Novel*. London: HarperCollins, 1997.

Fackenheim, Emil. *God's Presence in History: Jewish Affirmations and Philosophical Reflections*. New York: Harper and Row, 1970.

———. *To Mend the World: Foundations of Post-Holocaust Jewish Thought*. Bloomington/Indianapolis: Indiana University Press, 1994 (1982).

Fowler, Douglas. *Understanding E.L. Doctorow*. Columbia: University of South Carolina Press, 1992.

Frisch, Ralf. *Theologie im Augenblick ihres Sturzes: Theodor W. Adorno und Karl Barth; zwei Gestalten einer kritischen Theorie der Moderne.*Wien: Passagen-Verlag, 1999.

Gonzalez, Madelena. *Fiction after the Fatwa: Salman Rushdie and the Charm of Catastrophe*. Amsterdam/New York: Rodopi, 2005.

Griffiths, Paul J. *Religious Reading: The Place of Reading in the Practice of Religion*. New York/Oxford: Oxford University Press, 1999.

Grimes, Ronald J. *Beginnings in Ritual Studies*. Washington: University Press of America, 1982.

———. *Research in Ritual Studies: A Programmatic Essay and Biography*. Chicago/Metuchen: American Theological Library Association/Scarecrow Press, 1985; revised ed. Columbia: University of South Carolina Press, 1994.

———. *Reading, Writing and Ritualizing: Ritual in Fictive, Liturgical and Public Spaces*. Washington: Pastoral Press, 1993.

———. Ed. *Reading in Ritual Studies*. Upper Saddle River: Prentice Hall, 1996.

Harpham, Geoffrey G. "Ethics and Literary Study." In *Shadows of Ethics: Criticism and the Just Society*, ed. Geoffrey G. Harpham. Durham/London: Duke University Press, 1999. 18–37.

Hassumani, Sabrina. *Salman Rushdie: A Postmodern Reading of his Major Works*. Madison/London: Fairleigh Dickinson University Press/Associated University Presses, 2002.

Kamuf, Peggy. "Introduction: Event of Resistance." In Jacques Derrida. *Without Alibi*. Ed. and trans. Peggy Kamuf. Stanford: Stanford University Press, 2002. 1–27.

Manemann, Jürgen. *Monotheismus* (Jahrbuch Politische Theologie, 4). Münster: Lit, 2002.

Martinez, J. Garcia. *Confronting the Mystery of God: Political, Liberation and Public Theologies*. New York: Continuum, 2001.

Martinson, Matthias. *Perseverance Without Doctrine: Adorno, Self-critique, and the Ends of Academic Theology*. Frankfurt: Peter Lang, 2000.

Metz, Johann Baptist. *Zur Theologie der Welt*. Mainz: Matthias-Grünenwald-Verlag, 1968.

———. *Glaube in Geschichte und Gesellschaft: Studien zu einer praktische Fundamentaltheologie*. Mainz: Matthias-Grünenwald-Verlag, 1977.

———. "Theologie versus Polymythie oder: Kleine Apologie des biblischen Monotheismus." In *Einheit und Vielheit*. Ed. Odo Marquard. Hamburg: Meiner Verlag, 1990. 170–186.

Metz, Johann Baptist. "Im Eingedenken fremden Leids: Zu einer Basiskategorie christlicher Gottesrede." In *Gottesrede*. Ed. J.B. Metz, J. Reikerstorfer, and J. Werblick. Münster: Lit, 1996. 3–20.

———. *Zum Begrif der neuen Politischen Theologie 1967–1997.* Mainz: Matthias-Grünenwald-Verlag, 1997.

Parks, John. *G. E.L. Docotorow.* New York: Continuum. 1991.

Peters, Tiemo Rainer. " 'Eine Religion beweist sich stets selbst'—Zur Aktualität Overbecks und seine theologiekritischen Anfragen." In *Mystik und Politik: Theologie im Ringen um Geschichte und Gesellschaft.* Ed. E. Schillebeeckx. Mainz: Matthias Grünenwald-Verlag, 1988. 218–234.

———. "Evangelische Räte—therapeutische Räte." *Gottespassion: Zur Ordensexistenz heute.* Ed. Johann Baptist Metz and Tiemo Rainer Peters. Freiburg/Basel/Wien: Herder 1991. 68–103.

———. *Johann Baptist Metz: Theologie des vermissten Gottes.* Mainz: Matthias-Grünenwald-Verlag, 1998.

Rappaport, Roy A. *Ritual and Religion in the Making of Humanity.* Cambridge: Cambridge University Press, 1999.

Reikerstorfer, Joahnn. Ed. *Vom Wagnis der Nichtidentität.* Münster: Lit, 1998.

Rushdie, Salman. *The Satanic Verses.* Harmondsworth: Viking, 1989.

———. *Woede.* Amsterdam: Contact, 2001.

———. *Fury.* London: Vintage, 2002 (2001).

Sacks, Jonathan. *The Dignity of Difference: How to Avoid the Clash of Civilizations.* New York: Continuum, 2003.

Sloterdijk, Peter. "Die kritische Theorie ist Tod." *Die Zeit.* September 9, 1999.

———. "Regeln für den Menschenpark." In *Nicht gerettet: Versuche nach Heidegger.* Frankfurt am Main: Suhrkamp, 2001. 302–337.

———. *Regeln für den Menschenpark.* Frankfurt am Main: Suhrkamp, 1999.

Traubel, Michel. Die Religion in der kritische Theorie bei Max Horkheimer und Theodor W. Adorno. Unpublished dissertation, Freiburg in Breisgau, 1978.

Vattimo, Gianni. *Belief.* Oxford: Polity, 1999 (1996).

———. *After Christianity.* New York: Colombia University Press, 2002.

CHAPTER TEN

The "Indian" Character of Modern Hindi Drama: Neo-Sanskritic, Pro-Western Naturalistic, or Nativistic Dramas?

DIANA DIMITROVA

Introduction

This essay deals with the notion of "Indian" character of naturalistic Hindi drama, as revealed in the plays of Mohan Rākeś (1925–1972), Bhuvaneśvar (1912–1957), and Upendranāth Aśk (1910–1996) who wrote in the wake of Western theater and who were opposed to the influential theatrical school of Prasād (1889–1937). It reflects on the Indian character of Hindi drama by raising the question: what is Indian tradition? Does it comprise only Western (British), or Brahmanic (Sanskritic), or indigenous (folk) elements and influences, or is it informed by all of them simultaneously? Does the fact that naturalistic Hindi drama is meant for the proscenium theater, which came from abroad, mean that its character is "non-Indian"? How is the issue of ideology related to the concept of "Indian" character of modern Hindi drama and to the making of its canon?

In the following, I will with the origins and development of modern Hindi theater and drama, and will proceed to discuss some aspects of naturalistic Hindi drama, which was discarded as "pro-Western" by Indian criticism. In the last section of this essay, I show how the issue of ideology is related to defining the Indian character of modern Hindi drama and how it accounts for the exclusion of playwrights Bhuvaneśvar and Aśk from the literary canon. Thus, this essay studies the extent to which the interpretation and evaluation of Hindi drama and the making of its canon have been determined by ideology. This reflects the general tendency of reader-response criticism to stress cultural and political factors in the study of literature.[1]

Modern Hindi Theatre and Drama

The beginnings of professional (i.e., noncommercial) theater in North India are connected with the establishment of British colonial state.[2] The Englishmen brought to India their language and literature. In this way, Indian elite could get acquainted with major works of European theater through English translations. Interest in European dramatic literature had as a consequence the establishment of several professional theatrical groups in Calcutta in 1835. Soon thereafter, the growing Bengali audience could see not only European plays in Bengali translation, but original Bengali dramas as well.[3]

During the nineteenth century and up to Independence in 1947 there existed, however, no professional Hindi theater. Peter Gaeffke points out the following three reasons for this development. He argues that the British had influenced the Hindi-speaking area less in the sphere of education and economics than the regions of Bengal and Maharashtra. Gaeffke also observes that the strong presence of Muslims in North India in the previous centuries may have resulted in a culture that showed no interest in drama. As a third reason for the lack of professional Hindi theater, Gaeffke points to the circumstance that the living folk tradition of *nauṭaṅkī* ("name of a type of folk-drama in Brajbhāṣā or Kharī Bolī languages on legendary themes with music") was ignored by Hindi playwrights up to the 1960s and the material it provided was not reworked into new modern dramas.[4]

Gaeffke also argues that apart from folk theater and the tradition of *rāslīlā* ("Krishna's round love-dance with the cowherd girls of Braj") and *nauṭaṅkī* the Parsi theater represented the only living theatrical tradition during the nineteenth century. It was mainly interested in being commercially successful and could not stimulate the growth of professional theater in Hindi. Moreover, the language of the plays that were staged by the Parsi companies was not Hindi, but a very simplified Hindustani that was closer to Urdu than to Hindi. Only in 1910, under the growing influence of the Hindus, did the Parsi theater directors begin to perform dramas in Hindi as well.[5]

Therefore, the influence of Western drama, the spread of Western education and the consolidation of Hindi as a literary language were a prerequisite for the growth of professional theater in Hindi.[6]

In this respect, the work of Bhāratendu Hariścandra (1850–1885),[7] who understood the necessity of presenting his contemporaries with an alternative to the Parsi performances, played a decisive role in the development of modern Hindi theater. Whereas Bhāratendu set the beginnings of modern Hindi drama by emancipating it from the conventions of both classical Indian and commercial Parsi theater, Prasād broadened its expressive potential.[8] The power of his language and the depth of the psychological characterization of his dramatic figures marked a new phase in the development of the play of Hindi. While Bhāratendu wrote satirical, lyrical, and historical plays, Prasād established the historical play as the main dramatic genre of Hindi. The employment of highly Sanskritized vocabulary and the glorification of the great Hindu past together with the introduction of stylistic devices of classical Sanskrit drama gave birth to the neo-Sanskritic play of Hindi, which has been influential up to the present day and has received much acclaim from the critics.

In the 1930s, a generation of playwrights appeared who rebelled against Prasād's authority and the domination of historical drama. They followed the tradition of Western dramatists Ibsen and Strindberg, and wrote not only historical, but also social plays which handled immediate problems of contemporary Indian society. Their main representative in the 1930s was Lakṣmīnārāyaṇ Miśra.[9]

After Independence, the influence of Western drama grew and social problem play, or naturalistic Hindi drama, thrived. The British were gone; social injustice, however, remained. This prompted even more playwrights to stop writing historical plays that glorified the past. The predominantly social message of modern Hindi drama was in perfect conformity with the ideology of progressivism, with the ideas of Gandhi and Indian National Congress, and with the political orientation of the Nehru government toward the Soviet Union and socialism. Thus, problems in the family were seen in their relation to social evils. The plays of Upendranāth Aśk, Jagdiścandra Māthur, Bhuvaneśvar, and Mohan Rākeś are most representative of this time.[10]

Preoccupation with social issues in turn led to a new "rebellion" in the 1960s and a new shift in subject matter. Playwrights of the new generation approached problems of the relationships between man and woman in the family from a more personal perspective. Social issues became less and less topical. In this sense, the plays of Lakṣmīnārāyaṇ Lāl, Hamīdullā, and many others should be taken into consideration. Dramaturgically, new techniques were employed. Many Hindi playwrights sought for an alternative to the all-pervading influence of Western drama and began writing nativistic dramas by taking up the folk dramatic tradition as a model for their plays. In this respect, Habīb Tanvīr's and Śāntā Gāndhī's plays should be mentioned.

Hindi Naturalistic Drama: Vide ī Drama? Defining the "Indian" Character of Modern Hindi Drama: Ideological Implications

Western dramatic school and naturalistic Hindi drama as its recipient were of crucial importance to the beginning and further development of contemporary theater in Hindi. However, the ideological apparatus of Indian criticism associated the notion of "Western" with the hegemonic position of the British in India. Because of political controversies with the British, "Western" influence also came to be understood as "non-Indian" in the sphere of literature. This resulted in a negative stance toward the naturalistic play of Hindi and those dramatists who adhered to it.

How does the issue of Western influence[11] refer to naturalistic Hindi drama and to its "Indian" character?

Modern Hindi drama was indebted to Western tradition for its origination and development, as Bhāratendu's plays would not have been possible without his knowledge of Western drama. This influence concerned mainly the new dramatic form, meant for a new type of theater, namely, the proscenium theater. Hindi playwrights Bhuvaneśvar, Upendranāth Aśk and Mohan Rākeś wrote in the wake of Western naturalism. Western school also inspired the employment of understandable dramatic language, which contrasted with Prasād's Sanskritized Hindi. Ibsen influenced the open-ended quality of their plays, and Strindberg, the cyclical composition. For the psychological characterization of the protagonists, naturalistic Hindi playwrights were indebted to Chechov's mode of writing.[12]

Naturalistic Western theater sought to portray the social milieu of the protagonists in a realistic way. In this sense, the influence of Western dramatic tradition is also revealed in the fact that all authors discussed expose social evils of contemporary Indian society, and criticize social injustice and corruption in their plays.

In the play of Hindi, Bhuvaneśvar was the first mature recipient of Strindberg's work. In his plays *Śyāmā: ek vaivāhik viḍambnā (Śyāmā: A Marriage Anomaly)*, 1933, *Śaitān (Satan)*, 1934, *Lāṭrī (Lottery)*, 1935, and *Romāns: romāñc (Romance: Horripilation)*, 1935, he explores the difficult relationship between man and woman in marriage.[13] Most often, there is an eternal triangle, where it is not man, but woman who has both a husband and a lover, or doubts between two marriage partners and needs

rn Hindi drama, as reflected in the works of the three authors dis-
l. Dominance of Western or *videśī* ("foreign") ideas was soon con-
by the counter-dominance of Sanskritic or Brahmanic revivalism.
, British (cultural) imperialism was replaced by Sanskritic (cultural)
.mperialism.

'hat did this shift in ideology[19] mean to the future of modern Hindi
1a and theater and how did it affect the reception of the work of nat-
.stic playwrights Bhuvaneśvar and Aśk by Indian drama criticism?
1 the first place, it meant that Prasād's dramatic work, which was
o-Sanskritic"[20] both in its subject matter, and in the employed lange and dramaturgical form, was considered exemplary and was set as
andard by the institutional ideological apparatus of Indian drama crit-
m. The Academy of Music and Drama and the National School of
1ma, which were founded in the late 1950s, did not seek to encour-
contemporary plays dealing with contemporary subject matters and
itten by contemporary playwrights, such as Bhuvaneśvar and Aśk,
10 pronounced openly their admiration for Western dramatists. Thus,
eological discourse considered the neo-Sanskritic and the nativistic
ay of Hindi "Indian" in character, while naturalistic drama was discarded
pro-Western, and therefore *videśī* ("foreign").

The dramaturgical form of Rākeś's work was influenced by Western
1eater, too. The subject matter of his historical plays, however, could
laim to be in conformity with the standard set by Prasād. Therefore, his
1ramatic production was included in the canon of modern Hindi drama.
Aśk and Bhuvaneśvar had no such alternative to offer.[21] Consequently,
the two authors could not fit into the making of "Indian" canon of
modern Hindi drama, as envisaged by its makers in the 1950s.

An additional argument for the acceptance of Rākeś's plays and the
exclusion of those of Aśk and Bhuvaneśvar is the different interpretation
of women's issues. Whereas Rākeś's female characters are cast rather
conservatively and traditionally and are depicted as being dependent on
men in their lives, Bhuvaneśvar and Aśk portray women as free and
independent individuals who can make their own decisions and oppose
conservative male authority.[22]

Thus, in the play *Āṣāṛh kā ek din*, Mallikā exists only for her love for
the poet Kālidāsa. She spends her whole life waiting for him at home. She
does not dare to protest or forget him even though he betrays their love,
marries another woman, and never visits her throughout the years. At
the end of the play, he fails to recommit himself to her, this time because
he finds out that she has a baby. The final scene shows her crying and
tending to her child. Thus, the only way out that Rākeś envisages for her

to make up her mind. A parallel can be made be
plays and Strindberg's *Play with Fire*, 1892, and *Da*

Similarly, Aśk's admiration for the subject of the
revealed in the dramas *Taulie* (*Towels*), 1943, and *J*
Sister Añjo), 1955, can also be traced back to Strindberg'
the dramatist could develop further the tradition set
Bhuvaneśvar. Besides, Aśk followed in Ibsen's :
women's oppression by the social system and ad
rights. He sought to do in Hindi what Ibsen had dc
Norwegian. Thus, we can draw parallels between Aś
(*The Primordial Way*), 1943, *Uṛān* (*Flight*), 1950, an
(*Separate Ways*), 1954, and Ibsen's *A Doll House*, 1879.[1]

In his first two plays, *Āṣāṛh kā ek din* (*One Day in th*
1958, and *Lahroṃ ke rājhaṃs* (*Swans of the Waves*), 1963
follows the tradition of employing historical subject ma
address contemporary issues.[16] It is characteristic of his
that he does not seek to establish a link with classical In
this, he differs decisively from Prasād, who sees modern H
successor to the plays of classical Sanskrit theater. Rākeś
himself in favor of a genuine Indian theater, which was t
different from Western theatrical institution, and in accc
cultural expectations of Indian audience. His main aesthet
however, are *yathārth, saṃgharṣ* and *dvandva*, and they corresp
to notions of reality, struggle, and conflict, inherent in Western

Similar to Bhuvaneśvar and Aśk, in Rākeś's dramatic c
author's creative encounter with Western theater is manifeste
play *Āṣāṛh kā ek din* explores the dilemma of the artist betweer
art, and relationships between man and woman. His last play *Ā*
(*Incomplete Halves*), 1969, shows the impossibility of commu
between them.[18] Dramaturgically, the dramas are closer to the
of Western drama than to Prasād's work or to the legacy of
Sanskrit theater.

Consequently, Western drama and theater have cont
immensely to the rise and further development of naturalistic
drama and theater. Bhuvaneśvar, Aśk, and Rākeś, who were th
mature recipients of Western school, were most prolific as dramat
the immediate decades before and after Indian independence. Histoi
and politically, this time was marked by the struggle for national free
which expressed itself in nationalistic movements, and a wave of a
British and anti-European sentiments.

In this sense, the endeavors to create a cultural *svarāj* ("independ
state") could not have had a liking for the pro-Western school

is motherhood and acceptance of fate, in this case of Kālidāsa's will, who also makes decisions for her. Similarly, in the play *Ādhe adhūre*, Sāvitrī works in a company and is financially independent. However, though she is really ambitious and wants her family to progress, she does not consider the possibility of having a career of her own. Instead, she is desperate in her attempt to find realization for herself through the men around her, be it her husband, her son, or her former friend Jagmohan. In all cases, she fails. In the last scene, Rākeś prompts the audience to take sides with the male characters by implying that it is woman's high requirements and her dissatisfaction with men that account for the problems.

Conversely, in Bhuvaneśvar's play *Strāīk* (*Strike*), the female character goes on a "strike" and thus protests against the rules of marital life set by her husband.[23] Similarly, in Aśk's *Alag alag rāste*, Rānī rebels against the existing orthodox order by defying both the authority of her father and her husband. In both plays, we are made to sympathize with the female characters and approve of their courage. Moreover, the freedom of Bhuvaneśvar's heroines to choose or change a partner, as revealed in *Śyāmā: ek vaivāhik viḍambnā*, 1933, and *Lātṛī*, 1935, is unprecedented in modern Hindi drama. Aśk developed it further in the play *Bhaṃvar (Whirlpool)*, 1961.[24] While this interpretation is in harmony with Western ideals, it does not reflect the objective reality of Indian societies of the 1940s and 1950s, and could not appeal to the dominating critical discourse.

Thus, though naturalistic and pro-Western in form, Rākeś's work was in conformity with the neo-Sanskritic play of Hindi with regard to the historical subject matter and the interpretation of female characters along the lines of traditional Hindu values. All this accounted for the "Indian" character of his dramas and their inclusion in the literary canon of Hindi.

Aśk's and Bhuvaneśvar's plays did not reflect idealistic reworking of traditional Hindu values. This is why their dramatic achievement did not fit into the present-day critical discourse on modern Hindi drama. Consequently, the reception of their dramatic oeuvre by contemporary Indian drama criticism and their position in the Hindi world of letters was marked by neglect and exclusion from the canon. Thus, the issues of interpretation, evaluation, reading, and response are closely linked with the notion of ideological discourse. Critics as readers and makers of the literary canon have seen it as their responsibility to select for the literary canon dramatic works, which uphold traditional values, and this accounts for the negative reception of authors who seek to subvert Indian (read: orthodox Hindu) tradition.

Resentment of Western ideas in critical discourse gave birth to a new cultural and literary movement in the post-Independence period. In the

1960s, the notion of creating Indian art and writing Indian plays changed. The prevalent cultural movement was *deśivād*, or nativism.[25] Nativism opposed both the Anglicized and the Sanskritized elites of contemporary society. It emphasized the primacy of the language of the masses in the production of culture. Many Indian intellectuals have seen it as a form of "indigenism" and an expression of cultural nationalism, and self-assertion of a marginalized literary culture. They have also viewed it as an attempt to emancipate a formerly colonized nation from the hegemony of Anglo-American universalistic critical discourse.[26]

What did the ideology underlying nativism mean to the development of modern Hindi drama and theater?

The attempt to create national Indian theater in the 1960s was dogmatic and normative in character. Playwrights were made to write in the mode of folk theater traditions, and influential critics propagated this new theatrical policy.[27] The National School of Drama and the Academy of Music and Drama organized seminars and awarded prizes to playwrights who complied with the new directives of creating a *deśi* ("national") theater. As dramatist Prasanna tells in his essay, one could be successful as a playwright only if one limited one's artistic quest to the requirements defined by the institutional theatrical apparatus: "if you are a Karnataka applicant [for a seminar or an award], choose from these forms: Yakshagana, Jogarata and X, Y, Z. If you are from Bengal, Jatra, and X, Y, Z."[28]

Conclusion

In his essay *Theatre in India*, Girish Karnad discusses the main reasons for the absence of a thriving theatrical tradition in modern India in the light of authorial ethics and reader responsibility.[29]

In his opinion, modern Hindi drama cannot have the impact on the heart of contemporary Indian society, the way Western drama has in Western society, because it is not honest about the core of Indian reality. Drama has remained trivial in modern India because of the double set of values underlying the life of the urban middle class "professing faith in Western values of equality, individualism, secularism, or free competition in public while sticking to caste and family loyalties at home."[30]

Karnad argues that whereas the taking over of proscenium stage and the sale of tickets from the Western school marked the beginning of a new kind of "modern," proscenium Indian theater based on the Western model, it brought about the mechanical and literal borrowing of Western interior for the description of an Indian home setting. Karnad points out that most modern Indian plays are set, similar to Western models, in the living room. However, the role the living-room plays in the home life of a Western individual or family is different from that in India. Important issues in an Indian home are discussed not in the living-room, but in the kitchen and in the prayer room, beyond the living room.

Moreover, Karnad refers to the fact that by imitating Western models, modern Indian plays fail to be honest about the nature and direction of communication in India, where social and family life is defined by hierarchies. He states that it is not common that women sit together with men and discuss their most private affairs openly in front of total strangers, the way it happens in Western plays. Such a situation is unthinkable in a traditional Indian home. Thus, Karnad emphasizes the importance of playwrights' ethics and reader responsibility when constructing the meanings of a dramatic text.

Karnad implies that Indian drama that plays against an alien background cannot address native issues, that is, speak to the spectators' hearts. It cannot convince people that it is about them and cannot have the desired impact on contemporary Indian society. While I agree with Karnad's argumentation to a certain extent, I am of the opinion that we should also take into account the responsibility of critics as readers and makers of the canon. In my view, one major reason for the lack of popularity of modern Hindi theater is the normative approach of Indian criticism, which sets deliberately certain dramas as a standard while excluding others from the literary canon on the grounds of ideology.

The dogmatism of this theatrical policy has ignored the plurality of cultural tradition in India. In my opinion, Indian theatrical tradition comprises neither only Western (or English), nor only Brahmanic (or Sanskritic), or indigenous (or folk) elements and influences. Rather, it is informed by all these influences and elements simultaneously. Therefore, I hold that the assumption underlying the ideology of nativistic discourse that "if you want to be an Indian you should reject proscenium theatre because we think that proscenium came from abroad"[31] has played a negative role in the development of modern Hindi theater. It has suppressed and excluded from literary histories, critical studies, and potential theatrical performances many playwrights and dramas worth consideration.

Notes

1. M.H. Abrams, "Reader-Response Criticism," in *A Glossary of Literary Terms* (Fort Worth: Harcourt Brace College Publishers, 1993), 268–272.
2. P. Gaeffke, *Hindi Literature in the 20th Century: A History of Indian Literature*, vol. VII.5 (Wiesbaden: Otto Harrassowitz, 1978), 93–95.
3. Ibid.
4. Ibid.

5. Some of the most famous Parsi companies, e.g., Orijinal Vikṭoriya, Empres Vikṭoriya, Elfinsṭan Thiyeṭrikal Kampanī, Alfred Thiyeṭrikal, and Nyū Alfred Kampanī were established in Mumbai (Bombay), Lucknow, Varanasi, Delhi, and so on. They traveled from place to place in order to perform Hindi plays. See Gaeffke, *Hindi Literature in the 20th Century*, 94–95.

6. Ibid.

7. On Bhāratendu, see D. Dimitrova, *Western Tradition and Naturalistic Hindi Theatre* (New York: Peter Lang, 2004) 14–15.

8. Ibid., 15–20.

9. Ibid., 20–22.

10. Ibid., 22–50.

11. I will use the critical term "influence" in its traditional meaning, namely, as designating the affiliative relations between past and present literary texts and/or their authors. See Louis A. Renza, "Influence," in *Critical Terms for Literary Study*, ed. Frank Lentricchia and Thomas McLaughlin (Chicago: University of Chicago Press, 1990). 186–203.

12. See Dimitrova, *Western Tradition*, 11–37.

13. R. Bedār and Rājkumār Śarmā, eds., *Bhuvaneśvar Sāhitya* (śāhjahāṃpur: Bhuvaneśvar Prasād śodh sansthān, 1992), 45–51, 53–61, 95–103, and 87–93.

14. U. Aśk, *Añjo Dīdī: do aṅkoṃ kā ek sāmājik nāṭak*, 1955 (Ilāhābād: Nīlābh, 1983); U. Aśk, "Taulie," in *Paccīs śreṣṭh ekāṅkī* by U. Aśk (Ilāhābād: Nīlābh, 1969) 79–102.

15. ———, "*Ādi mārg*," in *Ādi mārg: cār sāmājik nāṭakoṃ kā raṅgmañc saṃskaraṇ*, by U. Aśk, 1943 (Ilāhābād: Nīlābh, 1961) 11–59; U. Aśk, *Alag alag rāste*, 1954 (Ilāhābād: Nīlābh, 1986);———, *Kaid aur uṛān*, 1950 (Ilāhābād: Nīlābh, 1972).

16. M. Rākeś, *Ā ṣāṛh kā ek din*, 1958 (Dillī: Rājpāl eṇḍ sanẓ, 1963); M. Rākeś, *Lahroṃ ke rājhaṃs*, 1953 (Nayī Dillī: Rājkamal, 1990).

17. See also Vasudha Dalmia, "Neither Half nor Whole. Dialogue and Disjunction in the Plays of Mohan Rakesh," *Tender Ironies: A Tribute to Lothar Lutze*, ed. Dilip Chitre et al. (New Delhi: Manohar, 1994) 189.

18. M. Rākeś, *Ādhe adhūre*, 1969 (Nayī Dillī: Rādhākṛṣṇa, 1985).

19. As James Kavanagh points out in his essay on ideology, the term should not be understood narrowly, i.e., as it is used in the mass media. "Ideology offers the social subject not a set of narrowly 'political' ideas but a fundamental framework of assumptions that defines the parameters of the real and the self." See James H. Kavanagh, "Ideology," in *Critical Terms for Literary Study*, ed. Frank Lentricchia and Thomas McLaughlin (Chicago: University of Chicago Press, 1990)———, 310.

20. The term "neo-sanskritic" refers to dramas written in Prasad's style and exploring subject matter inherent in his work. See the previous subsection of this essay.

21. Aśk wrote just one historical play, *Jay parājay* (*Victory and Defeat*) in 1937 and announced publicly that he did not intend to write historical dramas any more because the new time required modern plays discussing topical subject matter.See U.Aśk, *Jay parājay*, 1937 (Ilāhābād: Nīlābh, 1984); ———, "Hindi ekāṅkī aur jīvānt raṅgmañc: ek lambī ḍhalān ke donoṃ chor," in *Paccīs śreṣṭh ekāṅkī*, by U. Aśk (Ilāhābād: Nīlābh, 1969), 9.

22. On the treatment of women and gender in Mohan Rākeś's work, see D. Dimitrova, "The Treatment of Women and Gender in the Plays *Āṣāṛh kā ek din* and *Ādhe adhūre* by Mohan Rākeś (1925–1972)" in *Tohwa-e-dil: Festschrift Helmut Nespital.*, ed. Dirk W. Loenne (Reinbek: Wezler, 2001), 177–188.

23. Bedār and Rājkumār, *Bhuvaneśvar Sāhitya*, 107–117.

24. U. Aśk, *Bhaṃvar* (Ilāhābād: Nīlābh, 1961).

25. Bhalchandra Nemade coined the term "nativism" in his Marathi essay "Sahityateel Deshiyata" (1983). For more information, see Makarand Paranjape, ed., *Nativism: Essays in Criticism* (New Delhi: Sahitya Akademi, 1997).

26. See Prasanna, "A Critique of Nativism in Contemporary Indian Theater," in *Nativism: Essays in Criticism*, ed. Makarand Paranjape (New Delhi: Sahitya Akademi, 1997), 95–100.

27. Prasanna mentions Sureś Avāsthī and Nemicandra Jain. See Prasanna, "A Critique of Nativism in Contemporary Indian Theatre," in *Nativism: Essays in Criticism*, ed. Makarand Paranjape (New Delhi: Sahitya Akademi, 1997), 95.

28. Ibid., 95–101.

29. See G. Karnad, "Theatre in India," *Daedalus: Journal of the American Academy of Arts and Sciences*, Fall 1989: 331–353.

30. Ibid., 336.

31. See Prasanna, "A Critique of Nativism in Contemporary Indian Theatre," in *Nativism: Essays in Criticism*, ed. Makarand Paranjape (New Delhi: Sahitya Akademi, 1997), 99–100.

Works Cited

Abrams, M.H. "Reader-Response Criticism." In *A Glossary of Literary Terms*. Fort Worth: Harcourt Brace College Publishers, 1993. 268–272.

Aśk, Upendranāth. "Ādi mārg." In *Ādi mārg: cār sāmājik nāṭakoṃ kā raṅgmañc saṃskaraṇ*. By U. Aśk. 1943. Ilāhābād: Nīlābh, 1961. 11–59.

———. *Alag alag rāste*. 1954. Ilāhābād: Nīlābh, 1986.

———. *Añjo Dīdī; do aṅkoṃ kā ek sāmājik nāṭak*. 1955. Ilāhābād: Nīlābh, 1983.

———. *Bhaṃvar*. 1961. Ilāhābād: Nīlābh, 1961.

———. *Jay parājay*. 1937. Ilāhābād: Nīlābh, 1984.

———. "Hindī ekāṅkī aur jīvānt raṅgmañc: ek lambī ḍhalān ke donoṃ chor." In *Paccīs śreṣṭh ekāṅkī*. By U. Aśk. Ilāhābād: Nīlābh, 1969. 9.

———. *Kaid aur uṛān*. 1950. Ilāhābād: Nīlābh, 1972.

———. "Taulie." by U. Aśk. *Paccīs śreṣṭh ekāṅkī*. 1943. Ilāhābād: Nīlābh, 1969. 79–102. Eds. R. Bedār and Rājkumār Śarmā. *Bhuvaneśvar Sāhitya*. Śāhjanāṃpur: Bhuvaneśvar Prasād śodh saṃsthān, 1992. 45–51, 53–61, 95–103, 87–93, 107–117.

Gaeffke, Peter. *Hindi Literature in the 20th Century: A History of Indian Literature*. Vol. VII.5. Wiesbaden: Otto Harrassowitz, 1978. 94–95.

Dalmia, Vasudha. "Neither Half nor Whole. Dialogue and Disjunction in the Plays of Mohan Rakesh." In *Tender Ironies: A Tribute to Lothar Lutze*. Ed. Dilip Chitre et al. New Delhi: Manohar, 1994. 189.

Dimitrova, Diana. "The Treatment of Women and Gender in the Plays *Āṣāṛh kā ek din* and *Ādhe adhūre* by Mohan Rākeś (1925–1972)." In *Topwa-e-dil: Festschrift Helmut Nespital*. Ed. Dirk W. Lönne. Reinbek: Wezler, 2001. 177–188.

———. *Western Tradition and Naturalistic Hindi Theatre*. New York: Peter Lang, 2004.

Karnad, Girish. "Theatre in India." *Daedalus. Journal of the American Academy of Arts and Sciences*. Fall 1989: 331–353.

Kavanagh, James H. "Ideology." In *Critical Terms for Literary Study*. Ed. Frank Lentricchia and Thomas McLaughlin. Chicago: University of Chicago Press, 1990. 310.

Paranjape, Makarand. Ed. *Nativism: Essays in Criticism*. New Delhi: Sahitya Akademi, 1997.

Prasanna. "A Critique of Nativism in Contemporary Indian Theatre." In *Nativism: Essays in Criticism*. Ed. Makarand Paranjape. New Delhi: Sahitya Akademi, 1997. 95, 99–100.

Rākeś, Mohan. *Ādhe adhūre*. 1969. Nayī Dillī: Rādhākṛṣṇa, 1985.

———. *Āṣāṛh kā ek din*. 1958. Dillī: Rājpāl eṇḍ sanz, 1963.

———. *Lahroṃ ke rājhaṃs*. 1963. Nayī Dillī: Rājkamal, 1990.

Renza, Louis A. "Influence." In *Critical Terms for Literary Study*. Ed. Frank Lentricchia and Thomas McLaughlin. Chicago: University of Chicago Press, 1990. 186–203.

CHAPTER ELEVEN

Film and Apocryphal Imitation of the Feminine—Judith of Bethulia

ELIZABETH PHILPOT

Introduction

Shot on location in 1913 in Chatsworth, California, *Judith of Bethulia* was released in 1914. The film was produced and directed by the legendary American producer D.W. Griffith and starred the actress Blanche Sweet as Judith and Henry B. Walthall as Holofernes. This essay examines the role of both Judith and Holofernes as depicted in the film and relates it to feminist thought of the time just prior to the World War I. It discusses how far the filmmaker distorts facts from the biblical narrative for chauvinistic theatrical effects, in the same way that artists have changed the emphasis of their images through the centuries for differing reasons. In this film, Holofernes occupies the traditional male role of masculine pride, strength, and superiority while Judith is represented as the love-lost maiden who falls in love with him. However, in the end she turns the tables and in true warrior fashion, decapitates him and saves her hometown of Bethulia.

Key Words

Griffith D.W., Hollywood, Judith, salvation history (*Heilsgeschichte*), silent movies.

★ ★ ★

The Book of Judith described by Margarita Stocker as "one of the most striking stories of the Old Testament Apocrypha,"[1] as a tale exemplifying "the perennial battle of the sexes" by Alan Dundes,[2] and "as a poem and an allegorical passion play" by Martin Luther[3], the Protestant reformer, lends itself to be turned into visual cinematic terms. In art, this subject has been copiously illustrated right through the centuries, beginning with the fragment of the eighth-century wall painting in the church of Santa Maria Antiqua in Rome[4] and ending with the brilliantly colored contemporary oil painting executed in 2001 by Vivienne Licudi-Fry,[5] now in a private collection.[6] And yet there has been only one early spectacular "silent movie" entitled *Judith of Bethulia*, produced by D.W. Griffith in 1913.

Griffith's *Judith of Bethulia* makes several significant deviations from and returns to the Book of Judith. These deviations and returns as well as their reception by twentieth-century Western audiences can be usefully submitted to a Western feminist analysis. The story of Judith, which presents us with a forceful heroine, is the ideal vehicle for feminists because here is a woman in control, a frightening and unsettling prospect for many men. In the biblical text she comes over as an androgynous woman displaying both male and female characteristics. On the one hand, she is courageous, mentally strong, and able to make her own decisions, stand up to men and look after her husband's estate after his death from sunstroke. She is also well thought of by the elders of her town, takes responsibility for her own actions, and in the end kills the enemy of her people, with a little help from her maid, and saves her hometown—a veritable *Heilsgeschichte* ("Salvation History"). At the same time she also expresses a very feminine side of her nature by wanting to dress alluringly in her festive clothes in order "to entice the eyes of all the men who might see her" (Judith 10:4). The apocryphal account describes her as "beautiful in appearance," and "very lovely to behold" (Judith 8:7).[7] She was virtuous, chaste, and pious, praying to God, fasting and wearing sackcloth around her waist. In this respect the biblical account states "no one spoke ill of her, for she feared God with great devotion" (Judith 8:8). She was also wise, charitable, and good. In other words, she possessed all those "good" virtues and characteristics of womanhood that have been defined by Gilbert and Guber[8] as the "eternal feminine virtues of modesty, gracefulness, purity, delicacy, civility, compliancy, reticence, chastity, affability, politeness." However, she also exhibited other more contentious aspects of womanhood by showing herself not only to be cunning, but also a deceiver, a schemer, a shameless flatterer, a liar, a seductress, and a ruthless assassin. Yet as we know from the biblical text, she needed all these qualities to perform her act of heroism.

Let us now consider the film and see how far these characteristics are defined. This ambitious and expensive four-reel film was produced by the Biograph Studio, New York, under the direction of the legendary American producer David Wark (D.W.) Griffith (1875–1948) and starred the actress Blanche Sweet (1895–1986) as Judith and Henry B. Walthall (1878–1936) as Holofernes. Lillian and Dorothy Gish and Lionel Barrymore play other smaller parts.

Shot secretly on location in 1913 in Chatsworth, California, it was released in 1914. It is still considered to be one of the best films ever produced by this director. At the time, the production cost $50,000, a fortune in those days. However, by persuading most of the actors to play several parts in different beards and by filming from the distance, Griffith was able to film within his budget. It is therefore not surprising that one of the criticisms levied against it is that there are no close-ups of individual actors, except for the main protagonists.

To modern viewers, this film might seem rather slow, ponderous, lacking in tension, and even rather comical, but we must remember that it was issued at a time when other studios in Europe were producing epic films. This was the epoch of blockbusters, such as the eight-reel Italian *Quo Vadis?* of 1912, based on a popular novel about Romans and Christians, which was playing to eager audiences in New York where it was first shown, and subsequently in Chicago, Baltimore, and Philadelphia. Griffith, who extended the range of subjects for films, having turned to Alfred, Lord Tennyson, Robert Browning, Thomas Hood, and Edgar Alan Poe, based his epic of Judith not only on the bible story, as recounted in the Book of Judith, but also on a play entitled *Judith of Bethulia: A Tragedy* by the American Thomas Bailey Aldrich (1836–1907).[9] He was also the editor of the monthly magazine *The Atlantic* and author of *The Story of a Bad Boy* published in 1870.

Although the film takes the biblical narrative as its starting point, it also has a subplot running concurrently with the main story line. This is the tale of a handsome warrior (Nathan) played by Robert Harron (1893–1920) who is loved by the beautiful Naomi, played by Mae Marsh (1895–1968). We first meet Nathan at one of the wells situated outside the city walls of Bethulia, helping Naomi to draw water. Doe-eyed, they both exchange fond glances as they part at the entrance to the city, and we are left in no doubt of their love for each other. Later on in the film Naomi is captured by the Assyrians and then rescued, in true Griffith fashion, by Nathan from a burning tent from the camp of the Assyrians. She is the archetypal weak and helpless maiden, fluttering her eyelashes, while Nathan represents the strong male figure that audiences expected to see in 1914 films.[10] They were accustomed to watching nonconfrontational love stories, which, Griffith knew, would always bring in the public. This subplot neatly demonstrates the two contrasting women: the ultra-vulnerable and feminine Naomi and the brave and brutal Judith. Similar to the biblical tale, this film is also a story of murder, deceit, loyalty, bloody battles, love, loyalty, triumph, and bravery. Griffith exploits these themes to maximum effect. Nowadays, this hour-long film is almost forgotten, but at the time of its release it was very popular, receiving mixed reviews. *The Moving Picture World* of March 7, 1914 considered it to be "A fascinating work of high artistry . . ." that ". . . will not only rank as an achievement in this country, but will make foreign producers sit up and take notice." In her Museum of Modern Art monograph, Iris Barry says that the film was "a real landmark."[11] Compared to the other epic films of the time, Griffith's *Judith of Bethulia* has a freshness and new dynamism not to be seen in other films. Whatever praise or criticisms we lavish on this film, it must be put into its historical context. No doubt David Shipman is correct in his assessment when he says, in the introduction to the second volume of his book *The Story of Cinema*, that "most viewers today find his (Griffith's) films quaint at best and at worst unwatchable."[12]

The film, which demonstrates the *mis-en scène*[13] technique for which Griffith became famous, begins with the subplot of Nathan and Naomi meeting at the well (mentioned earlier); a poignant reminder that without water the citizens of Bethulia could not survive. We are quickly introduced to Judith, the wealthy, beautiful, and devout widow of Manasseh walking on the rooftop of her house. She summons her maid (the character actress, Kate Bunce (1858–1946)) and together they descend majestically to the marketplace where Judith generously gives alms to the poor and crippled. She stops to bless the child of a young mother, played by Lillian Gish (1893–1993), thereby greatly amplifying the theme of motherhood which Griffith adopts from the Aldrich play.[14] By turning away with a look of sad resignation, we are also made aware of Judith's unhappiness at her own childlessness.

Soon the film turns to the war waged by Nebuchadnezzar,[15] king of Babylonia against Arphaxad,[16] king of the Medes, and to the siege of the hilltop town of Bethulia by the Assyrians. Holofernes, the general in command of the armies who is second in command to Nebuchadnezzar himself,[17] has been laying waste the countryside by looting, plundering, slaughtering, killing, and tearing down the holy Israelite sanctuaries and ordering the citizens to worship Nebuchadnezzar as their god. It is in these shots of battles and skirmishes that the film can be said to excel, but these scenes have also met with criticism. William K. Everson writes in his book *American Silent Film*, "the garb of the opposing armies was virtually indistinguishable, and the action scenes became directionless skirmishes in which identical extras were absorbed into a background of dust, rocks and sun-dried grass and foliage."[18] In my opinion, these battle scenes, with their explosive energy, are remarkable for the sheer volume of men and weapons. On the other hand, the audience do not feel part of the combat, because, unlike in many later epic films, there are no clips of single men fighting to the death, horses being felled or other scenes of tragedy making the audience gasp. More successful close-ups show the Assyrians trying to ram the gates of the city, running ladders up against the walls, only to have them pushed down again, and sheltering beneath transportable roofs, while the citizens of Bethulia display their prowess by throwing down rocks and spears onto the enemy below. In contrast, David Shipman severely criticizes the film and says that it "is a shambles—much rushing about and barnstorming, amidst which may be discerned the Bible story of Judith and Holofernes."[19]

It is here that the film is grossly in error because in the biblical story the Assyrians do not storm the town of Bethulia, but no doubt Griffith saw this as his great opportunity to demonstrate his ability to stage an epic, historical battle scene.[20] What actually happens in the narrative is that having laid bare the countryside, Holofernes now orders "his whole army, and all the allies who had joined him, to break camp and move against Bethulia, and to seize the passes up into the hill country and make war on the Israelites" (Judith 7:1). However, at no time do they attack the town. The apocryphal account says that on the second day, Holofernes leads all his cavalry out in full view of the Israelites in Bethulia. Instead of launching a full-scale assault on the town, he reconnoitres the approaches to it, visits the springs that supplied their water, seizes them, and returns to his army. The Ammonites camp in the valley and they then seize the water supply and springs of the Israelites. Others encamp in the hill country, then rest in the plain, while they await the surrender of the thirsty and starving citizens of Bethulia. Contrary to the film, no one has died and no blood has, as yet, been shed. Had Griffith stuck to the text of the Book of Judith his whole raison d'être would have vanished overnight. Much of what follows differs between the film and the Book of Judith.

The whole Assyrian army surrounds the town for thirty-four days until all the cisterns are empty. It is at this point, when the citizens are collapsing and dying in the streets that we see Judith looking indignantly out of her window dressed in an old cardigan, "her heart bleeding at the distress of her people." The Apocrypha informs us (Judith 8:9) that having heard that Uzziah, the elder, is about to surrender the town to the opposing forces within five days if the salvation the Bethulians have been praying for does not materialize, she decides to take matters in to her own hands. In the film, the caption informs us that "a vision came from the Lord." Judith sends her maid to summon the elders Uzziah, Chabris, and Charmis to her house. Here Judith demonstrates the masculine, assertive side of her character. And what is more, these three bizarre looking elders with false beards meekly arrive at her home and listen as she derides them for their lack of faith. In the biblical text she tells them she is "about to do something that will go down through all generations of our descendants" (Judith 8:32) and that the town will be delivered within the allotted time of five days. She adds "only, do not try to find out what I am doing; for I will not tell you until I have finished what I am about to do" (Judith 8:34). Shrugging their shoulders, the elders glance knowingly at each other having given their permission, probably because they felt that they had nothing to lose. Judith exhibits the qualities of rebelliousness, single-mindedness, concentration, and tenaciousness, which the feminist art historian Linda Nochlin says are essential if women are to succeed in a man's world.[21] The biblical account is so pro-women, even to the extent of casting men in a foolish role, that Toni Craven asks whether the biblical account could, in fact, have been written by a woman.[22] Although she acts like a man in this instance, Judith also expresses the feminine trait of mystery or secrecy, perhaps as a way of covering up her uncertainty because she herself is not entirely sure what action she is going to take.

It is now that she prays to the Lord before undertaking her dangerous mission. In the film, we witness her praying. We know from the biblical text that she is asking God to grant her a beguiling tongue and strength. Dressed in sackcloth she clutches her breast, places ashes on her head, gesticulates, and casts her eyes to heaven. To us, Blanche Sweet's acting seems stilted, melodramatic, and exaggerated and we might be tempted to think she has based her performance on some sixteenth- or seventeenth-century painting where a female saint rolls her eyes heavenwards in a gesture of spiritual inspiration.[23] Yet actually there are very few scenes in art showing Judith at prayer. Some viewers might even find her outward display of torment and prayer painful to watch; others are reputedly moved by it.

The narrative continues with Judith removing her widow's garment, bathing, arranging her hair, anointing herself with perfume, and adorning herself in her finest clothes, sandals and jewellery, including bracelets, rings, earrings, and anklets, so as "to entice the eyes of all the men who might see her" (Judith 10:4). It is in a scene like this that Judith shows the other side of her character. She is no longer the innocent and defenceless woman of prayer but a sexual vampire, a *femme fatale* irresistibly glamorous and desirable wielding her sexual power, bent on seducing Holofernes and thereby accomplishing her mission of salvation.

In the film she reappears mysteriously veiled, fully clothed in all her regalia with an extravagant peacock-feathered headdress. And now "dressed to kill" she sets off bravely to the camp of the Assyrians, accompanied by her maid clutching an enormous food bag, which will conveniently be used to carry off the decapitated head of Holofernes. The elders watch the two women depart. We see Judith arriving at the camp being escorted by just two soldiers (not the one hundred mentioned in the apocryphal story (Judith 10:17)), to the quarters of Holofernes. In this way Griffith manages to save money by using only a small number of actors. However, as far as the audience are concerned the drama is lost because they cannot share any fear that Judith might have felt as she was accompanied by this large masculine force. Yet we know from the biblical narrative that she was fearless because she "feared God with great devotion" (Judith 8:7).

The film now concentrates on the central theme of the biblical story, namely that of Judith and Holofernes and the veritable story of the battle of the sexes. We have already encountered the powerful and despotic Holofernes in small vignettes. These include, his arrival by chariot at the camp of the Assyrians, ferociously punishing those who have disobeyed him, crucifying those who have betrayed him, shouting out orders to his underlings and revelling in bacchanalian festivities, while his effeminate eunuch tries to ingratiate himself with Holofernes. He is depicted with dark long curly hair and a swarthy beard befitting an Assyrian, resting in his tent on his bed, from which he rarely moves, covered with an exotic carpet.[24] Little attention has been paid to the issues of authenticity of the costumes of this film although much thought has been lavished on the settings and props. Significantly Holofernes appears for only sixteen minutes on screen, having been given a second billing. He is shown wearing a distinctly Oriental costume with an elaborate hat, part Saracen, part Assyrian, and part imaginative. We can say that the ideals of nationalism have not been explored. In her book *Undressing Cinema* (1997), Stella Bruzzi examines this issue and proposes that film directors should seriously consider the strong links which exist between history, costume, and fashion. Holofernes, on seeing Judith clothed in a clinging diaphanous low-cut dress, her hair falling loosely and seductively about her shoulders, is mesmerized by her beauty and loses his head before it is cut off.[25] Judith beguiles him by cunningly promising, "to deliver all Judea into his hands." He thinks only of her and gives no heed to "the artful women from the great Temple of Nin" performing The Dance of the Fishes—an entertaining interlude. Judith, on being shown in to Holofernes, simpers and rolls her eyes at him in true silent film style. The biblical text tells us that Holofernes is beside himself with desire and is eager to seduce her. We read how his passions were aroused, how "her sandal ravished his eyes, her beauty captivated his mind" (Judith 16:9), but in the film he "suddenly seemed noble in her eyes" and she is the one who falls in love with him, perhaps lured on by Holofernes' promises of a life of riches "in Nineveh, the city of the gods." This sexual attraction might seem rather odd considering that he has almost annihilated her hometown. He strokes her shoulders and caresses her cheek and just when she appears to be succumbing to his passionate, masculine charms, her conscience and the object of her mission finally dawns on her and she encourages him to drink the wine. Conveniently he falls onto the bed in a drunken stupor. Hovering over the sleeping Holofernes, she takes the sword from the bedpost, raises it, hesitates because of her "love" for Holofernes, struggles "to cast away her sinful passion" but then pulls herself together and with one swift blow decapitates "the blood-reeking monster"[26]—not the two blows as mentioned in the apocryphal story. It is interesting to note that Griffith who, on the whole, prefers to depict Judith from a feminine aspect, should in this instance choose to show her on equal male terms with the strength of a warrior and not as a physically weak woman needing two strikes in order to sever the head of Holofernes from his body.

Throughout this scene, according to Jack Lodge Blanche Sweet "looks beautiful and acting with splendid authority, she generates a formidable erotic charge."[27] The most striking images in the film are those where Judith tries to seduce the lecherous Holofernes. In the biblical account we are told that Judith lies, no doubt, temptingly, on the lambskins which Bagoas, Holofernes' servant, had provided for her to recline on while eating[28] but this has been ignored in the film perhaps because such sexually explicit antics might have been too much for the audiences of 1914. The Symbolist period when women were shown as vampires was over by this date and provocative images were therefore less acceptable by society.[29] Instead, Judith twists and turns her body and gazes adoringly at Holofernes inflaming his ardor. Griffith could have turned away from the narrative approach as many later film directors did, but he took an imaginative stance wherever possible. The silence of the film means that actors have to rely on mime and facial expression, grimaces, exaggerated gestures, and bravura actions. We would be under a misconception if we should think that this film with so few main characters fails in the psychological interaction of the characters but by gesture we are made aware of the closeness of, for example, Judith and her maid and Nathan and Naomi. The audience is well aware of the distress, frustrations, love, anger, and other emotions expressed between the characters. In silent films the audience cannot be wooed by a voice;

instead they have to be overwhelmed by the sheer excitement of the spectacle before them. It is therefore not surprising that this type of acting stood some actresses in good stead. Lillian Gish, for example, who went on to become one of the leading stars of the silent screen, pays tribute to David Griffith in her autobiography, *The Movies, Mr. Griffith and Me* first published in 1970 when she states "Mr Griffith always emphasized that the way to tell a story was with one's body and facial expressions" and says, "I learned from him to use my body and face quite impersonally to create effects, much as a painter uses paint on canvas." In this film, Blanche Sweet expresses her sexuality, not only for political reasons in saving her town, but also for erotic purposes arousing male sexual fantasies. It is not clear from her actions if she is personally taking a feminist stand and is making fun of the male fantasies of her audience.

While Judith has been engaged in the tent of Holofernes, we have been shown further tedious fighting scenes where a young warrior of Bethulia leads a brave dash for water at the wells, only to be attacked by the Assyrians with chariots and horses. This incident, inserted by Griffith, only serves to emphasize his idea of the bravery of male supremacy, but is not recorded in the Book of Judith. We are also given glimpses of the citizens starving and dying in Bethulia. In the film Judith's dramatic return to the town, accompanied by her maid with the head, the elders greeting her at the town gates and the excitement of the crowds, are all treated in a rather low key. We are not shown the bloody head of Holofernes hanging from the walls of the town which as the ultimate objective of her endeavors acted not only as a trophy of war but as a deterrent to the Assyrians. This act had been accomplished, as she herself said, "by the hand of a woman" (Judith 13:15), and the head hung there on her instructions. Griffith omitted this gruesome image because he probably did not wish to stress the feistiness of this coura-geous heroine but wanted to concentrate on the meek and feminine aspects of her demeanor. The film ends with the citizens paying homage to Judith while she smiles triumphantly at the cinema audience.

Judith, having delivered her town from the Assyrians and killed the enemy, can be regarded as the savior of her people. We would therefore have expected to find a much more triumphal ending to the film. Certainly the last chapters of the Book of Judith give us a very full account of the joy and relief of the citizens; the women blessing her, performing dances in her honor, crowning themselves with olive branches, wearing garlands, and singing hymns. It is significant that the women and Judith have been specifically singled out in the biblical story and that it was they who led the dance, the men of Israel following. Judith is observing the precedent and tradition set by Miriam, sister of Moses and Aaron, who after having defeated their enemies (Exodus 15:20) took a tambourine and went out with all the women following her with tambourines and dancing. Sadly there is no real sense of triumph or rejoicing expressed in the film, so that much of the triumphant nature of the narrative is lost.

How far does this film investigate the issues of gender and sexuality? How should we assess this film from a feminist point of view? On analysis, I do not think that it makes any concessions to women and can in no way be described as "feminist," although the heroine is an inspiration to women. She is not "subordinated, oppressed or exploited"[30] as many women are in films up to as late as the 1970s. The film is still deeply rooted into the old-fashioned clichés that women are here for men's pleasure. This is most obvious in the scene where Holofernes lusts after Judith and she falls in love with him. She is represented as the ideal image of womanhood, beautiful, young, glamorous, and shapely— immaculately dressed, bedecked in gorgeous jewels, while Holofernes remains the dominant patriarchal figure. That is, until she turns the tables on him and decapitates him, but even then her feminine persona never slips. Judith transgresses the male role but this is not translated into cinematic terms. The silent films of the time were not intended specifically for women but for mixed and mainly male audiences. The main characters do not engage much with the audience and their presence is more or less ignored. The days of Sigmund Freud's ideas on scopophilia which refers predominantly to the male gaze of Hollywood films and the joy of objectifying women as objects to be gazed at and the pleasure which they derive from looking (especially in the cinema) was not discussed by Freud until he wrote about it in his book *Instinct and their Vicissitudes* in 1915. The film, it can be said, uses the standard images of masculinity and femininity of the time with Holofernes as the bold and strong leader and Judith as the sexual temptress, albeit rather vapidly portrayed. This is what we would expect, because the producer was male, identifying with the male rather than with the virtuous female heroine Judith. The Judith here can never be convincing to modern day feminists because Sweet lacks the necessary toughness which we associate with this apocryphal heroine. This Judith is in no way the sexually aware, devouring female (castrating female) that Sigmund Freud wrote about. In some quarters the story of Judith and Holofernes can be seen as one symbolizing the fear of castration (a basic masculine fear). This becomes more poignant when it is the woman who is cast in the role of the aggressor. In this connection we must not forget that the hero of male masochism in Leopold von Sacher-Masoch's story *Venus in Furs*

(1870) has a fantasy where he imagines that he is Holofernes, victimized by the sensuous Judith.[31] Nevertheless, there is perhaps a message here directed at the male in the audience, namely that "he must resist the allure of women who will seduce, betray, humiliate and destroy him."[32]

We now also need to consider what part Judith played to the women in society at the end of the nineteenth and beginning of the twentieth century. What role did she occupy in the women's movement of the time? Was she an inspiration and would a film such as *Judith of Bethulia* have had any relevance? Yet no attempt has been made to explore contemporary social issues or gender roles at a time when the women's suffragette movement was at its height. Joanna Southcote stands almost alone in acknowledging Judith as an icon of womanhood. We have accounts of women writing to the "Sisterhood" at the turn of the nineteenth century about the freedom of being able go out alone or with friends unchaperoned, of swimming and even daringly venturing out at night.[33] These emancipated women who ventured out into the domain of men showed the same sense of freedom and daring as Judith did when she left the camp of the Assyrians with the head of Holofernes in the early morning just as dawn was breaking. This was also the era when many intrepid women explored the world under very harsh and inhospitable conditions, braving the weather and wild animals, like Mary Kingsley, who travelled up the Gabonese Ogowe River in 1894 fighting off crocodiles. Judith should have been a prototype to Victorian women feminists but they did not take her as an example. One of the main reasons was that the Apocrypha was omitted from all Anglo-American Bibles by 1860 and subsequently banished from the liturgy when the Book of Prayer was revised.[34] The Book of Judith was therefore no longer read and had it not been for Aldrich's play of 1904, Griffith may not have been inspired to produce his film *Judith of Bethulia*. It was not until the 1970s that feminist writers such as Germaine Greer[35] and women art historians—Linda Nochlin,[36] Griselda Pollock, and Mary D. Garrard amongst others—began to question how women were perceived both as artists and subjects in an art historical context. Such questioning also included studies on the female biblical figures: Judith,[37] Delilah,[38] Susanna,[39] Esther,[40] and Bathsheba.[41]

So why was this film based on the biblical narrative ever made? In the first instance, we have seen that it was produced to challenge other epic films coming out of Europe; it was a personal feat for D.W. Griffith: it was spectacular in its use of horses, chariots, costumes, props, and scenery and it employed the best American actors of the day. Margarita Stocker suggests that it was "the lost pastoral world of the Old South, and the war that ruined her" which attracted Griffith to the story of Judith.[42]

Although this film is silent it speaks to the audience, not so much through the captions, which often bear little resemblance to the text and dialogue, written in a kind of pseudo-biblical language, for example, when Holofernes says to Judith "come with me to Nineveh, the city of the Gods" and she replies "let me be thy hand maid alone for tonight" but through psychological realism expressed by the actors, especially Blanche Sweet. The filming of her faltering gestures, as she wrestles with her conscience in the decapitation scene, must rank as one of the most sublime moments of early film photography. Judith masterly diffuses the tension motivated by her sense of justice and the audience are able to heave a sigh of relief and relax. She has now successfully completed her task with masculine strength and the female Hollywood audiences of 1914 were now happy that they had "the feisty heroines (role models)" which they craved.[43] The film features very effective organ music which creates an atmosphere echoing the mood of the actions of the film—fast and loud for the battle scenes, sensuously Oriental for the bacchanalian revelries and slower for the more moving and touching moments— composed and arranged by Gaylord Carter and performed on a Preston M. Fleet Wurlitzer Organ.

For all its faults, this film, which "was the first ever full length Hollywood motion picture,"[44] certainly makes a contribution to twentieth-century visual culture: its historical importance should not be overlooked. Without it, would we have had the magnificent biblical films such as *Samson and Delilah* (1949) and *The Ten Commandments* (1950) by directors and producers like Cecil B. de Mille in the format in which they were produced? The unique challenge of the Judith film was to compete with other films coming out of Europe at this time. So why have there been no other films about Judith? Once this silent film had been released and seen, it was shelved. European directors were now producing longer and more exhilarating talking films. The simple truth is that the Judith story proved to be too short. D.W. Griffith had done his best to spin out the narrative with a non-biblical subplot and bloody scenes of battle and sieges; however, audiences were now much more exacting and wanted longer films with a greater basis of historical facts. However, we must not forget that in the end Griffith gave the film punters of the time what they wanted: namely, action, attempted seduction, vengeance, deception, and the despatching of schemers and villains.

Notes

1. Margarita Stocker, *Judith Sexual Warrior Women and Power in Western Culture* (New Haven/London: Yale University Press, 1998), 1.

2. Alan Dundes, *Narrative Structure in the Book of Judith*, ed. Luis Alonso-Schökel, Protocol Series of the Colloquies of the Center for Hermeneutical Studies in Hellenistic and Modern Culture (Berkley: Graduate Theological Union), 1974, 28–29.

3. Quoted in Carey A. Moore, *The Anchor Bible, Judith, a New Translation with Introduction and Commentary* (New York: Doubleday and Company, 1985), 46.

4. See my unpublished thesis: A Comparative Study between the Images of Judith and Holofernes and David and Goliath in the History of European Art with Special Reference to the Period 1400–1700, University of Glasgow, 1999 and Per Jonas Nordhagen, *The Frescoes of John VII (A.D. 705–707 in Santa Maria Antiqua in Rome* (Rome: "L'Erma" di Bretschneider, 1968).

5. The artist Vivienne Licudi-Fry studied at the Heatherley School of Fine Art and has exhibited in Europe.

6. There may, of course, be other more recent paintings of Judith of which I am unaware.

7. All the quotations from the Book of Judith are taken from *The Holy Bible containing the Old and New Testaments with the Apocryphal/Deuterocanonical Books*, New Revised Standard Version (Glasgow: Collins, 1989).

8. Sandra M. Gilbert and Susan Guber, *The Madwoman in the Attic: The Woman Writer and the Nineteenth-Century Literary Imagination* (New Haven/London: Yale University Press, 1979), 23.

9. Thomas B. Aldrich, *Judith of Bethulia: A Tragedy* (Boston/New York: Houghton Mifflin & Co., 1904).

10. To our twenty-first-century eyes Harron may appear puny but with his photogenic good looks he was considered one of the leading "movie" stars of his time and a favorite of D.W. Griffith.

11. David Shipman, *The Story of Cinema: An illustrated history*, Vol. 1, *From the Beginnings to Gone with the Wind* (London: Hodder and Stoughton, 1982), 45.

12. David Shipman, *The Story of Cinema: An illustrated history*, Vol. 2, *From Citizen Kane to the Present Day* (London: Hodder and Stoughton, 1984), 537.

13. In cinematic terms this means the settings, costumes, props, composition, and the way in which the action moves within the frame.

14. Margarita Stocker, "On the Frontier: Judith and Esther in the Myths of America," essay in *Borders, Boundaries and the Bible*, ed. Martin O'Kane (Sheffield: Sheffield Academic Press, 2002), 252.

15. Here the biblical story is inaccurate because the historical Nebuchadnezzar did not rule the Assyrians. He was the Babylonian king who took Jerusalem in 587 BC.

16. Arphaxad was never king of the Medes.

17. He is referred to as "prince" in the captions throughout the film.

18. William K. Everson, *American Silent Film* (New York: Oxford University Press, 1978 [originally published]). Paperback edition—New York: Da Capo Press, 1998, 73.

19. Shipman, *The Story of Cinema*, Vol. 1, 45.

20. I extend my thanks to Dr. Jan Willem van Henten of Amsterdam University for his stimulating thoughts on the fighting scenes in the film and for drawing my attention to his essay "Judith as an Alternative Leader: A Rereading of Judith 7–13," in *A Feminist Companion to Esther, Judith and Susanna, The Feminist Companion to the Bible 7*, ed. A. Brenner (Sheffield: Sheffield Academic Press, 1995), 224–252.

21. Linda Nochlin, *Women, Art, and Power and Other Essays* (London: Thames and Hudson, 1991), 170.

22. See Toni Craven, *Artistry and Faith in the Book of Judith* (California: Scholars Press, 1983), 121.

23. Such as the painting entitled "The Penance of the Magdalene" by the Spanish artist El Greco executed between 1579 and 1586, now in the Nelson-Atkins Museum and Art Gallery in Kansas City, U.S.A. For an illustration see Santiago Alcoplea, *El Greco* (Barcelona: Ediciones Poligrafa, S.A., 1990), plate 26.

24. This was Griffith's brilliant way of disguising the difference in height between the small stature of Henry B. Walthall and the tall Blanche Sweet.

25. Comment made by Paul Winter, *The Interpreter's Dictionary of the Bible*, ed. G. A. Buttrick, 4 vols. (Nashville: Abingdon Press, 1962), 1024.

26. Karl Brown, *Adventures with D.W. Griffith* (New York: Signet, 1973), 21.

27. Jack Lodge, *Movies of the Silent Years* (New York: Orbis, 1984), 27.

28. This is an example of an element that shows that the narrative dates from the Hellenistic period.
29. See Alessandra Comini, "Vampires, Virgins and Voyeurs in Imperial Vienna," in *Women as Sex Object*, ed. T. Hess and L. Nochlin (New York: Newsweek, 1972), 206–221.
30. Annette Kuhn, *Women's Pictures: Feminism and Cinema* (London/Boston: Routledge and K. Paul, 1982), 4.
31. Leopold von Sacher-Masoch, *Venus in Furs*, English translation (London: Merlin Press, 1969), 21–22.
32. See Norma Broude and Mary D. Garrard, "Introduction: Feminism and Art History," in *Feminism and Art History Questioning the Litany*, ed. Norma Broude and Mary D. Garrard (New York: Harper & Row, 1982), 6.
33. Deborah Cherry, *Beyond the Frame, Feminism and Visual Culture, Britain 1850–1900* (London: Routledge, 2000), 28.
34. See R.C.D. Jasper, *Prayer Book Revision in England 1800–1900* (London: SPCK, 1954).
35. Germaine Greer, *The Obstacle Race: The Fortunes of Women Painters and Their Work* (New York: Secker and Warburg, 1979).
36. This movement was led by Linda Nochlin with her essay "Why Have There Been No Great Women Artists?" in *Women, Art, and Power and Other Essays* (London: Thames and Hudson, 1991), 145–178. There had been earlier studies. For a full bibliography and sources see Whitney Chadwick, *Women, Art, and Society*, 3rd edition (London: Thames and Hudson, 2002), 467–485.
37. Elizabeth Philpot, essay "Judith and Holofernes: Changing Images in the History of Art" in *Translating Religious Texts*, ed. D. Jasper (New York: Macmillan Press, 1993) and Elizabeth Philpot, essay "The Triumph of Judith—Power and Display in Art," in *Talking it Over: Perspectives on Women and Religion 1993–95*, ed. Alison Jasper and Alastair Hunter (Glasgow: St. Mungo Press, 1993).
38. Madlyn Millner Kahr, essay "Delilah," in *Feminism and Art History, Questioning the Litany*, ed. Norma Broude and Mary D. Garrard (New York: Harper & Row, 1982).
39. Mieke Bal, *Reading "Rembrandt": Beyond the Word-Image Opposition* (Cambridge: Cambridge University Press, 1991) and Elizabeth Philpot, essay "Susanna: Indecent Attraction/Fatal Exposure," in *Believing in the Text*, Religions and Discourse Series, ed. David Jasper and George Newlands with Darlene Bird Peter (Bern: Lang, 2004).
40. Linda Day, *Three Faces of a Queen, Characterisation in the Books of Esther* (Sheffield: Sheffield Academic Press, 1995).
41. See Mary D. Garrard, *Artemisia Gentileschi The Image of the Female Hero in Italian Baroque Art* (Princeton: Princeton University Press, 1989).
42. Griffith's own father had been a general who had fought in the American Civil War and had been wounded five times. See J. Hart, ed., *The Man Who Invented Hollywood: The Autobiography of D.W. Griffith* (Louisville, KY: Touchstone Publishing Company, 1972).
43. Stocker, *Judith Sexual Warrior Women*, 213.
44. Stocker, "On the Frontier," 229.

Works Cited

Aldrich, Thomas B. *Judith of Bethulia: A Tragedy*. Boston/New York: Houghton Mifflin & Co., 1904.
Alcoplea, Santiago. *El Greco*. Barcelona: Ediciones Poligrafa, S.A., 1990.
The Holy Bible. New Revised Standard Version. Glasgow: Collins, 1989.
Bal, Mieke. *Reading "Rembrandt": Beyond the Word-Image Oposition*. Cambridge: Cambridge University Press, 1991.
Broude, Norma, and Mary D. Garrard. "Introduction: Feminism and Art History." In *Feminism and Art History Questioning the Litany*. Ed. N. Broude and M.D. Garrard. New York: Harper & Row, 1982.
Brown, Karl. *Adventures with D.W. Griffith*. New York: Signet, 1973.
Bruzzi, Stella. *Undressing Cinema*. London: Routledge, 1997.
Chadwick, Whitney. *Women, Art, and Society*. London: Thames and Hudson, 1990.

Cherry, Deborah. *Beyond the Frame, Feminism and Visual Culture, Britain 1850–1900*. London: Routledge, 2000.

Comini, Alessandra. "Vampires, Virgins and Voyeurs in Imperial Vienna." In *Women as Sex Object*. Art News Annual XXXVIII. Ed. T. Hess and L. Nochlin. New York: Newsweek, 1972.

Craven, Toni. *Artistry and Faith in the Book of Judith*. Chico, CA: Scholars Press, 1983.

Day, Linda. *Three Faces of a Queen, Characterisation in the Books of Esther*. Sheffield: Sheffield Academic Press, 1995.

Everson, William K. *American Silent Film*. New York: Oxford University Press, 1978.

Freud, Sigmund. "Instincts and Their Vicissitudes." In *The Standard Edition of the Works of Sigmund Freud*. Ed. James Strachey. 24 vols. London: Hogarth, 1953–1974.

Garrard, Mary D. *Artemisia Gentileschi the Image of the Female Hero in Italian Baroque Art*. Princeton: Princeton University Press, 1989.

Gilbert, Sandra M., and Susan Guber. *The Madwoman in the Attic: The Woman Writer and the Nineteenth-Century Literary Imagination*. New Haven/London: Yale University Press, 1979.

Gish, Lillian. *The Movies, Mr. Griffith and Me*. London: Columbus, 1988.

Greer, Germaine. *The Obstacle Race: The Fortunes of Women Painters and Their Work*. New York: Secker and Warburg, 1979.

Hart, J. Ed. *The Man Who Invented Hollywood: The Autobiography of D. W. Griffith*. Louisville, KY: Touchstone Publishing Company,1972.

van Henten, J.W. "Judith as an Alternative Leader: A Rereading of Judith 7–13." In *A Feminist Companion to Esther, Judith and Susanna, The Feminist Companion to the Bible 7*, ed. A. Brenner. Sheffield: Sheffield Academic Press, 1995.

Jasper, R.C.D. *Prayer Book Revision in England 1800–1900*. London: SPCK, 1954.

Kahr, Madlyn Millner. "Delilah." In *Feminism and Art History, Questioning the Litany*. Ed. N. Broude and M.D. Garrard. New York: Harper & Row, 1982.

Kuhn, Annette. *Women's Pictures: Feminism and Cinema*. London/Boston: Routledge and K. Paul, 1982.

Lodge, Jack. *Movies of the Silent Years*. New York: Orbis, 1984.

Moore, Carey A. *The Anchor Bible, Judith, a New Translation with Introduction and Commentary*. New York: Doubleday and Company, 1985.

Nochlin, Linda. *Women, Art, and Power and Other Essays*. London: Thames and Hudson, 1991.

Nordhagen, Per Jonas. *The Frescoes of John VII (A.D. 705–707 in Santa Maria Antigua in Rome*. Rome: "L'Erma" di Bretschneider, 1968.

Philpot, Elizabeth. "Judith and Holofernes: Changing Images in the History of Art." In *Translating Religious Texts*. Ed. D. Jasper. New York: Macmillan Press, 1993.

——. "The Triumph of Judith—Power and Display in Art." In *Talking it Over: Perspectives on Women and Religion 1993–95*. Ed. Alison Jasper and Alastair Hunter. Glasgow: St. Mungo Press, 1996.

——. A Comparitive Study between the Images of Judith and Holofernes and David and Goliath in the History of European Art with Special Reference to the period 1400–1700. Unpublished thesis. Glasgow: University of Glasgow, 1999.

——. "Susanna: Indecent Attraction/Fatal Exposure." In *Believing in the Text*. Religions and Discourse Series. Ed. David Jasper and George Newlands with Darlene Bird. Bern: Peter Lang, 2004.

von Sacher Masoch, Leopold. *Venus in Furs*. English translation. London: Merlin Press, 1969.

Shipman, David. *The Story of Cinema: an illustrated history*. Vol. 1. *From the Beginnings to Gone with the Wind*. London: Hodder and Stoughton, 1982.

——. *The Story of Cinema: an illustrated history*. Vol. 2. *From Citizen Kane to the Present Day*. London: Hodder and Stoughton, 1984.

Stocker, Margarita. *Judith Sexual Warrior Women and Power in Western Culture*. New Haven/London: Yale University Press, 1998.

——. "On the Frontier: Judith and Esther in the Myths of America." In *Borders, Boundaries and the Bible*. Ed. Martin O'Kane. Sheffield: Sheffield Academic Press, 2002.

CHAPTER TWELVE

Revolting Fantasies: Reviewing the Cinematic Image as Fruitful Ground for Creative, Theological Interpretations in the Company of Julia Kristeva

ALISON JASPER

Introduction

Are the movies good for us? In her book, *Intimate Revolt: The Powers and Limits of Psychoanalysis*, Julia Kristeva (2002a) defends what she calls a revolutionary culture whose mode and purpose is a liberating process of questioning and interpretation, derived from both philosophy and psychoanalysis, which challenges what Guy Debord has defined as the "society of the spectacle"—a society dominated by deadening, stereotypical images or representations which paralyze our imagination and lead to the banalization of evil and horror in the service of global capitalism. In this piece I attempt to apply some of Kristeva's insights about a revolutionary culture of interrogation and interpretation to two commercially successful films—*The Silence of the Lambs* (Jonathan Demme 1991) and *Interview with the Vampire* (Neil Jordan 1994)—in order to test her conclusions. I argue that Kristeva's understanding of revolution or revolutionary culture contributes to what I have described as a "theological" process of making—provisional—meaning.

Key Words

Fantasy, intertextuality, revolution, society of the spectacle, subject/
speaking subject/*sujet en process.*

★ ★ ★

What makes sense today is not the future (as communism and providential
religions claimed) but revolt: that is the questioning and displacement of
the past. The future, if it exists, depends on it (Kristeva 2002a, 5).

> by displaying evil, does the cinema take part in another mystification,
> another banalization of evil? (Kristeva 2002a, 79)

Introduction: Kristeva and Revolution

The French writer Julia Kristeva connects the intimate, therapeutic
encounter of psychoanalysis with the process of challenge and change
that also describes political revolution (Kristeva 2002a, 3; 2002b, 38).
She suggests that the work done by the analyst and analysand can
become the means of "revolting"[1] the imagination and healing, to some
degree, our psychic maladies, by creating and interpreting a language of
fantasy in order to contain or at least mediate otherwise inexpressible,
destructive emotions. Kristeva's psychoanalytical approach builds on
theoretical assumptions also familiar within reader-response theory.
In the most general terms reader-response theory shifts the emphasis
from the text—essay, performance, narrative, film—to the reader or
interpreter who *engages with* the text[2]. In her psychoanalytical work,
Kristeva focuses on the importance of creating both stories or fantasies[3]
and interpretation, balancing in her references to intertextuality[4] the
claims of writer/artist, reader, and context. But her work is distinctively
psychoanalytical in the sense that these processes of creation and interpretation are never merely a matter of literary analysis. For her, language
is always under pressure from the semiotic,[5] nonlinguistic, bodily
energies and drives of the human psyche; therefore, telling stories, interpretation and response to the text all reveal something about a human
subjectivity that is stressed and formed at the boundaries between conscious fantasies and other imaginative projects, and the realm of the
unconscious. Interpretation is no simple debate about authorial intent
versus readerly reception but, more significantly, it is a means for dealing
with, decoding or redirecting the desires, fears, and aggressions of the
unconscious in creative ways that account for these unresolved tensions.

However, Kristeva goes beyond the hope, as a practicing psychoanalyst herself, that she can help the analysand maintain a subjective integrity and make some sense of their life. In her more philosophical work, she describes this process of revolution and fomenting revolt, of question and critique, as also a vital cultural necessity. The subjective richness and revolutionary possibilities of the imagination—sustained for all of us by the work of writers and artists for example—are well worth exploring on their own terms, but more than this they are vital for our cultural survival. Kristeva's objectives are themselves political and revolutionary. Confronted both in clinical practice and more widely by a psychic malaise expressed in terms of passive consumerism and nameless anxiety,[6] she champions the culture of revolution[7]: "The future, if it exists, depends on it" (Kristeva 2002a, 5).

Could contemporary theology have something to gain from this revolutionary approach rather than regarding the work of psychoanalysis as invariably antagonistic as has been one tendency in the past?[8] If we can accept theology as a process of articulating and interpreting/reading fantasies as Kristeva understands the term, then perhaps we could see some analogy at the very least with the task of articulating meanings and truths that has, in fact, always been the work of theologians. Moreover, this theological work has itself always been characterized by upheaval and revolution, interrogation, critique, and reformation as "revolting" theologians dispute passionately with each other. Of course, Kristeva's own work is unambiguously non-realist.[9] But her discussion nevertheless reflects authentically theological concerns with meaning, truth, and freedom. Anti-transcendentalist, atheistic philosopher through she is, Kristeva herself continually weaves dazzling theological fragments into her language and images, returning readers to a revolting, nauseating, and dizzying sphere of loose theological ends they might have thought would be finished and tied off by such a "secular" figure. But of course language is never merely incidental as Kristeva and all other good psychoanalysts, poets, and novelists know. The interpreter and analyst must take note when Kristeva speaks of revolution in terms of a "return" which she compares to St. Augustine's focus on consciousness as self-knowledge or return to oneself (Kristeva 2002a, 6), or when she writes about the process of introspection as "strictly speaking, resurrectional" (125). Elsewhere in her work—in her extraordinary essay on the Virgin Mary and motherhood (Kristeva 1986), in her discussion of love and psychoanalysis (Kristeva 1987) as well as in her conversations with Catherine Clément (Clément and Kristeva 2001)—the saints and the doctors of the Catholic Church are visible and recurring threads in the matrix she weaves. Ultimately it is liberation (both for and from) she seeks to achieve (Kristeva 2002a, 67). And the means to this end is a liturgy of revolt/return which begins and begins again in the polyvalent intertextualities of the literary or, perhaps sometimes, of the cinematic imagination.

What theologians should be able to take from her work, I believe, is an urgent impetus to attend to the stories and fantasies of contemporary culture with a little more confidence, recognizing their potential to describe a meaningful process and support a theological interpretation, even if they do not appear to be directly concerned with either the narratives or moral framework of a particular religious tradition. In order to begin to sketch out the powers and limitations of a theological approach on these terms, I want to discuss the extent to which the cinema—as one important expression of contemporary culture—can be a fruitful ground for developing revolutionary fantasies and theological interpretations.

My question then, in the broadest terms, is whether popular films— narratives that are widely familiar today to wo/men across the globe—can help us to live well by giving us the means to articulate our individual and collective motivations and subject them to interpretation; to engage with them in the process of making or making better and more adequate meanings. Or, alternatively, do they merely contribute to Debord's "society of the spectacle"? In other words, do popular films deal in the kind of empty and boring images or representations that reflect not a lively human struggle with tough resilient structures born out of genuine human experience and a previous revolutionary imagination—for example, the Christian Church or democratic politics—but rather the needs of a mindless, disembodied, alienating process of capitalist production? As case studies, I focus on two commercially successful and widely re/viewed films *The Silence of the Lambs*, (Jonathan Demme 1991) and *Interview with the Vampire* (Neil Jordan 1994). Kristeva suggests that cinematic images potentially allow us to formulate fantasies more subtly than any other media. Cinematic, specular images provide the means to "more supple, less controlled, riskier" (Kristeva 2002a, 69) representations of these fantasies, closer to primal and unconscious desires, because the visual is the first articulation of the drives.[10] Kristeva responds to the subtlety and riskiness of cinematic images with the hope that they will invite a more intense and far-reaching interpretation. Taking in all aspects of sound, light, music, rhythm, and the somatic responses they generate, she hopes they will bring about an engagement between film and viewer and by "formulating the phantasmatic narrative and interpreting it . . . dissolve the symptom" (64) which is the passive resistance to revolution that leaves us impoverished as both individuals and societies.

However, what is crucial for Kristeva is the relationship between the nonlinguistic affective and bodily dimensions of human subjectivity and the role of language. What qualifies her enthusiasm about the cinematic image is the fear that by evading the verbal path (68), images which invoke these nonverbal elements can sometimes seduce the viewer, merely appeasing our desire for happiness or its "sadomasochistic flip side" (79). Finding that a presentation of desire, evil or sadomasochistic motivations resonates strongly, there is a danger that the viewer will be trapped at the level of this response rather than moving outside the affect rooted in a nonlinguistic and somatic context into language (67)[11] in order to give that affect symbolic significance and allow the viewer to become involved in the processes of giving and challenging meanings. So within this theoretical approach, a film or a series of cinematic images succeeds in being truly revolutionary only in so far as it does not merely mesmerise and pacify.[12] Superficial, stereotypical, boring, and banal representations fail to provide the viewer with the means to engage symbolically—that is fundamentally in terms of language—with their otherwise inexpressible fears and desires. These exhausted representations serve simply to trap us, and we remain, in respect of our viewing, alienated from ourselves and our society. Currently, without ideology or strong structures of family, church or political party to frame discussions, Kristeva believes that people literally have no language to "express what they feel about life, about sex, about their friends" so that there can be "no conversation to absorb the psychic malaise" (Riding 2001, B11). In other words, in her reservations about film, Kristeva fears that in "the society of the spectacle" the images produced simply do not "revolt" the imagination sufficiently to stimulate us into finding new symbolic forms to compensate for these losses. All they do is—effectively—squeeze out of discredited structures the last drops of affective content while taking no measures to create new ones. Cinematic images can be seen as fantasies— their construction comparable with the way in which we mold and contain the emotional traumas of our lives as subjects. But she argues that what we need in order to construct useful fantasies is not a series of ready-made, off the peg images but the kind of interrogative vocation she identifies in the work of many European philosophers. It is, she says, an intuition found in Descartes, Leibniz, Heidegger, and Sartre, all of whom are driven to ask and answer—in different ways, of course— fundamental questions about being and nothingness (Kristeva 2002a, 142). Tentatively drawing connections between this search for meaning on the grander philosophical scale with her own experience of psycho-analysis, she concludes that our fundamental conduct and freedom is to question the "substrata of nothingness" (142) to which the philosophers give varied systematic expression. It is this questioning of and resultant risky freedom in interpretation to which she aspires in her own revolutionary work.

One way to look at the positive potential of the specular image of the cinema, then, is as a way of conjuring up and then demystifying potentially destructive emotions by bringing them to consciousness in a form of fantastic representation and subjecting them to interpretation as questioning. In the process, structures—albeit provisional and challengeable—of meaning are formed. Within the context of cinema, Kristeva suggests that this takes place most effectively when there is a kind of "distancing" established for the viewer, for example, by irony or satire; the demystification of Hitler's anti-Semitic "acting out" in Charlie Chaplin's *The Great Dictator* (1940) for example, ". . . when the image, saturated with evil, also allows itself to laugh, identity collapses and all dictators are toppled" (Kristeva 2002a, 79–80). In the end, though Kristeva remains suspicious of cinematic representations, she also thinks that films—at least some films—do have the potential to free us, "[p]rovided that, saturated with evil, the cinema does not only take us for a ride but makes us keep our distance" (79).

The Silence of the Lambs

So can we say that Demme's very popular film *Silence of the Lambs*[13] has what it takes to inspire creative responses in terms of a contemporary discourse about embodiment and death, for example, perhaps stimulating the imagination and interrogating and interpreting an inherited Christian theology of these things? Or does it merely serve up exhausted images that lock us in the seductive gaze of appeasement and prevent us from articulating anything to compensate and console us for our underlying anxieties and losses? Does the film encourage revolution by making us keep our distance, keep our eyes open, keep our feet on the ground? This film was based on Thomas Harris' 1988 novel, *Silence of the Lambs* and is one in a steady stream of films and TV docudramas about serial killers. This cinematic genre probably owes its origins to Alfred Hitchcock who, in *Psycho*[14] (1960), first brought together the elements of a psychological thriller and a horror film. Hannibal Lecter, a sociopathic ex-psychiatrist, kills without remorse and eats bodies or, at least, the organs he extracts from his victims as trophies. Buffalo Bill, a serial killer, following a murderously misogynistic impulse, sets traps like a hunter and covets the transformational abilities of the moth. He wants to transform himself into a woman not by shedding his own skin but by harvesting the hide, shedding the skin of his female victims. Clarice Starling, a trainee FBI agent, orphaned as a youngster, recounts her poignant childhood fantasy of saving a lamb from slaughter that seems to reflect a traumatic response to her father's undeserved and violent death. In other words, the film doesn't, on the surface of things, seem to shy away from the darker or deeper emotions that motivate our actions and relationships. But if we are to keep our distance as viewer, we need a skilfully crafted film which makes us engage on every level. We need to respond to the images as they invoke the unconscious, semiotic, nonlinguistic realm out of which rich fantasies arise, but we need to be encouraged or enabled to articulate or consciously to organize our responses, to demystify what we see and give it—provisional—meaning.

In *Silence of the Lambs* the language of psychology or behavioral science is used self-consciously. This discourse is now widely recognised in Eurocentric cultures as a means of understanding and interpreting human actions and motivations that seem, on the surface of things, inexplicable, or monstrous. In other words, it does appear to provide us with a structure for making meaning. The FBI investigation that represents the film's main narrative structure focuses on Starling's attempts to get Lecter to provide her with a psychological profile of the serial murderer called Buffalo Bill and Lecter's attempts to get Starling to trade intimate details of her own life in return. So Lecter's "analysis" of both Buffalo Bill and Starling encourage us, to some extent, to demystify the images of horror and evil presented in the film by seeing them as symptoms of psychological tendencies or disturbances. However, arguably, this presentation does not challenge us to reinterpret or change our way of viewing and interpreting to any great extent. There is little attempt, for example, in the film actually to link the appalling Lecter to more sympathetic human emotions or motivations in a way that would make his human complexity more evident or the definitions of "insanity" or "criminal" more provisional and challenging. Though he is sometimes shown as the tormented victim of sadistic officials, or publicly restrained within a harness that has the appearance of a medieval instrument of torture, this, arguably, contributes as much to the pleasures of seeing him eventually get his revenge on his tormentors than it does to making him seem a less monstrous or a more complex human figure. Perhaps we are being encouraged to see some human significance in the bond that develops between Lecter and Starling in the course of the hunt for the killer. But this contributes equally well to the picture of him as a dangerous, manipulative, and inhumanly prescient predator. Much less effort is put into the characterization of Buffalo Bill who comes across as irredeemably evil, inarticulate, leering, and ugly, a stereotypical Beast! So, in the end, psychological profiling seems more like an aid to building narrative tension and increasing the fascination of horror—by providing us as viewers with a lot more evidence of Buffalo Bill's murderous career—than as a means of helping us keep our distance by problematizing a stereotypical mystification of evil. Moreover there is no attempt to question or give meaning to our motivations as viewers as in a much more off-beat serial killer film of 1987, *Henry: Portrait of a Serial Killer*. In this far less comfortable film, the murderers are seen filming their violent murder of a whole family and subsequently rerunning the tape for a second view (Taubin 1993, 126–127). This forces viewers into a challenging self-reflexivity which is more likely to pose the question "Why am I watching this?"!

On the other hand Starling interviews the psychopathic psychiatrist Hannibal Lecter with the conviction that she can know the answers, that she can solve the riddles he sets before her and come to such understanding that she can liberate the latest victim from death, which is one of the reasons, of course, why Kristeva adopted the genre of the detective story in her own ventures as a novelist.[15] It preserves the vision of a question that is worth asking and that can, in some sense, be answered. Moreover, as both a young woman in a man's world and as a persistent and independent-minded police officer, Starling's role, in the context of this darkly sexualized material, does, in some ways, resist representation in predictably pornographic terms. To some degree it does take up a revolutionary modality, challenging the political representations of patriarchy. Certainly it is made abundantly clear within the film that Starling's initial involvement with Lecter is highly exploitative in sexual terms; she is set up as bait to tempt Lecter to give up the information the FBI need. Starling's resistance both to female stereotypes in general and to these exploitative moves within the story is heightened within the film version by the strong and focused representation of actress Jodi Foster. As Starling, Foster is a thought-provoking combination of female vulnerability and strength. The film revisits, returns to, and to some extent revolves around her fantasies of traumatic loss—which refer centrally to the death of her father caused by a violent attack which is sustained in the course of his work as a night marshal—and alongside the violent brutal images of death and dismemberment, there are also images of Starling as a child with her father's body in an open coffin. Another illustration of this in some ways "counter-stereotypical" combination of vulnerability and strength has her seeking out conversation with a dangerous criminal, and she takes considerable risks to gain information in the context of her complex emotional need to save this new victim from death. So, in the sense that Foster's representation of Starling opens up a gap between the predictable exploitation of women's sexuality and a more nuanced discussion of female strengths, women's roles, and individual emotional motivations, the film does effectively employ types of distancing irony and analysis. Yet this distancing is not sustained throughout. The film ends with Dr. Lecter on the loose in pursuit of new ways to satisfy his unresolved and fascinating oral impulses rather than with the viewer having any greater understanding of Dr. Lecter or Buffalo Bill in their own psychic recesses or of the meaning of these impulses in human lives. Though we have built up quite a sympathetic picture of the police officer who chases the criminals, the mad men are still essentially just mad men. And neither, in a film overburdened with images of tortured, devoured bodies and death, are we any clearer about these matters. Though the possibility exists for exploring the perverse images of transformation and rebirth that characterize the Buffalo Bill themes of the film, their poetic, revolutionary, and theological possibilities are swamped in this narrative by the horror and ultimately the banality—empty because urelated to anything else—of the evil he enacts.

Interview with the Vampire

In Ann Rice's 1976 novel, *Interview with the Vampire*, adapted for cinema by Neil Jordan (1994), we once again track contemporary fantasies about death and the body. Like serial killers, vampires have featured frequently in the history of the cinema. Similarly, there has been a stream of vampire films, many of them versions or adaptations of Bram Stoker's 1897 novel, *Dracula*, beginning, perhaps, with the silent, *Nosferatu: A Symphony in Terror* (F. W. Murnau 1922). Fictional vampires and their needs are typically eroticized and frequently opposed in a very conscious way to the prohibitions of conventional Christian sexual morality. Blood figures in abundance, an endlessly fascinating, seeping, contaminating, death- and life-bearing bodily substance,[16] and apart from endless TV and cinematic vampire narratives, its erotic and/or death-driven attraction is attested in contemporary society, for example, both by the practice of consensual feeding on blood for sexual pleasure[17] and cutting as a form of self-harming. Vampires in *Interview with the Vampire* are promiscuously indiscriminate in choosing their victims, their drive to feed on the warm blood of the living lustfully overwhelming every other human impulse. The film heightens the play of this guiltily erotic preoccupation by setting the action against elaborate and sensuous eighteenth and nineteenth-century sets, with elegant, decorative costumes, interiors and mannered interactions, which by their very restraint seem to intensify their sensual promise and the impact of the

vampires' wildly unrestrained appetites. The same purpose of erotic inten-
sification seems powerfully signalled in the casting of Brad Pitt, Tom
Cruise, and Antonio Banderas, from Hollywood's first division of male sex
symbols in the early 1990s, as leading vampire characters.

In addition, of course, any vampire story invites us, theoretically
at any rate, to fantasize and thus explore our feelings about death.
In *Interview with the Vampire*, for example, the figure of Claudia, a child
rescued from a plague-ridden slum in New Orleans, only to be made a
child vampire by her monstrous guardians combines dark fantasies of
eternal death in life, with the revolutionary modality of feminist thinking and, in this case, feminist thinking about bodies as a primary site of
patriarchal oppression. Trapped in a child's body, Claudia is forced to
live out, as it seems in some sort of hellish perpetuity, the infantilization
of the stereotypically desirable female so incommensurate with her adult
mind and conscious desires. She enacts powerfully the experience of
limitation and frustration within a world dominated by masculinist
values and the male gaze, which it might not be too much to describe in
some cases precisely as "death in life."

The vampire story seems then, superficially at any rate, a suitable fantasy
with which to articulate any number of exciting, excluded, and frightening aspects of ourselves. Jordan's subject matter seems a potentially fruitful
place for fantasy and interrogation, dealing as it does so seductively with
desire and fear. But the question, once again, has to be whether the
director and his team of cinematographers, actors, and editors can help us
not simply to invoke the unconscious, semiotic, nonlinguistic realm out of
which rich fantasies arise, but to organize our responses, questioning and
demystifying what we see and giving it at least provisional meaning. Or is
this film, in the end, much more a collection of journalistic stereotypes
which deprive us "of the possibility of creating our own imagery, our
own imaginary scenarios" (Kristeva 2002a, 67), immobilizing us with a
fascinating trace of nonrepresented drives (Kristeva 2002a, 74)?

Both the film and the book appear to be concerned, to different degrees,
with questioning values and making provisional meanings, although in
Rice's novel an explicitly theological dimension—in a traditional Christian
sense—is far more in evidence than in the film. For example, the grief and
pain that drives Louis into the arms of his first vampire encounter is occa-
sioned in the book by the death of his brother, who sees visions of the
Virgin and the saints, and wants his brother to sell everything he has so that
he can give to the poor. When Louis refuses to take him seriously he takes
his own life and condemns Louis to all the intensity of revulsion, guilt, and
self-doubt amplified by doubts about any ultimate principle of goodness.

The narrative of the book, in other words, is concerned from the very beginning with Louis' crisis of faith. His life as vampire might be seen as an extended, obscene yet tragic salute toward the figure of a nonexistent God who alone can guarantee the innate nobility of his human nature. God is utterly abolished by a vampire who exists, meaninglessly, outside theological but not supernatural/paranormal parameters that condemn him to eternal life, mimicking divine immortality and Christian resurrection. Louis, the religious doubter, still struggles with the tempter in a world without God, in language echoing the words of 1 Corinthians 13: "You do not know your vampire nature. You are like an adult who, looking back on his childhood realizes that he never appreciated it . . . You no longer look 'through a glass darkly.' But you cannot pass back to the world of human warmth with your new eyes" (Rice 1996, 91).

However, although the film does not frame the discussion in such overtly Christian terms, it is clearly attempting to grapple with the more broadly interpretative, theological questions of making meaning in a world of collapsing values. This too is a narrative concerned with constant interrogation; it believes in asking questions in spite of every encouragement to give up and give in to meaninglessness. During the course of the film, the main narrator, the vampire of the title, describes his quest to discover others like himself and thus to discover whether he is human or vampire or something different from both. It is, like *The Silence of the Lambs*, or Kristeva's novel, *Possessions* (1999), an adventure of detection begun in the determination that the main protagonist can know. In this case the interiority of the vampire not only as a figure of evil but also of considerable complexity, who returns to his own motivations over and over again, is a much more central element within this film than is the case of *The Silence of the Lambs*. We are given the opportunity in this film to ask questions about what it means to be human rather than an exploitative, unscrupulous, remorseless vampire-like creature who uses others, draining them of warmth and sympathy and giving little if anything in return. We are drawn into this interior complexity partly through Brad Pitt's sympathetic portrayal of the vampire character Louis, which expresses both passionate self-doubt and loathing as well as tenderness and hope. But most obviously we find a way into the process of revolution and meaning-making by means of the distancing which is achieved by through the dramatic device of the title's interview. The narrative we watch is the visual counterpoint of an aural record we first see being recorded on tape by a young reporter one hot New Orleans night at the beginning of the film. We are invited, as both narrator and interviewer interrupt the narrative with reflection and conversation, continually to assess the status of the account and the sincerity of the participants and to assign them provisional meanings, rather than simply to abide within the film's powerful and highly seductive images of death and perverse desire in the constant darkness and artificial light of the vampires' world. In this way we can put some distance between ourselves and the cinematic images and engage in the more theological task of interrogating the subject in process and in flux (Kristeva 2002a, 124).

But once again, as in *Silence of the Lambs*, the distancing is not maintained consistently. At the end of *Interview with the Vampire*, a character from Louis' vampire narrative breaks into the account of the interview, dispelling its ambiguity and thus shaking us loose from the interpretative mode in which the fantasy of the vampire could be read and interrogated perhaps as a representation of the modern wo/man in search of meaning. Instead, it becomes one more representation of meaningless evil which thrills us with horror, but, wrenched out of its more subtly "distanced" context, no longer directs us to examine our own motivations or those of the film's characters.

Conclusion

The two films I have reviewed were chosen deliberately because they were commercially successful and reached a wide audience. They therefore seemed particularly suitable for interrogating Kristeva's argument that the specular images of cinema, as often as not, contribute more to the "society of the spectacle" as defined by Debord, than to generating revolt and revolution as a means of either cultural survival or acquiring self-knowledge. Ultimately, the application of Kristeva's critique to these two popular films reveals how they can and do invoke the unconscious, semiotic, nonlinguistic realm out of which rich fantasies arise, but that they do not always succeed in helping the viewer to organize their responses, through questioning and demystifying, in order to give these fantasies at least provisional meaning. Sometimes all they do is immobilize and disempower us with their presentation of the banality of evil, desire, fear, or aggression. The success of Kristeva's revolutionary methodology, which I also link with what I call a theological project of making provisional meaning, depends, within the context of cinematic images, upon the skill of the filmmakers in helping us to "keep our distance." This can be done through irony, humor, or by drawing the viewer's attention explicitly to their own role, allowing them consciously to appreciate the need for and to own the process of "readerly" interpretation. In other words, Kristeva's notion of revolution includes or assumes the revolutionary vocation of readers, since it is essentially the reader—understood in the broadest terms as the one who engages with or responds to the text—who calls something existing into question and brings about upheaval, but also a new and potentially healing and theological sense of provisional meaning or value:

> The telling moment in an individual's psychic life, as in the life of societies at large, is when you call into question laws, norms and values. You can't deplore the "death of values" and discount the movements that question them as some are doing. Because it's precisely by putting things into question that "values" stop being frozen dividends and acquire a sense of mobility, polyvalence and life. (Kristeva 2002b, 12)

Notes

1. In French as in English the word "revolution" implies a turning over; a new beginning, but also a going around again, a re-turn (Julia Kristeva, *Intimate Revolt: The Powers and Limits of Psychoanalysis*, vol. 2., trans. Jeanine Herman [New York: Columbia University Press, 2002a], 3–4). And this is the task Kristeva takes on as both reader and analyst, that is to say the fomenting of revolt between intimately familiar principles, like the analyst and analysand returning and returning again to the same issues with a new layer of interpretation, a new set of intertexts, a new question or the old question reformulated. This revolutionary process through which we put the "text" of our own subjectivity may often be conflict-ridden and painful but, says Kristeva, it is also fundamental to being truly alive at all (Kristeva, *Intimate Revolt*, 125).

2. See, e.g., the introduction to Tompkins' edited collection on Reader-Response theory: "The objectivity of the text is the concept that these essays, whether they intended it or not, eventually destroy. What that destruction yields, ultimately, is not a criticism based on the concept of the reader, but a way of conceiving texts and readers that reorganizes the distinctions between them. Reading and writing join hands, change places, and finally become distinguishable, only as two names for the same activity" (Jane P. Tompkins, ed., *Reader-Response Criticism: From Formalism to Post-structuralism* [Baltimore/London: Johns Hopkins University Press, 1980], x).

3. Kristeva uses the term "fantasy" to describe those emotions and desires which, in terms of psychoanalytic theory, more generally are said to have been repressed. These are the unconscious fantasies (Kristeva, *Intimate Revolt*, 64) of our "psychic reality" (Kristeva, *Intimate Revolt*, 65) whose content is yet too disturbing for us to be able to deal with directly. "Fantasy" also describes the way in which those repressed emotions, in a modified sense, return to consciousness, as illusory formations—erotic, fearful, hostile, sadomasochistic—in dreams or even, to some extent, in daydreams (Ibid., 65) and which may be said to cause symptoms of psychic ill-being; depression, paranoia, hysteria, acting out of one kind or another. Fantasies of different kinds are inevitable (Ibid., 63 and 66).

4. For example, in the essay translated as "Word, Dialogue and Novel" (Toril Moi, The *Kristeva Reader* [Oxford: Basil Blackwell Ltd, 1986], 34–61), Kristeva uses Mikhail Bakhtin's classification of words within a narrative to explore the sense in which such words work on different levels, and possess varying degrees of ambivalence, in order to contest any notion that narrative can be regarded as monologic, or univocal. "What allows a dynamic dimension of structuralism

is [Bakhtin's] conception of the "literary word" as an intersection of textual surfaces rather than a point (a fixed meaning), as a dialogue among several writings: that of the writer, the addressee (or the character) and the contemporary or earlier cultural context" (Moi, *Kristeva Reader*, 36).

5. The term "semiotic" has a specific reference in Kristeva's work. Following, in the broadest sense, the psycho-linguistics of Jacques Lacan, she develops the gendered distinction between the feminine "semiotic," a pre-verbal space which precedes any form of subjectivity, and a masculine "thetic" or "symbolic" time of language and law.

6. ". . . a city filled with people steeped in their own image who rush about with overdone make-up on and who are cloaked in gold, pearls, and fine leather, while in the next street over, heaps of filth abound and drugs accompany the sleep or the fury of the social outcasts. . . . the current onslaught of psychological illness . . . seems to call out to psychoanalysis, "Tell us the meaning of our inner turmoil, show us a way out of it' . . ." (Julia Kristeva, *New Maladies of the Soul*, trans. Ross Guberman [New York: Columbia University Press, 1995], 27–29).

7. The culture of revolution, fashioned "by doubt and critique" has in the past, according to Kristeva, provided Europeans with moral and aesthetic grounding strong and flexible enough to facilitate freedom and revolution without itself disintegrating (Kristeva, *Intimate Revolt*, 4). Going beyond her concern for any individual client, Kristeva sees a prevailing tendency toward passive consumerism, in the "society of the spectacle" as the threat to a European culture of revolution. Kristeva's use of the term "The Society of the Spectacle" is a direct reference to Guy Debord's 1967 classic of the same title. Guy Debord was an intellectual and a filmmaker, whose Situationist ideas were inspirational in the student revolts in France in 1968. In *The Society of the Spectacle*, Debord argued that in societies characterized by modern processes of production, there is a shift toward a system of evaluation that focuses on representations or images rather than on essences or things in themselves. In other words, rather than attempting to live our lives on their own terms, we are more and more concerned with how they match up to the images produced by a mechanics of capitalist consumerism. Rather than seeking our own authentic ways of being happy or of finding meaning in our lives, we are mesmerized and seduced by the images of happiness or style or desirability the capitalist society of the spectacle produces to control and contain our desires in order to entice us to consume. These images—frequently banal and boring—begin to mediate the way in which we relate to each other. The illusion, the idol becomes more important than the real.

8. "Kristeva . . . makes clear her adhesion to the Freudian position that religious beliefs and practices are 'illusions,' that is wish-fulfilments whose truth-context cannot be verified. Whereas Freud regarded such illusions as personally and socially damaging, however, Kristeva who does not share his empiricism, ascribes a higher value to them. She writes that the function of psychoanalysis itself is in part . . . to reawaken the imagination and to permit illusion to exist" (Luke Ferretter, "Histoires de l'Église: The Body of Christ in the Thought of Julia Kristeva," in *Writing the Bodies of Christ: The Church from Carlyle to Derrida*, ed. John Schad [Aldershot: Ashgate 2001], 149).

9. The difference Kristeva might make between herself and more traditionally Christian readers, however, is that while for her "psychoanalysis offers a negotiation of unconscious traumas that recognizes their imaginary quality. . . . the church offers such a negotiation in the deluded belief that its content is true" (Ferretter, "Histoires de l'Église," 145).

10. This is a matter which gains credence in clinical practice, she suggests, when patients who cannot communicate psychic or somatic ill-being through words may sometimes only be able to approach traumatic emotions at first through gesture and image as in the action of a psychodrama (Kristeva, *Intimate Revolt*, 69).

11. "The role of language is essential for the formation of fantasies: without the possibility of telling them to someone (even if 'I' do not use this possibility), 'my' desires do not become fantasies but remain encysted at a prepsychical level and risk spilling over into somaticization and acting-out (from crime to drug addiction)" (Kristeva 2002a, 68).

12. In psychoanalytic terms, trapped in a condition where we are unwilling to give up the autoerotic pleasures of not separating seeing from being seen.
13. See Jill Bernstein, " 'But Dino, I don't want to make a film about elephants. . . . ,' " *The Guardian*, Friday, February 9, 2001. The film made $131million and was awarded 5 Oscars including best actor, best actress, and best picture.
14. An adaptation of a novel written in 1959 by the horror fiction writer, Robert Bloch.
15. Outside the therapeutic relationship between analyst and analysand, Kristeva sees the novel, not the cinema, as the "privileged terrain" (Kristeva, *Intimate Revolt*, 5) for the vital processes of revolution. Revolution means constantly engaging with and questioning old values and old conclusions in order to produce new ones. Novels are densely filled with ambivalent images and conflicts over values and established conclusions. They belong to the thetic realm of language but they still give expression to semiotic stress by their use of language, e.g., in linguistic rhythms, metonymies, and metaphors, elipses and disjunctions which indicate the unnameable realm beyond. Moroever, novels have what Kristeva describes as an open, incomplete "adolescent" structure and pre-eminently in the novel, she sees the possibility of a working out not unlike that found in transference and analytic interpretation (Kristeva, *New Maladies*, 152). Kristeva has herself written three novels: *The Samurai: A Novel* (1992), *The Old Man and the Wolves: A Novel* (1994), and *Possessions* (1999). Possessions takes the form of a detective novel and begins conventionally with a body and a murder investigation. Yet she invests this conventional genre with a purpose. In "the criminal and virtual universe of Santa Vavara, a police investigation is still possible" (Kristeva, *Intimate Revolt*, 4): The detective novel, she says, is a popular genre that keeps alive, albeit minimally, the possibility of questioning—doubt and critique.
16. The powerful and ancient symbolism of blood as both sacred and contaminating has been discussed at length by anthropologists like Mary Douglas and Victor Turner.
17. See, e.g., "Safe Blood Feeding" at <http://groups.msn.com/NightfiresRealVampireHaven/safebloodfeeding.msnw>.

Works Cited

Bernstein, Jill. " 'But Dino, I don't want to make a film about elephants. . . .' " *The Guardian*. Friday, February 9, 2001.

Clément, Catherine, and Julia Kristeva. *The Feminine and the Sacred*. Trans. Jane Marie Todd. New York: Columbia University Press, 2001.

Debord, Guy. *The Society of the Spectacle*. Trans. Donald Nicholson-Smith. New York: Zone Books, 1995.

Ferretter, Luke. "Histoires de l'Église: The Body of Christ in the Thought of Julia Kristeva." In *Writing the Bodies of Christ: The Church from Carlyle to Derrida*. Ed. John Schad. Aldershot: Ashgate, 2001, 145–158.

Harris, Thomas. *The Silence of the Lambs*. New York: St Martin's Press, 1988.

Kristeva, Julia. *Powers of Horror: An Essay on Abjection*. Trans. Leon S. Roudiez. New York: Columbia University Press, 1982.

———. "Stabat Mater." In *The Kristeva Reader*. Ed. Toril Moi. Oxford: Basil Blackwell, 1986, 160–186.

———. *In the beginning was love: Psychoanalysis and Faith*. Trans. Arthur Goldhammer. New York: Columbia University Press, 1987.

———. *The Samurai: A Novel*. Trans. Barbara Bray. New York: Columbia University Press, 1992.

———. *The Old Man and the Wolves: A Novel*. Trans. Barbara Bray. New York: Columbia University Press, 1994.

Kristeva, Julia. *New Maladies of the Soul*. Trans. Ross Guberman. New York: Columbia University Press, 1995.

———. *Possessions*. Trans. Barbara Bray. New York: Columbia University Press, 1999.

———. *The Sense and Non-sense of Revolt: The Powers and Limits of Psychoanalysis*. Vol. 1. Trans. Jeanine Herman. New York: Columbia University Press, 2000.

———. *Intimate Revolt: The Powers and Limits of Psychoanalysis*, Vol. 2. Trans. Jeanine Herman. New York: Columbia University Press, 2002a.

———. *Revolt, She Said: An Interview by Philippe Petit*. Trans. Brian O'Keeffe. Los Angeles/New York: Semiotext(e), 2002b.

Moi, Toril. *The Kristeva Reader*. Oxford: Basil Blackwell Ltd., 1986.

Nowell-Smith, Geoffrey. Ed. *The Oxford History of World Cinema*. Oxford: Oxford University Press, 1996.

Rice, Anne. *Interview with the Vampire: First Volume of the Vampire Chronicles*. [1976] London: Warner Books, 1996.

Riding, Alan. "A French Thinker Corrects her Idea of Political Correctness." *The New York Times* Arts & Ideas. Saturday July 14, 2001.

Taubin, Amy. "Grabbing the knife: 'The Silence of the Lambs' and the History of the Serial Killer Movie." In *Women and Film: A Sight and Sound Reader*. Ed. Pam Cook and Philip Dodd. London: British Film Institute (Scarlet Press), 1993. 123–131.

Tompkins, Jane P. Ed. *Reader-Response Criticism: From Formalism to Post-structuralism*. Baltimore/London: Johns Hopkins University Press, 1980.

CHAPTER THIRTEEN

Literature as Resistance: Hannah Arendt on Storytelling

DIRK DE SCHUTTER

Introduction

In *The Origins of Totalitarianism* Hannah Arendt expresses her distrust of literature, in *Eichmann in Jerusalem* she unequivocally states that one man will always be left alive to tell the story. What accounts for this development and change of view? Yet, Arendt will never overcome her lack of confidence in literature and will always stick to the difference between storytelling and fabricating fiction. The fictional character of totalitarian regimes is mirrored by the totalitarian character of fiction. That explains why telling the truth can become an act of dissidence. Arendt's warning to the reader is to beware of believing those who corrupt language and who are alienated from the world.

Key Words

Totalitarianism, holocaust, testimony, remembrance, fact, fiction.

★   ★   ★

"We do not need Homer": these confident words are spoken by Pericles in his famous *Funeral Oration* in an attempt to convince the Athenians that their city has developed a unique political structure and that they will acquire immortal fame when they have fallen in battle. At any rate, these words are put into the mouth of Pericles by Thucydides, who cites in full Pericles' oration in the second book of *The Peloponnesian Wars*. Arendt refers to the Greek historian in the fourth chapter of *The Human Condition*, which offers an analysis of "action" when she explains how the Greek polis found a solution for the transitory nature of actions. The polis, Arendt says, was founded to keep great deeds in memory: it organized public memory. It provided a space where mortal man, whose action and speech leave behind a barely tangible trace, could partake of immortality. The polis did so by creating a public forum for the performed actions so that these would never escape attention nor sink back in oblivion. Whereas the heroes of the Trojan War lived on in memory thanks to the epic talent of Homer, the polis now takes over the task of the bard and warrants the remembrance of great actions. Arendt writes:

> The *polis*—if we trust the words of Pericles in the Funeral Oration—gives a guaranty that those who forced every sea and land to become the scene of their daring will not remain without witness and will need neither Homer nor anyone else who knows how to turn words to praise them. (Arendt 1989, 197)

Arendt's approval of Thucydides (and Pericles) appears to be so complete that she does not even bother to quote their words; she inserts these words without quotation marks in her own text and as such appropriates them. The only reservation she makes is hidden in the conditional clause "if we trust the words of Pericles." But at no moment does she elucidate whether she truly believes these words and what such a belief would entail.

Arendt, who often dwells on the figure of Pericles, does not pay any attention to the remarkable opening of the *Funeral Oration* either. The latter opens in a remarkable way, because in it Pericles states that he dissociates himself from the tradition that he nevertheless carries on. He starts with the remark that he sincerely respects the Athenian tradition according to which the soldiers fallen in combat are annually honoured with a ceremonial burial, but he adds that he does not agree with the initiators according to whom a ceremony needs a proper eulogy. So, he opens his oration with the remark that he would rather not give a talk and that words in this case could be superfluous. He underpins his point of view with the argument that the dead have distinguished themselves by a glorious deed and that therefore only deeds can honor them.

This argument must have surprised Arendt as well for at least four reasons. First, the fundamental discovery of the Athenian polis and politics is freedom and this freedom is made concrete in a freedom of speech. Arendt points out that the Greeks had no less than three words for what we call freedom of speech: *isonomia, isègoria* and *isologia*. The political activity *par excellence* is the discussion (Arendt 1993a, 40).

Second, this primordial, Greek experience is laid down in Aristotle's double definition of man: *zoon logon echon* and *zoon politikon*. Arendt emphasizes time and again that both definitions belong together: man is engaged in politics because he is a linguistic animal, and he is a linguistic animal because he is engaged in politics. That is why the Greeks held the opinion that *logos* is denied not only to slaves, who by definition are bereft of their freedom and do not participate in political life, but also to barbarians subjected to a despot. Both slaves and barbarians are *aneu logou*: bereft of the free word, of the possibility to discuss with equals. So, Aristotle's definition of man as *zoon logon echon* is a political definition, not an ontological one. With this interpretation Arendt distances herself from Heidegger, who understands Aristotle's formula as a description of man's essence, as if according to Aristotle *logos* would constitute man's highest characteristic. Arendt disagrees: according to her Aristotle considers *nous* (let us say, the faculty to think) as man's highest characteristic, and man has been given *logos* to do politics.

Third, *logos*, characterizing man as political being, is the meaningful word. It is not aimed at revealing truth, but rather at bestowing meaning to what has happened and to giving an account: "*logon didonai.*" As Arendt emphasizes time and again, politics is first and foremost about well-considered opinions and persuasions, *doxai*.

Fourth, in the eyes of Arendt the attempt to get rid of Homer does not want to bar the word from the political domain, but paradoxically enough strives at a higher respect for the value of the word. Arendt points out that the Greeks were looking for a way to preserve the experiences gained during the siege of Troy and praised by Homer. These experiences circled around freedom, but also around the desire to excel, to be the best of one's peers. Homer has been the first to give expression to what has been called after Jacob Burckhardt: the Greek spirit of *agon*. The Greeks themselves coined for this spirit the word "*aristeia,*" in which we hear "*aristos*" (the best) and which can be translated as excellence. Arendt writes: "It is as if the Homeric army does not dissolve, but after its return home gathers again, founds the polis and has found a space where it can stay together permanently" (47). But whereas the Greeks in the Trojan War tried to excel in heroic deeds, the gathering on the *agora* will concentrate on speaking great words. "At the same time, freedom moves away from action to speech, from the free act to the free word." Speech turns into an action; in both activities man reveals who he is. Ultimately, this experience lies also at the basis of the Greek tragedy, in which people are brought to ruin, but not without speaking great words. Nietzsche, who unlike many others was sensitive for the dignity of the word, called the Greeks "a people of insatiable chatters," because they exercised daily the strange power of the spoken word that surely does not avert calamities, but still faces them.

But let us go back to Pericles and ask ourselves why Arendt makes so little reservations concerning his oration, in which the word is disparaged and the narrative treated as dead wood. Is there a reason why Arendt distrusts literature? We find the answer in *The Origins of Totalitarianism*.

Both the second part, which deals with imperialism, and the third part, which deals with totalitarianism proper, carry out an analysis of what can be called with Julien Benda: "*la trahison des clercs*." ("betrayal by the learned") Arendt blames the intellectuals in general and the writers in particular for being alienated from the world and for being unable to experience reality. The origin of this lack of experience and this "worldlessness" that can be circumscribed as "barbarism" (Arendt 1995, 13), lies in a corruption of language. Arendt situates the beginning of this corruption in the romantic age and romanticism. In that time originated the idea that in literature it is possible and permitted to say anything and that words can mean anything. Arendt seems to be touching on an issue that is also brought up in a conversation between Derek Attridge and Jacques Derrida. In an attempt to elucidate what has urged him on in his philosophical investigations, Derrida propounds the statement that, since romanticism, literature has been granted the liberty to say anything. In French "*tout dire*" means to say everything and to say anything. Derrida describes this freedom as "a very powerful political weapon," but he immediately adds that this powerful freedom conceals some impotence, vulnerability, and even irresponsibility. Whoever says anything and refuses to account for what he says, whoever withdraws from every form of *logon didonai*, does not assume responsibility. We could say that he or she does not answer for what is uttered, that he or she does not give an answer or that he or she flees the dialectic of word and counterword, or proposal and rebuttal: he does not consider his words as answers to a given context, and he deprives them at the same time of the possibility of being countered. But Derrida goes one step further: this irresponsibility may hide the highest form of responsibility. For such words are pledged to the future, they promise a future: they are called to account not by an instance in the present, but by an absence suspending every presentation and withdrawing from the present, by a future that keeps coming and is for ever reserved. To this promise that of essence is not to be fulfilled Derrida gives the name "democracy." He says: "The institution of literature in the West, in its relatively modern form, is linked to an authorization to say everything, and doubtless too to the coming about of the modern idea of democracy. Not that it depends on a democracy in place, but it seems inseparable to me from what calls forth a democracy, in the most open sense."[1]

Arendt would agree with this. Nevertheless, the freedom to say anything is worrisome to her. She relates this freedom to the desire to be original that has obsessed Western culture since romanticism. This obsession is characterized by the lack of any obligation toward the world and an exclusive interest in one's self. Whimsicality, arbitrariness, unaccountability do not form an objection; on the contrary, they prove in their own way the originality, or even the genius of the person in question. What counts is not to say sensible things about the world or to explain events from a sound, well-founded point of view; what counts is rather to come up with an original, surprising vision and afterward to surprise once again with an ingenuous refutation of the first vision. Any opinion can be defended, on the condition that it is witty and equivocal. Any event can be sacrificed to this desire to stress one's stylistic talents, no event is spared from this cynical self-complacency that destroys the world not in deeds, but in words.[2] Arendt does not dissemble her vexation for this vampirism that sucks the meaning from the world. Two theoreticians of romanticism are named—Adam Mueller and Friedrich Schlegel. She writes:

> Adam Mueller and Friedrich Schlegel are symptomatic in the highest degree of a general playfulness of modern thought in which almost any opinion can gain ground temporarily. No real thing, no historical event, no political idea was safe from the all-embracing and all-destroying mania by which these first literati could always find new and original opportunities for new and fascinating opinions. (Arendt 1976, 167)

Arendt's indignation about this romantic attitude is inspired by three judgments. First, this attitude surrenders to the cruel insanities that tear the world apart. If you say no matter what, you deprive yourself of the right to press charges against the world. Ultimately, the world and what goes on in it is never at stake in these witticisms, but only a sterile insistence on being right, a malevolent lust to criticize, a contempt that spares nothing but one's own malicious and inventive puns.

Second, Arendt is highly upset by the indifference toward the falsification of history that is expressed by this attitude. The romantic intellectual seems to be convinced that any historiography is a falsification, because it tells the story of the winners and forgets about the losers and the downtrodden. But once one begins to reduce official history to a farcical tale, one will ultimately believe that historical reality as it is known is only a façade put up to fool people, and will ultimately believe that there is more truth to pompous conspiracy theories swearing that the world is secretly ruled by the Jews or the freemasons or the Jesuits.

Third, these two attitudes, both the contempt for the meaningful word and the disdain for historiography, lay bare a fearsome resemblance with totalitarianism. Arendt quotes a text by Mussolini, entitled *Relativismo e Fascismo*, in which the latter describes himself as both "aristocrat and democrat, revolutionary and reactionary, proletarian and antiproletarian, pacifist and antipacifist" (168). Mussolini's utterance bears witness to an appalling cynicism: whoever says that he is both aristocrat and democrat, or revolutionary and reactionary, actually gives to understand that he thinks nothing is important, that he is willing to defend every possible point of view if that suits him, and that only one thing really counts, that is, his own career, his own position in society. But Mussolini's statement also demonstrates that totalitarianism is not only characterized by a monolithic rigidity but also and even more by a radical relativism. The mobilization to which all aspects of society are subjected affects language as well: words and their meaning are taken up in a *perpetuum mobile* that enables totalitarian discourse to transform itself unceasingly. When words have lost every reference to reality and to the world, they can order reality at their whim and ultimately dissolve it. Anyway, Arendt's diagnosis that denounces the unceasing shift of meaning to which words are submitted is confirmed by the language-political observations of Victor Klemperer in his study *Lingua Tertii Imperii*. A striking example elaborated in detail by Klemperer is the word "fanatic," which until 1930 signified an inadmissible quality, something in between illness and crime. According to national socialism, however, people had to be brought up to fanaticism: the word melted together in a glorious way notions like "brave," "devoted," and "uncompromising." Other well-known examples are the word "*Endlösung*," which presents the complete annihilation of the Jewish people as a solution of the Jewish question, or the word "*Figuren*," which leaves the humiliated corpses of the camps maimed beyond recognition to be transfigured without redemption. This implosion of every signification reaches a climax in the falsification of history that is carried out by the totalitarianism of Hitler and of Stalin. This falsification affects both the movement itself and the history that precedes the movement. So, Arendt does not agree with Slavoj Zizek nor with Alain Badiou, who both claim that Stalinism is still inherently linked to a true and authentic event, whereas Nazism would be deprived of every truth and authenticity.[3] She refuses to make that distinction; on the contrary, she points out that both forms of totalitarianism have cut themselves loose from their past and their sources. Nazism has attached more importance to the completely unbelievable concoctions about a Zionist conspiracy than to the dubious racial theories of Gobineau that no matter how still contained a grain of scholarly nature; likewise, Stalinism has renounced the albeit doubtful, yet academically accepted theory of Marx about the dialectic-materialistic course of history and given preference to the troublesome gossip about the 300 richest families in the world. The step toward a falsification of history was quickly made: Trotsky has never played a role in the Russian revolution, has never been commander-in-chief of the Red Army; the Nazis have never done anything but return the enemy's fire in a Jewish war that was forced upon them, and in spring 1943, that is, after the carnage at Stalingrad, Goebbels admitted that "at the periphery of the war we have become somewhat susceptible."[4]

One of the most poignant discoveries when reading the third part of *The Origins of Totalitarianism*—the part that deals with totalitarianism proper—has to do with the high frequency of words denoting falsehood. On almost every page Arendt uses a variation from the series: "lying," "fiction," "forgery," "fictitious," "mendacious," "spurious." Her argumentation is aimed at a demonstration of the "essentially fictitious character of totalitarianism" (378).

Hitler made some fantastic discoveries: he discovered that a lie can only be successful if it is excessive. This explains why a phenomenon like revisionism or the denial of the Holocaust is possible: it is easier to believe the executioners who maintain their own innocence than to trust the victims and their utterly desperate stories. Hitler also discovered that people are prepared to live in a world of lies, because they detest nothing more than unpredictability and contingency. People—actually I should say the people from mass society—are not convinced by facts, nor by inconsistent fictions, but they are convinced by a consistent system that enables them to look at facts and events as if they obeyed a general rule and thus to get a grip on what is going on. Nothing revolts twentieth-century mass society more than the contingent, the thought that nobody rules and that nobody controls the console table of history. This fear for the chaotic, this aversion from the obscure complexity of action can only be conquered by a leader who guarantees a world of consistency. This world can only be mendacious and false, for in contradistinction from the world of work where an expert succeeds in explaining what he is doing or what is to be done, the world of politics and action is permeated by the unexpected and the unforeseen, because someone who acts never really knows what he is doing.

One of the major misconceptions held by the twentieth century lies in the identification of consistency with truth or in the definition of truth as consistency. If we take for granted that truth says something about the world, in other words that it has a revelatory character, we can conclude that consistency has nothing to do with truth. Consistency is the mental capacity to deduce cogent propositions from premises, but has no relation whatsoever with the world. Moreover, a consistent system can be worked out by someone who lacks every experience, it is a form of thinking that makes the world superfluous. That is why Arendt can round off her study on totalitarianism with the following, provocative remark: "The ideal subject of totalitarian rule is not the convinced Nazi or the convinced Communist, but people for whom the distinction between fact and fiction and the distinction between true and false no longer exist" (474). This remark is based on an insight in the psychology of brainwashing: the result of a consequential substitution of factual truth by lies is not that the lies are accepted as truth, but that the mental capacities with which people orient themselves in the world are broken down. One of these mental capacities is the capability to make a distinction between fact and fiction, or between true and false. Someone who is lied to unremittingly loses these faculties: he will not believe the lies he is told, but he will become completely indifferent and not believe anything anymore.

Totalitarianism is a fiction, that is, it is not a story, or it is a bad story. And "bad" in this context has an ethical and an aesthetical meaning. The distinction between storytelling and fabricating fiction plays a hidden, yet important role in Arendt's oeuvre. In *The Human Condition* she writes: "The distinction between a real and a fictional story is precisely that the latter was 'made up' and the former not made at all" (Arendt 1989, 186). She comes back to this distinction in her essay on Isak Dinesen, pseudonym of Karen Blixen, the author of *Out of Africa*, and repeats there that storytelling and fabricating fiction do not coincide, but on the contrary exclude one another to a certain degree. The story is according to Arendt true to life: not just because it gives an accurate reproduction of life, but also because it helps to live and above all to die. Without stories men cannot fulfill the task they have been allotted. That task involves: to be someone, to lead a life in which the quest for meaning gets a chance to transform the absurd cycle of life into a singular existence. We could say with two words borrowed from Greek: the story changes a *zoê* into a *bios*. The story repeats in imagination what life has given and thus brings about a reconciliation with what has happened. That is why the story in the long run confers a sort of serenity, not to be understood as paralyzing inertia, but as the capacity to let go. In a memorable passage Arendt writes: "Without repeating life in imagination you can never be fully alive, 'lack of imagination' prevents people from 'existing.' 'Be loyal to the story, be eternally and unswervingly loyal to the story' means no less than be loyal to life, don't create fiction but accept what life is giving you, show yourself worthy of whatever it may be by recollecting and pondering over it, thus repeating it in imagination" (Arendt 1995, 97). And she adds the following thought-provoking words: "The reward of storytelling is to be able to let go." We are granted the chance to let go of life, that is, to die, but to say yes to what has been as well, provided life has been told. Strangely enough, this favor is granted by life itself: "the reward of storytelling" talks about a reward offered by storytelling, but it is a reward that storytelling itself has been offered by life. Thanks to the story we are able to let go of life, but in actual fact life, as told in a story, has let go of us. Life lets go of us, sets us free, so that we can bid farewell in death or recommence. Arendt quotes a phrase from Isak Dinesen: "My life, I will not let you go except you bless me, but then I will let you go." Blessed by life, we succeed in letting go of life.

But this will only come to pass, if we resist the temptation to fabricate. "Don't create fiction" is Arendt's warning. The fictional blocks the story, it does not wait for the story to unfold, but thrusts itself forward with a preconceived pattern, a plan. Both the story and life are violated by fiction: the story is expected to tally, to be correct and consistent; life is expected to take its course as planned, to realize what fiction has preconceived.

In the foregoing we have paid attention to the essentially fictional structure of totalitarianism; now we may add that fiction has a totalitarian structure. The two structures, the fictional and the totalitarian, match because of their bent for consistency. We have also pointed out that consistency is undoubtedly an indispensable quality in the domain of logic, but that it is hardly recommendable in the domain of action and storytelling: consistency does not set free, in the way that the story confers the favor of letting go, but it binds, because it chains the future to the past and thus excludes every renewal or change.

Consistency is achieved and desired by someone who dreams of omnipotence. Whoever claims to be almighty cherishes the delusion that not only the future can be manipulated as if it were an extension of the present, but that the past can be denied as well. That is why omnipotence and the consistency it requires, of necessity, result in mendacity and an elimination of truth as revelation. Omnipotence misunderstands in a double way action and the power it needs. It does not understand that the power organized by action is of essence finite and limited, because it is shared. Nor does it understand that action can only be directed at the future and that it needs the stability of the past: omnipotence views the past as if it were part of the future, in other words as if it were stripped of every factuality and as if it were purely potential. Thus, omnipotence deprives itself of the indispensable stability that the past due to its ineradicable nature offers, and condemns itself to a hopeless series of groundless interventions. Omnipotence always raving about the absolute thus exposes itself to the most destructive form of relativism.

In *The Human Condition* Arendt ascribes to the Greek polis the power to organise public memory; yet, she knows from her study on totalitarianism that regimes can degenerate into a sort of organized lie or organized forgetfulness. In Nazi Germany and in Stalinist Russia forgetfulness was organized in the concentration camps. Arendt calls them the present-day "holes of oblivion." To the question of whether the camps are an accidental side-effect of the totalitarian system, Arendt answers emphatically in the negative: the camps are the true face of totalitarianism. They put into practice the idea that everything is possible, that the past can be obliterated and that people can disappear from the earth without leaving any trace: the camps are the laboratories of totalitarianism.

The relation between lying and politics has preoccupied Arendt until the last decade of her life. She comes back to this issue in two late essays: in "Truth and Politics," written in response to the controversy about her book on the Eichmann trial, and in "Lying in Politics," written in response to the Pentagon Papers on the Vietnam War. Before that, in 1959, she gave a speech in Hamburg, the city that awarded her the Lessing Prize. In this speech she sides with Lessing to fight the age-old metaphysical saying: "*Plato amicus, magis amica veritas*" ("Plato is my friend, but the truth even more"), and she explains that Lessing considers friendship to be the highest community-founding virtue, because he is convinced that what matters in politics is not truth, as most philosophers since Plato have argued, but the exchange of opinions. But why then is it so important for a political regime to speak the truth, and why is it that so many political regimes, not only totalitarian, but democratic regimes as well, have difficulties with this?

To gain insight in this problem Arendt starts from the conclusion that truth has something tyrannical, that it is supported by an element of coercion. This applies to any form of truth, to rational and to factual truths. Propositions like "The sum of the angles of a triangle equals 180°" or "The earth orbits the sun" or "In August 1914 Germany invaded Belgium" came to be in different ways, but as truths they withdraw from the domain of disputation and agreement. To recognize these truths does not require persuasion, nor has it anything to do with the number of people able to understand them. Truth is so compelling that philosophers at the dawn of the Modern Age asked the question whether truth restrained God's omnipotence; Grotius, for example, held that not even God can cause two times two not to make four.

Yet, there is a problematic difference. The proposition "Two times two makes four" is a rational truth; the sentence "In August 1914 Germany invaded Belgium" contains a factual truth. The problem is that denial affects these truths in a different way. It is rather hard, not to say impossible, to completely obliterate a rational truth. Even if Euclid's oeuvre had been lost in the fire of the library of Alexandria or even if all geometry books in the world were burnt, even then we might suppose that the human mind would always possess the capacity to discover or to reproduce these axioms. But this is not the case with factual truths: these risk tasting defeat in the onslaught by the totalitarian lie. And once they have been eliminated, no rational or spiritual effort can bring them back. In the words of Arendt herself:

> Perhaps the chances that Euclidean mathematics or Einstein's theory of relativity would have been reproduced in time if their authors had been prevented from handing them down to posterity are not very good either, yet they are infinitely better than the chance that a fact of importance, forgotten or, more likely, lied away, will one day be rediscovered. (Arendt 1993b, 232)

The foregoing immediately makes clear why political regimes have such a hard time in telling the truth. As we have said, truth is tyrannical: it is entitled to an unconditional recognition and precludes every discussion, whereas politics and the public domain are of essence constituted by discussion. But in spite of their shameless indestructibility facts and events keep something contingent: they might just as well not have happened or occurred differently. That is why politics, and especially political domination or totalitarianism, are tempted to deny and manipulate facts. Moreover, facts occur in the domain of human affairs and constitute the fabric of political space. So, they seem to lend themselves to agreement, controversy, objection, whereas their compelling truth can only be recognized and accepted. About the confusing relation between facts and opinions Arendt writes the following:

> Facts and opinions, though they must be kept apart, are not antagonistic to each other; they belong to the same realm. Facts inform opinions, and opinions, inspired by different interests and passions, can differ widely and still be legitimate as long as they respect factual truth. Freedom of opinion is a farce unless factual information is guaranteed and the facts themselves are not in dispute. (238)

Precisely because totalitarian regimes, driven by consistency, desire to prove their omnipotence by a falsification of facts, truth telling can turn into a political deed.

Arendt, who in *The Origin of Totalitarianism* declares that writers are superfluous and that the organization of political memory can be entrusted to the state, had every possible reason to question the utterance of Pericles. Indeed, in *The Origins of Totalitarianism* she had described and analyzed a political regime that was not at all at the service of remembrance, but that pursued the obliteration of memory and the organization of forgetfulness. On top of that, Arendt belongs to the select circle of philosophers who often and with an outspoken passion for the word insert quotations in their texts. Almost every classical author from European literature is mentioned in her oeuvre: Homer, Virgil, Dante, Shakespeare, and Goethe; in reference to modern times a prominent place is given to Melville, Faulkner, Kafka, Auden, René Char, and the Dutch novelist Harry Mulisch; she has written insightful essays on Heinrich Heine, Bertolt Brecht, Hermann Broch, Isak Dinesen, and Randall Jarrell. Last but not least, Arendt's philosophy is an always renewed meditation on the work of historians, on Homer, Herodotus, and Thucydides, on Livy and Virgil, on Machiavelli and Tocqueville. So, more than ever the question remains whether the proposition "we do not need Homer" would be endorsed by her. Maybe, this proposition expresses a threat rather than a relief, and maybe it gives to understand the burden of responsibility that rests on the shoulders of writers and the immense importance of the spoken and written word.

Arendt's judgment has not really changed in the course of years, but she seems to have become more and more aware of the role truth telling plays in the political scene. As has been indicated in the beginning of this text, the *logos* Aristotle ascribes to man as political being does not necessarily mean the true word but rather the meaningful word. The *logos* is used to assume responsibility and to exchange opinions. But this freedom of speech turns into a horrible farce as soon as the right to factual truth is no longer warranted. This guarantee becomes completely void in a totalitarian regime, but it can also be infringed upon in a democratic republic. That has been the case in the United States during the Vietnam War, when Pentagon spread lies on a large scale and deceived the American population about the number of American and Vietnamese casualties, the arms used, the objectives, and the war crimes. In these circumstances telling the truth becomes a deed of immense political importance. We could refer in this context to Vaclav Havel, who calls living in truth an act of dissidence.

The following paradox marks the facts from the past: they are at the same time indestructible and vulnerable, obtrusive and fragile. For its continued existence the past needs stories: it owes its factuality to a world of words. Where facts are not acknowledged, they vanish: only the nonfictional story accounts for what has happened. This does not imply that what has happened is approved of or excused or trivialized; on the contrary, as Arendt writes in the introduction to *The Origins of Totalitarianism*, such a story is the only way to bear the burden of the past, to come to grips with the past. Once again, this does not mean that the past is experienced as if it were unavoidable destiny, but it does mean that the contingency is recognized, that one does not shrink from the insight that things might have occurred differently and yet accepts what has been. Only in this way we can ultimately stand up to what is called reality. The context sketched by the introduction to *The Origins of Totalitarianism* makes a great deal of this thought: the facts Arendt mentions are Nazism, Stalinism, total war, the camps. Her words may be valid as principle for any form of historiography:

The conviction that everything that happens on earth must be comprehensible to man can lead to interpreting history by common-places. Comprehension does not mean denying the outrageous, deducing the unprecedented from precedents, or explaining phenomena by such analogies and generalities that the impact of reality and shock of experience are no longer felt. It means, rather, examining and bearing consciously the burden which our century has

placed on us—neither denying its existence nor submitting meekly
to its weight. Comprehension, in short, means the unpremeditated,
attentive facing up to, and resisting of, reality—whatever it may be.
(Arendt 1976, viii)

In this way Arendt enters her politico-philosophical project in the
history and historiography of the West, from Homer to Faulkner. She
praises Homer, not so much because he could make up these elaborated
comparisons, but rather because he reported as an impartial observer
about the siege of Troy. In the *Iliad* Homer does not intervene as Greek,
but as an unbiased, equitable spectator who pays as much attention to the
Greek Achilles, driven by faithfulness and fury, as to the noble Trojan
Hector. Homer is justifiably considered to be the father of Western
culture, for, as Arendt points out, he has been the first to incorporate that
attitude that eventually led to the development of the Western invention
par excellence: Homer has been the first to take up an objective standpoint
and has made the first step toward a scientific attitude. Herodotus has
followed in his footsteps: in *The Persian Wars* he intends to sing the praise
of both Greeks and barbarians in order to assure the remembrance of their
glorious deeds for posterity. And indeed, though Arendt does not go into
this, we could complete this list by adding Aeschylus. The latter fought in
the battle of Marathon, but in his historical tragedy *The Persians* keeps
away from any vindictive bickering; he does not get even with the
Persians, neither does he inappropriately toot the trumpet of the Greeks.
But he expresses a considerable lot of commiseration for the desperation
of Xerxes and his faithful followers. Perhaps we can bring up in passing
the latest conflict between the West and the Middle East, the Gulf War:
what Aeschylus describes as "*atê*" or "bewilderment" has undoubtedly
blinded both parties; and the socalled victor overindulges in brawny
onanism to such a degree that any compassion for the woe of the defeated
is seen as treason and that we can rightly ask with Baudrillard whether a
war has actually taken place. An admirable exception opposing the
twentieth-century disease of one-dimensionality and self-complacency is
William Faulkner: with his novel *A Fable* he erects a monument to the
Unknown Soldier, the victim of the enormous madness, who as we
know has no nationality. From Faulkner Arendt borrows the saying:
"The past is never dead, it is not even past" (Arendt 1993b, 10). Precisely
because the past does not belong to what has gone, but keeps coming to
us, it forces us to tell about it time and again. And, as Isak Dinesen has it,
only the narrated past will ultimately set us free.

To lend words to reality, to translate the world: a polyphony of stories guards us, human inhabitants of the earth, from barbarism. That is what the Greeks have understood, and what Herodotus had in mind, when he defined the task he set himself: "*legein ta eonta*," to say what is, to bear testimony to what is, only and justly because it is, to render in words what occurs, only and justly because it occurs.

While Arendt in *The Origins of Totalitarianism* profusely enumerates totalitarian measures that exclude these testimonies to what occurs, she elsewhere, for example, in *Eichmann in Jerusalem*, confesses her unconditional belief in the future of storytelling and the fall of totalitarianism. The latter rule of government is doomed to fail and to bring itself down, precisely because it is built on the delusion of omnipotence and consistency. The attempts to obliterate every trace of massive slaughter, to make opponents to the regime disappear in the anonymity of the camps, were doomed to fail for the very simple reason that there are far too many people on this planet to bring such a gigantic cover-up to a successful end. Totalitarianism presupposes a perfection that does not belong to this world. That is why Arendt concludes her book on the Eichmann trial with the prosaic considerations: "The holes of oblivion do not exist. One man will always be left alive to tell the story" (Arendt 1992, 233). This glad tiding does not express hope, but soberly states a fact, as if it were a natural phenomenon. Arendt does not write "one man should always be left alive" or "must always be left alive," but she uses "will" as if she was completely sure of the outcome and as if she was dealing with something predictable. Like one says in English: "Tomorrow the sun will rise at 6 o'clock."

Arendt's matter of factness in this issue contrasts sharply with the dramatic declarations accompanying most meditations on the Holocaust that are often influenced by theological speculations. Any call to a holy silence is alien to her philosophy, if only because she is above all inspired by obligations toward the world. Even Jean-François Lyotard was irritated by Arendt's laconic remark: "One man will always be left alive to tell the story." "Irritated" is the correct word, because all he does is shrug his shoulders. Hence, his caustic question: "What does she know?" This question is unmistakeably rhetorical, for the implied answer is known beforehand: "nothing." He adds, without apparently realizing that he agrees with Arendt: "The Shoah, an almost perfect annihilation, if it hadn't been for some small things, no one would have been able to tell about it."[5] Precisely: what counts, is that "almost." "Nothing human is that perfect": that is what the final pages of *Eichmann in Jerusalem* say. Let us add: what counts, are those "small things"; yes, small things matter.

So, Arendt asks us to resist and to come up with a story. Yet, she has one more warning. History will only be restored to honor, if historiography renounces its scientific character, that is, if it relinquishes its privilege to explain what has happened and to fit it into all-encompassing schemes and if it learns to tell stories. Science eliminates the meaning of occurrences by inserting them in impersonal processes and attributing them to the dynamics of historical movements, like progress or emancipation or class struggle. These explanative models are the scientific equivalent of fiction: they usurp the meaning of historical tale. They smother every singularity, because they view each event, no matter how momentous or how trivial, as the application of a general rule. Finally, these models intend to prove only one thing: there are no events, everything has already occurred, we have always been underway toward the end of history; or stories are superfluous, we have always already understood everything.

Here lies maybe the true greatness of the philosopher Hannah Arendt. She confronts the world and does not pretend to understand it, she dares to articulate that lack of comprehension. She dares not to have an explanation for the murderous madness of totalitarianism, not to know what politics is required in a world threatened by nuclear conflicts and environmental catastrophes, to fully experience the break with the past in which tradition, authority, and religion played a major role, to be frightened by a society in which man risks to become superfluous.

Conclusion

Arendt's political philosophy has strongly influenced the country that used to be called Czechoslovakia, especially the writers of Charta 77—I am thinking of Jan Patocka, Vaclav Havel, and Milan Kundera. The latter starts his novel *The Book of Laughter and Forgetfulness* with the following remark: "The battle of man against power is the battle of man against forgetfulness." The late Arendt would undoubtedly not have used the word "power" but rather "domination" or "totalitarianism." But let us leave this aside. Further on in the book Kundera alludes to the attempt of the Soviet regime to delete Trotsky from history, and he states that Prague is described in the novels of Kafka as a city without memory. In that context he has one character asking the question: "Is it true that a people cannot cross the desert of organised oblivion and still be alive?" Kundera borrows this image from Nietzsche: the image of

Western civilization as a desert; it is an image Heidegger and Arendt as well call upon. "The desert grows," Nietzsche writes. In *What is politics?* Arendt comes back to that image and expresses the hope that we will be able to cultivate oases in that desert. Heidegger too cites that image, and he adds in his well-known provocative style that the destruction or desertification of the earth is not simply caused by the annihilating violence of total war. The destruction that plagues the present-day world is, according to Heidegger, even more ominous than war, because it is linked with a high living standard. This destruction has nothing to do with the bombing of a country, but is due to the expulsion of Mnemosyne, the mother of the muses and the goddess of remembrance.[6] With Heidegger we may ask and conclude: did we expel Mnemosyne? Or did she withdraw? Have we perhaps been expelled from the land of Mnemosyne? And what does it mean that we live in oblivion, that no one remembers who we are?

Notes

1. Jacques Derrida, "This Strange Institution Called Literature," in *Acts of Literature*, ed. D. Attridge (New York/London: Routledge, 1992), 37.
2. This is also discussed by A.M. Roviello in "Les intellectuels modernes," in *Ontologie et Politique. Actes du colloque Hannah Arendt*, ed. M. Abensour (Paris: Tierce, 1989), 225–235.
3. I refer to A. Badiou, *L'éthique* (Paris: Hatier, 1993) and S. Zizek, *Het subject en zijn onbehagen* (Amsterdam: Boom, 1997).
4. As reported by Victor Klemperer.
5. J.F. Lyotard, *Lectures d'enfance* (Paris: Galilée, 1991), 75–76.
6. M. Heidegger, *Was heisst Denken?* (Tübingen: M. Niemeyer, 1971), 11.

Works Cited

Arendt, Hannah. *The Origins of Totalitarianism*. San Diego: HB&C, 1976.
———. *The Human Condition*. Chicago: Chicago University Press, 1989.
———. *Eichmann in Jerusalem*. Harmondsworth: Penguin, 1992.
———. *Between Past and Future*. Harmondsworth: Penguin, 1993.
———. *Was ist Politik?* Ed. U. Ludz. München/Zürich: Piper, 1993.
———. *Men in Dark Times*. San Diego/New York/London: HB&C, 1995.
Badiou, A. *L'éthique*. Paris: Hatier, 1993.
Derrida, Jacques. "This Strange Institution Called Literature." In *Acts of Literature*, Ed. D. Attridge. New York/London: Routledge, 1992, 37.
Heidegger, M. *Was heisst Denken?* (1953), Tübingen: M. Niemeyer, 1971.
Lyotard, J.F. *Lectures d'enfance*. Paris: Galilée, 1991.
Roviello, A.M. "Les intellectuels modernes." In *Ontologie et Politique. Actes du colloque Hannah Arendt*. Ed. M. Abensour. Paris: Tierce, 1989. 225–235.
Zizek, S. *Het subject en zijn onbehagen*. Amsterdam: Boom, 1997.

INDEX